The Margaret Powell Cookery Book

By the same author

Below Stairs
Climbing the Stairs

The Margaret Powell Cookery Book

Margaret Powell

THE COOKERY BOOK CLUB

This edition published by
The Cookery Book Club
St. Giles House, 49/50 Poland St., London W1A 2LG
by arrangement with
Peter Davies
© 1970 by Margaret Powell and Leigh Crutchley

*Chapter-head
designs by
Una Lindsay*

Printed in Great Britain by Butler & Tanner Ltd., Frome and London

Table of Contents

Contents contd.

*To
my Mother
with love*

Introduction

I have dedicated this book to my mother who, like my grand-mother, my great-grandmother and myself, was in domestic service, first as that lowest of the low, a kitchen maid, and later as a cook. Many of the recipes and hints I have inherited from them. The others are those I learnt in service from the cooks I served under, or invented myself and improved by trial and error.

You may wonder why I felt that a cookery book such as this needed to be written, or could possibly be of any interest now that one can produce meals in a matter of minutes. You may think that from time to time I go on a bit about present-day food, but don't think I'm decrying instant meals—far from it. I think that they are a great boon to a busy housewife, especially if she also works outside the home. I know from experience how hard it is to come home tired, exhausted from working in somebody else's house, office or factory and then have to start preparing and cooking a meal.

Again, I'm not going into the rights or wrongs of house-wives working outside the home. You can divide them up into two types: those who work because they really have to for financial reasons and those who are so bored with just being housewives that, even if they didn't need the money, they would go to work anyway. No, I'm all for freedom of choice and freedom of action and I bless the things that make these easier. When my family was young and I had to go out to work to earn more money there were no instant meals. You could buy some frozen foods but you certainly couldn't buy a meal which you could stick in the oven and in about twenty minutes' time it was edible; edible, that is, to the people who haven't been used to home cooking.

Mind you, even if there had been these instant pre-packed meals, I wouldn't have been able to afford them. It was then, and still is, cheaper to cook a meal at home. Look at the quantity to start with. Some of these packeted jobs say 'enough for three'—well, I can only think that the manufacturer must be basing people's appetites on those of sparrows, because I could eat the whole lot myself. There doesn't seem to be the same bulk in prepared food as there is in fresh food, even if you cook the same quantity. Perhaps because it's been dehydrated and hydrated back again (if that's the word for it)—it seems to lose something, something else, I mean, apart from flavour. And although bulk may not be the sort of thing to mention in a cookery book, it is important when you are feeding a family. For growing boys and girls and maybe a husband who does a manual job, bulk counts for something. It doesn't have to be bread and potatoes—bulk can be very tasty and very nourishing, but it requires time to prepare, you can't just open a packet and produce it.

Mention of bulk brings me to what is called a balanced diet, one that is sort of measured in scientific scales and worked out in calories. This is not a scientific cookery book. When I was a cook I didn't know anything about calories or vitamins, and people didn't seem to bother about diets. I've not written a book in which you weigh up the calories—I wouldn't dare with some of the recipes I've given. We didn't cook by science. We selected our menus by common sense and cooked food that was appetizing and nutritive.

Many's the time since I left service that I've gone through my tried and trusted recipes and wondered whether I should keep them. It didn't seem to me that anybody would ever take the time and trouble to prepare the meals that we did when I was a cook. But today there does seem to be a revival of interest in the culinary arts, and modern implements have provided satisfactory short cuts that make it possible to prepare the dishes in much less time than it took us. So I feel that, by giving you the chance to try some of my recipes, you will be able to turn back the pages of history and taste the meals of past generations.

Not that the people I worked for were fabulously wealthy—not by their standards, at any rate. But a considerable portion of their incomes went on food. It was considered absolutely necessary to have three large meals a day: breakfast, lunch and dinner; and the preparation of these occupied the cook and the kitchen maid all day and every day. They did nothing else. They didn't make beds, answer doors or wait on table—preparing food was the sole purpose of their lives.

People didn't eat out much, except when visiting each other's houses. They preferred to eat in the privacy and comfort of their homes, and you can't blame them for that; they had opulent houses, a large staff, tip-top food and service, and if we had those things today we should stay in and enjoy them. It's a way of life that's vanished for ever. Not that I think it's a fact to be mourned. By its nature it was a safe, solid and a secure existence for the few. It could never be emulated by the masses. Not that it worried us particularly, and it didn't rub off on to us. When I married the milkman, who earned a wage of £3.5.0 a week, I had to come down from eating butter to eating margarine, from rump steak to shin of beef or stewing steak, and from cream to evaporated milk, but I was able to accept it easily because we were taught that we were not with 'them' or of 'them', that our worlds were apart in every way; so we didn't ally ourselves to the kind of eating and comfort that they had. We were made to feel different and we *felt* different.

When I wander around London today and look at some of the very large houses where I and other servants that I knew worked, and where we spent so many hours in the dark basements, I find it hard to believe that two worlds could live in one house as we did. One world was a world of warmth, ease and plenty, and the other below stairs so different. Not only did we not count as individuals, but we *knew* we didn't count. We literally lived in the same house but in a world apart. But as I prepared this book I felt that what I was doing was salvaging something that was the best of both these worlds. I now look back on myself not as a skivvy, as we were so derogatively called, but as a person who was doing something that was really worth while, and something that, when I became a cook, I found great pleasure in doing and in having done well. Everyone has to work for a living, but there's a great difference between working at something that is a craft and working at something where you are just a cog in a vast machine and the end result shows nothing of you at all. All right, it's not like painting or sculpture; it isn't something that lives for ever—it's demolished within half an hour of your having prepared it. But nevertheless, there is the pride of achievement. There you are, with the ingredients on the table in front of you—eggs, butter, sugar, meat, fish or what have you—and it's up to you to transform them into something that bears no relation to the separate ingredients, something that isn't lasting, but something about which you hope people will say, 'That was marvellous.'

Food is more than just food. I never eat food because it does me good, I eat it because I like it. I like it to be prepared and cooked well, and I like trouble taken over it. I'm not fussy— I can eat sausages and mash, fish and chips, with the best of people. I'm not pretending that all my days are taken up spending hours over the stove—of course they're not. Nevertheless, there are the occasions, and very frequent occasions, when I spend a lot of time cooking just for the sheer pleasure it gives me.

I would like to make the point that all of the recipes I give have been tried out, and although I can't pretend that they're the sort of things that you can knock up in a few minutes, many of them can be adapted to a simpler pattern. Generally they are leisurely recipes, suiting the leisurely way of life that we had. Leisurely, I mean, for those who ate the food after we'd prepared it. It was a time when eating was a major pleasure in life. Meals were more than something to be enjoyed, they were something to plan, to relish and savour, to compare, criticize and recall. Many's the coroner's inquest we've had on meals next morning when the lady of the house has come down.

So, as I add this to the hundreds of cookery books already published, let me say that even if it is only history, it is history that can be brought to life and, who knows, with the way the world is going, with greater mechanization leading to more leisure, perhaps one day people will again find the time to give to cooking the attention that it deserves.

I

Learning to Cook

Lots of girls nowadays by the time that they get married know a great deal about cooking, because their mothers have let them learn it at home. Today people have got more money and can experiment, but when I was a girl money was so tight and food was so precious that my mother couldn't possibly let me practise at cooking. I used to peel the vegetables and do other odd jobs for her, but that was all. I'd get upset about it because I would have loved to make pastries and cakes. I was always anxious to learn. I knew that other mothers let their daughters cook and I thought Mum was being unkind. When you're young you don't really understand about the shortage of money.

So it was that when I went into domestic service as a kitchen maid at the age of fifteen I knew nothing about cooking at all. This surprised the cook. She was a Scot, and she told me that up there no mother would dream of bringing up a daughter without instructing her in the rudiments of cooking from a very early age, but she was quite kindly. 'Well, gal,' she said when I joined her, 'you're going to have to begin at the beginning. It may be no bad thing at that. At least you'll learn to do things my way. Just keep your eyes and ears open and do as I do or as I tell you.'

The first thing I learned was the utensils that she used and what she used them for: the knives, saucepans and the different kinds of basins and casseroles, the dishes and pie-dishes.

For instance, with pans: for sauces, and especially a sauce that had to be left on the heat, you chose one with a heavy base because sauces, by their very nature, can burn easily.

The size of a dish shouldn't be a matter of speculation. You must choose, for instance, a casserole dish that is large enough to contain all the ingredients that you are going to use, and it's important when you are making a soufflé to ensure that the dish is going to be high enough when the soufflé rises.

One of the first things I did in a practical way was to learn how to prepare vegetables. At home we were very rough and ready. I would take as little of the peel off the potatoes as possible because we needed to economize. I didn't bother about making them look perfectly round in shape or removing every piece of peel, and we cooked all the cabbage, including the stalk, to make it go as far as possible, but in this kitchen none of the outside leaves was used and every leaf was pulled from the stalk. The same with spinach: when my mother cooked spinach she would wash it once and then put the whole lot in. I didn't know that you had to pull off the stalk, wash what was left three or four times at least, and cook it in the smallest amount of water.

Again at home I'd only seen potatoes done three ways: roasted, boiled or mashed. I was astonished when I found the variety of methods there were of preparing them.

Asparagus I'd seen in shops but I'd never handled it. I didn't know that you had to scrape the bottom off each stick, put it into water with a dash of lemon to keep the bottom of the stalks white and then put another dash of lemon juice in the water when you cooked it.

There were (apart from asparagus) vegetables which were unknown to me. Things like artichokes: the Jerusalem ones were the foulest possible things to peel, and the other kind, the globe artichokes. I could never understand why they were both called artichokes, because two more dissimilar vegetables I'd never seen, and when I discovered the small amount that people

2

ate of globe artichokes, I just felt they were a waste of money, but I still had to find out how to prepare them. When the cook asked me whether I knew how to cook vegetables and I said, 'I have a rough idea,' I didn't realize how truthful I was being.

The elementary rules I learned about cooking were that many vegetables are enhanced by adding butter or cream, and that they can be ruined by bad cooking just as easily as any of the more expensive dishes. When she'd felt I'd learnt the rudiments of preparing and cooking vegetables, the cook showed me how to prepare birds for the table. In this particular place we used to have game sent down from Scotland: grouse, partridge and pheasant. All of which was, of course, new to me. The only bird we had at home was a chicken for Christmas.

Of course, I didn't know game had to be hung, unplucked and undrawn, with a hook through the head on a rail in the passage. Sometimes the birds hung there so long that I'd come down and find the heads on the hook and the bodies on the floor. Then the cook would say that they were ready. Plucking them had to be done with great care, because if you pulled the feathers the wrong way you broke the skin. I watched the cook do the first one. I've never seen anyone pluck a bird as quickly as she could. The feathers simply flew. Then I had to learn to gut them, pull the insides out. It was a horrible job, but I had to know how to do it, and finally how to singe them by holding them over the fire.

After this I was initiated into the rites of preparing fish. Often the fish were delivered to the door in a bucket alive, so I had to kill the poor things first. I didn't know where the vulnerable part of the fish was, but after one flapped up just as I was cutting its head off and scratched my nose, I became very wary of them. I used to get the heavy iron poker from the kitchen range and hit them about the head with it. I don't suggest that you do this today. Anyway, fish don't come like that any more. Cook showed me how to prepare fish, how to cut off the fins without cutting into the body, how to remove the head and clean the inside, how to get the black skin off without breaking the flesh and how to fillet. My first efforts weren't always successful, but I learned by trial and error, and when I made errors, that particular fish was given to the servants to eat.

3

The main thing is to have the right kind of knife. Any old knife won't do, and, like all knives, the one used should be kept very sharp. We had a man round every month to do ours.

Then I had to start preparing the meals for the other servants. The cook showed me how to prepare and cook beef that wasn't of the best quality, because naturally we servants didn't have rump or fillet steak. She used to soak it in vinegar and water, the quantity was about one gill of vinegar to one quart of water. It would soak for three or four hours, and this made it tender. Then it was cut up and placed in the dish and water added, barely covering the meat. It was put in the slowest part of the oven and left for an hour and a half before being covered with pastry. She showed me how to flavour it with herbs, rubbing them between the hands until they were fine powder. They weren't powdered in advance because that way they seemed to lose their flavour.

Most that I learned though came from taking the cook's advice to keep my eyes and ears open. As my mother and grandmother told me, very few cooks would explain to a kitchen maid how they made particular dishes. Not because it was a big secret, but with seven or eight people to cook for upstairs, they couldn't be bothered, and no doubt they thought that, as they'd had to learn as they went along, you'd have to do the same. Mind you, I chose my moments, and those moments were generally when the cook had to sit down to do a particular job. She would tell me then.

I remember once when she was making a sponge with just eggs, sugar and flour—no butter. I said, 'Why do you have to sit and beat that for twenty minutes with just a wire whisk?' She explained to me that it was to get as much air as possible into the mixture; that it was the air that made it rise. I'd thought it was just to mix the eggs with the sugar. But if it was an intricate dish I couldn't get anything out of her. So I used to watch. Fortunately, I was blessed with a very good memory, and when I got to my bedroom at night I used to jot down the things I'd seen her do. I didn't always know the proportions, but I learned these later by trial and error.

By the time I left my first place I had a whole notebook filled with dishes. The under-housemaid who I shared a room with used to say, 'I can't see why you bother, you don't get

4

paid any extra, sitting up half the night writing things out.' But when you're an under-housemaid the jobs are just routine; except for the basic things, cooking isn't.

Another thing that helped me was that in one place where I was a cook they used to give a lot of dinner parties with certain special dishes, and the madam would engage a chef to come in and cook these in my kitchen. After we'd served 'them' upstairs, the chef, the butler, myself and the head parlour maid would have our meal afterwards. The drinks would be brought out and the chef would begin to get mellow. Then I'd start to butter him up, flatter him and give him all the old flannel. I'd say that never in my life had I seen such a marvellous dish, and how I would love to be able to make it, but of course it was beyond the powers of poor little me. He would say, 'Oh, it's not as hard as all that.' Then I'd ask him how he got a certain texture and gradually, bit by bit, by the end of the evening I'd have got the recipe out of him.

Another thing I learned as I moved around was that cooks have different methods of doing things. In my first place, for instance, we never had such a thing as a tammy cloth, so that in my second place as kitchen maid, when cook said to me she was making a clear soup, get the tammy cloth out, I didn't know what she meant. 'Huh, fine sort of cook you must have had back at your last place,' she said. It appeared that a tammy cloth was a large piece of fine woollen material, and if you were making either clear soup or a purée, you emptied the mixture into it with a person at each end, and they then twisted the cloth in opposite directions so that the soup or purée would ooze out through it. I must say I thought a hair sieve was just as good. But I later used this bit of knowledge to impress my employer. When I took my first place as a cook, I said to the lady of the house who wanted a clear soup, 'Do you like it put through a hair sieve or a tammy cloth, madam?' I don't think she'd heard of either, but I could see I'd risen in her estimation.

Never, I found, should you say to a cook, 'Oh, but I've seen it done another way.' Nothing riled a cook more, because it sounded as though you were insinuating that it was done better than the way she did it. Husbands often make the same mistake. When I first got married, my husband would sometimes say that he would like a dish that his mother used to make. For instance, a roly-poly pudding with treacle. When I made a treacle pudding I put the treacle at the bottom of the basin and the mixture over it so that when I turned it out the treacle had been cooked with it, but no, he wanted it the way his mother made it, which was a roly-poly in a cloth and the treacle dolloped on afterwards. Easier, yes, but infuriating to a wife who's been a cook, and, of course, if you say anything it looks as if you are criticizing your mother-in-law.

So that's how I learned cooking. Watching, and by trial and error: what you would call the hard way. Just as at that time a farmer's boy learned to be a farm labourer. There was no method about it. You picked it up as you went along. Today, of course, practically every girl is taught at school, and if she shows any real interest, she knows a lot by the time she leaves. If she wants to take it up professionally, there are many ways she can go about it.

She can do it the way I did, by going into domestic service, and domestic service today has a great deal to offer. I know this because I've been back into it recently. Things have changed and changed fast. In my young days I was press-ganged into it by my mother saying it was quite different from when she was a girl; but that was a fallacy. It hadn't altered. The money was better, but as regards the amount of work, the inferiority feeling, the distinctions between 'them' and 'us' and the scarcity of time off, there was no difference at all. But now you've only got to read the advertisements to see that domestic service is a very different proposition.

You see: 'Kitchen maid wanted, £7 per week, own room, television, liberal outings.' Well, you can't say that you're going into 'service' as you were in my day. I'm sure there wouldn't be that difference in the social status between 'them' and you. You would be treated like a person in your own right, allowed to run your life, and there would be far more oppor-tunities to learn how to cook. As well as learning by doing, you could go to evening classes. Again, you wouldn't have the hard work of grating, mincing or beating by hand. You wouldn't be cooking on the kitchen range, lugging in coals from morn-ing till night, washing up with soda or soft soap and ruining your hands. You'd have rubber gloves to work in or barrier creams, you'd have gas or electric stoves, electric mixers, liquidizers, and you'd be sure to have these things because to-

6

day they go with servants, and servants go with money and well-run houses.

If you don't want to go into domestic service, then you can attend a technical college. You can have a complete course and learn every branch of cooking, or if you want to specialize in a particular subject, you can do so. For instance, if you want to be a pastry cook or to know how to make cakes and decorate them, you need only study that and it's possible to earn your living by specializing; and of course there are examinations to pass, then you've got qualifications. Qualifications today in any job are what references were in my day. You can't really get anywhere without them.

Not that I particularly wanted to get anywhere. I just wanted to find myself a husband and to get out of service. You didn't have to have a reference for that.

I think if I had been to a technical college and qualified I wouldn't have gone into service. I'd have gone into a hotel, as a vegetable cook to start with, and then worked my way up to being an assistant chef. I know you don't often hear of women chefs. Men have done their best to keep us out and they've succeeded, largely by bad language, temperamental behaviour (rudeness) and heavy drinking, if what I hear is true; but the quality of their work leaves much to be desired, and they seem to have lost the capacity for taking pains which women still have. So I can see another bastion of masculine superiority falling to us soon.

As I have said, my ambition in life was to find myself a husband and, as a result of the slaughter in the First World War, they weren't easy to come by. I knew the cliché that the way to a man's heart was through his stomach, but first I had to find the man, and having found one, I wasn't given the opportunity of catering for his stomach. Coffee and cake in the kitchen for a tradesman was all I dared chance, but even if I'd been able to offer him what they were getting upstairs, I don't think it would have made the slightest difference because the working class man's stomach couldn't appreciate that kind of food.

Today there are more opportunities for seduction through feeding. Opportunity to travel has titillated men's appetites. So if you have marital ambitions as I had, you're on to a good thing. There again, marriage and family need not be the end of your career. You can advertise yourself as willing to go out and cook dinners at night. There are a number of people who love to give dinner parties but don' t want the chore of doing the cooking. They want to play the hostess and they don't want to be dashing in and out of the kitchen. There's good money in this, and I think it's an ideal way of adding to the family income.

I've told you something about the way I learned to cook. It was a hard way but it wasn't a bad way. Still, it is one that nobody today has to endure because the facilities now for learning to cook are such that no one now getting married has an excuse for saying, 'I don't know how to boil an egg.' I believe that the ability to cook is as important as the roof over your head, the clothes you wear and the entertainments that you expect.

I would say that money spent on food, if you're prepared to take the trouble to choose and cook it well, is never money wasted. If your purse doesn't allow you to buy the expensive food, then find out how to cook the cheaper because, with a little know-how, a little money can go a very long way.

2

Choosing and Buying

One of the first things the cook told me about when I went into service was choosing and buying food. 'All you need, gal,' she said, 'is experience, forethought and common sense.' Well, I had no experience, not of her sort of food; forethought, indeed any sort of thinking, I'd found, was discouraged; but common sense I suppose I did have.

Although the tradesmen used to call for the orders, the cook would often shop around in the afternoon. She could go out every afternoon, not like the under-servants who only had the strict time allotted to them. She said that she went to compare prices, but I don't believe that she was interested in saving money for our employers. I think she went to keep her face in front of the shopkeepers because not only did she get some nice little Christmas boxes but every three months she went round paying the bills; and since about this time she would come back with a new hat or new clothes, it's my opinion she used to collect her percentages—cook's perks—and why not!

I must admit it was very necessary then to know when food was in season; now, with deep freezing, we get practically everything all the year round. In those days, particularly with

9

fruit and vegetables, if you didn't watch for the allotted time you didn't have them at all. And of course the season varied with the weather so that you couldn't fix the dates accurately. You did, of course, with pork: pork was never eaten out of season, and the season was when there was an 'r' in the month. It was the same with fish—particularly trout and salmon. You get them all the year round now, not that frozen salmon bears any resemblance to fresh, but nevertheless, it's there. Shopping wasn't done so much in bulk then; today people often buy enough for the whole week, and some items for even longer.

One thing I remember that was bought in bulk was soap. It was bought by the half-hundredweight in awful mottled grey bars. It was my job to cut them up in slices about two inches thick and lay them along the shelf over the range to harden, and they did harden—like concrete. The same thing happened with candles; we used to harden them too. None of it made much sense when you think how, on the one hand, people would bother about saving money by buying soap in bulk and hardening it so that it would last longer, and on the other, they would spend money on good food and later throw half of it away into the pig bins. 'Economies' like that drive me up the wall.

We also bought potatoes in bulk—sacks of them, and they were kept in one of the cellars that ran under the pavement, with manholes above them. One terrible day the coalman lifted up the wrong manhole and shot a ton of coal right down on top. I thought the cook would have gone stark staring mad. The coal had to stay there; the coalman couldn't possibly have shifted it, so we left it until we gradually worked our way through. By the time we got to the potatoes they weren't a pretty sight or a pretty smell.

Most food was ordered as we wanted it. This the cook did at least once a day by telephone. The tradesmen would deliver, and the cook was very particular that no one ever came with meat, fish or vegetables without her making them wait while she inspected the goods. By watching and listening to her I learned something about choosing.

Beef, she insisted, should always be bright red and very fine grained, with the fat white not yellow. She would prod the meat with her finger, and if it felt clammy or moist it had to be taken back. Mutton had to be dark-coloured otherwise it was returned. It's difficult today to tell what colour the meat is; it all seems to me to be a sort of dull grey. As for the red gravy we used to fight over as children, it's a thing of the past. All I seem to get now is a joint reposing in a pool of water. I suppose the freezing does something to the blood and turns it to water. Veal, unlike beef or mutton, had to be white-coloured, very close grained and dry. Never would cook have veal that was moist; if it was, she returned it saying it was stale.

Fish, too, was carefully examined. I remember her saying something about salmon which I've never heard from anyone else: that it should have a small head, small tail and thick shoulders. I remember smiling and saying, 'I didn't know a salmon had shoulders.' That, I found, was a mistake. I never tried to be funny again.

Regularly we had chickens. Fowl, cook said, had to have smooth legs and a smooth comb; if either the legs or the comb were rough, it was an old bird. Then white-legged fowls were for boiling and dark-legged ones for roasting. When we had duck they were chosen for their yellow feet and yellow bills; the feet had to be pliable, because if a duck had stiff feet, according to cook, it was stale.

Many people think, and it's probably because of the various hygiene laws that have been introduced in recent years, that there was a lot of dirty food around in the early twenties; and our methods of choosing food by handling it are considered unhygienic today. Perhaps they were, but if you want to make the right choice I can't believe that there's any other way of doing it. I think in the old days it was what happened to food after it had been taken home that caused the food poisoning.

Look at our supermarkets. There's the food arrayed on the racks and the public prod it. I have seen them pick up loaves and feel them to see if they're new or not and then put them back. I know many articles are wrapped in Cellophane, but someone is handling them when he wraps them and you don't see him do it. Whereas in my day you went into the shop and watched the assistant cut what you wanted of, say, cheese. You could see whether his hands were clean and you saw where the cheese came from. Today that kind of thing is done behind the scenes. I prefer seeing it done and seeing where it comes from. I was brought up on the motto that cleanliness was next to godliness—and when I was a cook I preached the same gospel.

The kitchen tables were witness to this. Talk about whiter than white. And larders—why, the smell of the larder in my first place was like a garden in spring. On the shelves were pieces of charcoal which kept it sweet. Although cook would select fresh meat she would keep it until she knew it was ready, and it would be sprinkled with herbs and powdered charcoal, which were washed from it before it was cooked, but the meat would taste like ambrosia or whatever comparison you may like to make. At any rate, whatever meat you ate you knew what it was, and if you were sat blindfold in front of meat today you'd have difficulty guessing.

The whole business of shopping has, of course, changed. Naturally, when I was in service we used the 'best' shops, and because we were good customers, we were given the best. When we weren't satisfied we were allowed to criticize and return the goods. We were on very friendly terms with the tradesmen and errand boys. Ideas would be exchanged and discussed between us so that choosing and ordering was a pleasant business.

Today for many of us shopping can be a chore. You set out with your two-wheel basket, battle your way round two or three supermarkets, pick up your tins, packets and Cellophane bags and try to work out how much you have spent. This operation makes me look like a lunatic because I have to add up out loud—I'm no good at mental arithmetic—so I stand there talking to myself while the other customers give me queer looks and a wide berth. You never get to know the staff— there's no friendly banter. Those that you do see standing round you feel sure are store detectives watching your every move. Then you queue up to pay the cashier, whose eyes are down on your basket and whose fingers click up the figures like some super bingo player. Then you're in the street and starting to regret half the things you've bought, but it's too late. There's no going back. You haven't the stamina or the courage.

Well, that's how it used to be for me. Then I saw I was becoming a nervous wreck so I decided to change my ways. Now what I do is what I call shopping around, and I look on it as an adventure. If you shop around you can save yourself up to twelve shillings a week or more if you've got a family of, say, yourself, your husband and four children. It's a matter of taking trouble looking and not buying everything that's in the one place because it happens to be convenient. (Most people have got more time to do the shopping in today because the housework isn't as tedious, nor does it take up the time that it used to.) You also want to make sure that you're getting what you're paying for. Don't pick up a packet and think to yourself that it holds half a pound or a pound, because it doesn't necessarily show. Manufacturers use various weights and measures to baffle the liveliest brains—and packets and cartons are, as the Bible says, 'a snare and a delusion'. And it's the same with jam. Most of the pots of jam that look exactly like the old pound pots did you'll find contain only fourteen ounces. So you want to swot up on weights like grams so that you've got some inkling of what the actual contents are.

I was in a supermarket the other day studying two bottles of sauce, one of fourteen grams and the other of twenty-five grams and trying to work out if it was cheaper to get the bigger bottle. An assistant came up and said, 'Can I help you?' so I said, 'Yes, how many ounces are there in fourteen grams and how many ounces in twenty-five grams?' He grinned at me and said, 'I don't know, mother; it's all Greek to me.'

One of the most important points when you're buying pre-packed things is to make sure they weigh what they say they weigh. Shops are compelled by law to provide scales for the customers to check the weight. I've found that very few customers take advantage of this. Perhaps they're afraid of the peculiar looks they'll get from the assistants. I'm not. I do it regardless of the way the other customers gawp at me as if I was a sort of freak. All too often I've found goods underweight, never over weight. This is cheating and I don't like being cheated.

Another imposition I ran across recently was over the price of sausages. They were 3s. 7d. a pound, but if you bought under a pound they were rated at 3s. 9d. a pound. I tackled the manager on this (managers make a beeline for the back of the shop now when they see me coming in, they've got to know me). He said it took longer to weigh them and wrap them. That's an absurd argument and a cheat, particularly in a town where there is a large percentage of old people who don't want a pound of sausages at a time.

I've advocated shopping around, but as far as meat is

concerned, my advice is find yourself a good small butcher and settle for him: if possible a man who owns his own shop and who takes pride in his meat and will do what you ask him. Once you've found him keep him happy, butter him up, flatter him, joke with him, play on the old masculine ego. It'll be worth the effort. For instance, if you want to make a liver pâté, he'll mince it for you—you won't get it done in a supermarket, they sell their own. He'll salt beef for you—you can choose the beef yourself and then he'll salt it. It's not like choosing a piece of salted beef in a shop when you don't know how long it's been out of the brine. He'll get to know your likes and dislikes and the depth of your pocket.

I've got a magnificent butcher. He took some finding; he's one of the old school—he still wears a straw hat. I've always found that a butcher who wears a straw hat is a good butcher; it's a symbol of the trade. My butcher's father was a butcher and so was his grandfather; they always wore straw hats so he wears a straw hat. It may not look very hygienic—but he never says that you or he should eat it. When I go there he knows I haven't a lot of money and that I like the best possible value and he advises me. He shows me not only what's good for today but things that are going to be ready in two or three days' time. All right, it costs a penny or two more than the supermarkets, but real service, advice and help save money every time.

Living as I do by a seaside town, the thought of buying frozen fish from the supermarkets has never entered my head. Even if I lived inland it wouldn't. It has the taste and consistency of cotton wool and it's expensive. Again, I know the fishmonger and I've made it my business to be friendly. I go in and tell him what I want and I add that I don't want it to come to more than two shillings. 'What do you think this is,' he says, 'a bloody draper's shop?' But he's prepared to play along and give you what he knows you want. He knows what's fresh and what's good. It pays you to stick to one man if you can. You can't expect anyone to take the same interest when they know that you're either a casual shopper, or you're making a convenience of them because you haven't got the time to get to your usual supermarket.

Again, although I don't always stick to the same one, I like to buy at a greengrocer's rather than a supermarket. I like to inspect a cabbage and make sure it's got a heart to it, to look at cauliflowers and to feel the sprouts. I don't want to find everything done up in tight Cellophane bags. I don't think I'm mean, but it worries me that they don't sell vegetables by weight; they sell them by the packet. It's the same with apples and tomatoes, you can't really tell what they're like. It stands to reason, doesn't it, that somebody has to be paid to clean and wrap things in bags, be it potatoes, cabbages, tomatoes, apples or what have you, and those wages are passed on to you. What's the point, because when you get home you cut the Cellophane off and you throw it away. So what have you paid for? Something that's no good to you at all.

I suppose I can be accused of clinging too much to the old ways of doing things. What I found a pleasure is looked on today as a chore, but shopping then was a pleasure because the shops were small, you were known and you were welcomed. You never had to look round to find and see what you wanted. The shopkeepers would tell you of any new lines they had in and you would have time to think, because you didn't do your shopping on just one day a week. You made a regular thing of it and it was a matter which concerned the shopkeepers and you. Today the shopkeepers have dropped out and it's a contest between the manufacturers and you as to whether they are going to capture your precious bit of money. They're at you with their advertising on television, in newspapers and on hoardings, through your letter-box and by door-to-door canvassing. The shop is just a collection depot for their goods. If you complain to a shop manager he tells you to write to the manufacturer.

Since choosing good materials is so much a part of good cooking, we've reached a very low state, but I still feel that there are a few shops left that cater for people who want to cook well, so it's worth while shopping around, pitting your wits against the manufacturers and making sure that you don't pay more than you should.

3
Kitchen Equipment

I remember when I first went into service as a kitchen maid the sense of amazement I had when I saw the kitchen range. It was a vast, black, shiny thing that took up the whole of one side of the room. This, although I didn't know it at the time, was to become a nightmare to me, with the endless stoking, cleaning and polishing that it required. But, like its modern counterparts, it was the most important item of kitchen equipment, and as such I was required to give it the respect the cook felt it deserved.

Despite its size there were only two main ovens on either side of the fire. The larger oven, owing to the way the flues were arranged, got much hotter than the smaller which was used to make cakes or anything that needed very slow cooking. The larger one was used to roast, for making pastry or for anything that wanted a quick oven.

To grill, you lifted the top off the fire and made it an open fire, put an iron plate over it and grilled the meat on that. Whatever you were cooking had to be watched the whole time and continually basted. You couldn't leave it because the heat of the fire was such that the outside would have become hard

16

and dry. Frying was also done on the middle part of the range. Again, you couldn't put things on and leave them; they needed constant watching.

When I look back I find it extraordinary how very little was ever spoilt using kitchen ranges. I remember cooking a wedding cake, four tiers. The bottom two tiers were cooked in the large oven and the two smaller tiers in the small oven. They didn't burn; indeed, they were cooked to perfection. But I don't think that cooking the way we did, the hard way, was better. Equally good results can be obtained by cooking on electricity, by gas or oil-fire stoves. It's only heat that cooks food. There's no special merit attached to coal as coal.

Equipping a kitchen in the twenties was a major operation. Four large saucepans were permanently in evidence—the stock pots. We always had four kinds of stock on the go: white, brown, clear soup stock and a fish stock, and every other day two of these were boiled up, so that each day we had two large iron saucepans on the kitchen range.

There was a large fish kettle with its perforated platform fitting inside which could be lifted straight out of the kettle and the fish rolled on to the plate without breaking the skin. There were countless copper saucepans for general use, and foul they were to clean. We must have had, too, at least half a dozen large enamel pans. And there was a thing called a bain-marie: a huge square pan which was filled with boiling water, and there were little saucepans fitted inside, and into these we poured the sauces. The bainmarie would then be put to one side of the stove and the sauces were kept hot and ready to serve. It wouldn't be very much good, though, on a gas or electric stove unless the stove was exceptionally large, because it took up a lot of room.

We had a three-tiered steamer, as many vegetables were just steamed, two frying pans which were made of iron, and an enamel omelet pan. I don't recommend enamel pans for omelets as they were always inclined to stick.

On the kitchen table there were two or three colanders, nutmeg graters, flour dredgers, mincing machines, a coffee mill, smaller mills in which we ground peppers, all worked by hand —very hard. There were two or three sieves—practically everything seemed to be put through sieves, a wire sieve or hair sieve, and of course an absolute necessity to most recipes in those days: pestles and mortars. We had two, one large, one small, and in the middle of the table were the scales.

In the cupboards and on the dresser were the other things for occasional use, the tins, pans for the joints, Yorkshire pudding tins, pastry tins, the flat tart tins and the dozens of basins of all shapes and sizes. And cook's knives: I was bewildered by the variety of knives cook used. There were knives for preparing meat, knives for fish, pastry knives, knives for gouging shapes out of vegetables, knives for peeling them, knives for removing eyes, knives for chopping, knives for cutting rind off the bacon—a separate knife for everything. And the same with scissors; the cook had four pairs of scissors always on the table. And of course toasting forks, because the only way we could toast was by holding the bread to the fire.

There were the fancy moulds—moulds to make borders for mashed potatoes, moulds for aspic jelly, and of course dish covers, because flies were in abundance. Flies, like fleas, seem to have disappeared from kitchens, but then nothing could be put in the larder without having its wire-mesh meat cover, and anything that was in a jug or cup had to have its own little muslin cover weighted down with beads.

Then there was a marble slab to roll pastry on. I use one even today. And there was a very heavy iron implement that flattened the steak out. Nowadays they make them with spikes on—perhaps the kind of steak you get now needs to be penetrated by spikes.

We didn't have a refrigerator, instead we had wooden tubs in which we kept the ice. Anything we wanted to freeze we stood in these. In my first place we even had an icehouse out in the garden. I can't quite remember how it was made, but it seemed to be after the style of the Eskimo igloos.

I'm often asked what I think has been the greatest invention for the kitchen since my early days, and have no hesitation in saying it's the non-stick saucepan and frying-pan. I say this because there are so many recipes which are very much improved if cooked with the smallest amount of grease, whether it's butter, lard or dripping. In the old days we couldn't cook anything in a frying-pan or a saucepan with only a little fat, it would have stuck like glue, no matter how we tried moving it around. So with these non-stick pans, greasy food is a thing of the past.

Another boon is the big number of Pyrex brand dishes in which you can cook and serve straight to the table. They are particularly useful if you are casserolling very delicate birds like quail, woodcock and snipe. We had to transfer these from our oven dishes into entrée dishes while trying to keep their shape and heat.

I very much enjoy using these new copper saucepans. Very unlike the ones that we had which had to be cleaned with a combination of silver sand, salt and lemon or vinegar every time they were used, and which ruined your hands and nails. I also like the heavy-bottomed aluminium pans—you can put them on the side of the stove and have the heat at the very minimum and they will go on cooking.

Then, of course, there are all the electric gadgets that are on the market now, the mixers and liquidizers. It seems to me that these things are very much a matter of opinion. I've worked for people who have them and wouldn't be without them, and for those who have them and never use them. I haven't got them, and it's not inverted snobbery when I say I don't want them. It's just that I enjoy cooking, and since I cook for the pleasure of it, and time is of no particular object, the possession of gadgets doesn't appeal to me. When I cook I sort of go to town on it. I often spend a whole day doing nothing else, and now one has the advantages of a refrigerator, it is amazing how much cooking can be done in advance. I can make up sauces and stocks and keep them for a week in the fridge. Perhaps to me cooking is a kind of therapy, because I enjoy using an ordinary mincer and I like rubbing things through a wire sieve and pounding away with my pestle and mortar. But if you don't like cooking and if you've got the money to buy the things that rid you of the chores, then I see no reason why you shouldn't use them because they help to cook meals quickly and well. I sometimes think, though, that I would like an electric beater for making Yorkshire puddings or to mash potatoes or mix a sponge, because as I get older I find I haven't the strength in my arms that I had when I was young, and there's no short cut if you're doing it by hand.

Another thing I'm asked is, if I was able to design a kitchen, what would it be like. I'm best able to answer that question by saying what it wouldn't be like. By that I mean one of those places with built-in sink units, wall cupboards, formica-topped fittings, plastic curtains and strip lighting, in which you prepare a meal in rubber gloves and white housecoat—only needing a face mask to make quite certain you're in a hospital operating theatre.

No, I'd like a kitchen-cum-dining-room. A place where the food is cooked, served and eaten, and a kind of liaison kept between the act of cooking and the act of eating. A lot of love, even devotion, goes into preparing and cooking good food, and I think that this can be lost when it is transferred to a separate dining-room.

I would like the kitchen to be the focal point of the house—the epitome of home—a place that looks good, smells good and where things taste good.

4

Hors d'oeuvre

Hors d'œuvre in my time have become very fashionable. My grandmother and my mother were both cooks and neither prepared hors d'œuvre when they were in domestic service. I don't think they were served in my first place as kitchen maid in Brighton, but they were when I moved to London. Now, of course, everyone has hors d'œuvre, or 'starters' as they call them. I must admit that it's an ideal course to begin with, especially if you've a substantial main dish. When I was a cook and we had hors d'œuvre, we always had soup as well—'them' upstairs would no more dream of leaving out the soup course than the main meat course. I think that this hors d'œuvre type of food has come in more because of the shortage of time and the shortage of servants. Now the hostess who is giving a small dinner party has got to do almost everything herself, so it's ideal for her. Then again, people give these buffet type of parties where the guests all stand up and help themselves; so again everything can be prepared well in advance.

Before I gave up working I often used to go in the evenings to where I worked in the mornings when they were giving a small dinner party for, say, six to seven people. Ostensibly I was there to do the washing-up afterwards, but naturally I used to help beforehand. Preparing hors d'œuvre is great fun because you can really go to town on them. It gives you a marvellous opportunity to be original. Maybe you get the recipe out of a book, but there are so many things that you can do to suit yourself or express yourself, not only in the composition of the dish but in garnishing it. Hors d'œuvre lend themselves to decoration more than any dish I know. The whole idea of them is surely to stimulate the appetite, so that the more tempting you make them look, the more they're serving their purpose. You can make a colour symphony with hors d'œuvre, and I found that I became quite an artist with fish, meat and veg; also I used to enjoy doing hors d'œuvre as I didn't have to rush them—not like those last-minute dishes that you've got to send up elaborately garnished and hot as well.

Perhaps the reason hors d'œuvre weren't so popular when I was in service was that then people didn't need anything to stimulate their appetites. They'd got enormous ones, otherwise they couldn't have got through a four-course lunch and a six-course dinner each day. Then perhaps the most popular starter was oysters, just as they were, with lemon and brown bread and butter. They didn't need decorating: they looked lovely on their own in their shells on a bed of ice and surrounded by lemon.

Caviare was another favourite. We used to serve it in various ways, and I've given one or two recipes, but I still think that the best way to serve it is in its original jar. We used to stand the jar in a silver container with slivers of ice all the way round.

Today people seem to have gone mad on smoked salmon, but unless you buy it by the side and keep it well or select it very carefully, it can look and taste as if it's been hanging on a clothes-line to dry. Restaurants nowadays seem to be very conservative with their hors d'œuvre, which means that your guest will appreciate the kind you can put on your table at very little expense.

Then there are fancy butters: you can make them with anchovy, lobster, and the coral from the crab. I give recipes for these in the chapter on Sauces and Garnishes. While hot hors d'œuvre are perhaps more complicated, if you're missing the soup course it can be a good thing to serve. For example, small patties of puff pastry filled with crab, lobster or game, and served with a sauce, or chicken livers. It has always amused me that you can get chicken livers without the chicken. What happens to the bird! Or do some chickens have spare livers!

To sum up, then, if you are giving a party, whether it's a formal sit-down one or a buffet-type, it's good to start off with hors d'œuvre, but remember they need to be very small to excite the eye and to stimulate the appetite. The greater the variety the better, and try combining hot with cold. Don't just stick to the usual things that you get in restaurants, like smoked salmon, prawn cocktail or melon—be original, and this is not difficult as there are so many things on the market today. Even forty years ago I've prepared as many as a dozen cold and half a dozen hot: and there can be no better reason for serving them than that people love them.

Anchovy Canapés

Makes ½ dozen. Time: 20 minutes

6 whole anchovies
1 hardboiled egg
2 teaspoons olive oil

1 teaspoon chopped parsley
paprika pepper

Wash the anchovies, remove the backbone; sieve the egg. Put into a mortar the anchovies, egg, parsley, pinch of pepper and 1 teaspoon of the olive oil. Pound well together; put a teaspoon or more of the mixture on to rounds of buttered brown bread. Just before serving put a drop or two of the oil on each round.

Anchovy Salad

6 persons. Time: 20 minutes

6 whole anchovies
1 lettuce
1 hardboiled egg

3 teaspoons olive oil
1 teaspoon chopped chervil
paprika pepper

Wash the anchovies, dry them on a soft cloth and carefully remove the backbone. Wash and dry the lettuce and pick 6 leaves from the heart. Arrange these in an hors d'œuvre dish, place an anchovy in each and sprinkle the sieved egg and chervil and a shake of pepper on each one. Pour about ½ teaspoon of olive oil over just before serving.

Cantaloup Salad

Time: 20 minutes

1 ripe cantaloup melon
1 glass white wine
pinch powdered ginger

2 tablespoons tarragon
  vinegar
paprika pepper

Peel the melon and cut the flesh into small cubes. Put into a bowl, add the ginger and a shake of pepper. Mix the wine and vinegar together and pour it over the melon. Serve very cold.

Caviare with Smoked Salmon

1 per person. Time: 15 minutes

smoked salmon (Scotch)
1 jar caviare
lemon

chopped gherkins
chervil
tarragon vinegar

Cut the smoked salmon into very thin slices—allow one small slice per person; on each slice place 1 teaspoon of caviare, roll up the slice. Place in an hors d'œuvre dish and sprinkle with a few drops of tarragon vinegar. Garnish with the gherkins, chervil and slices of lemon; hand thin slices of brown bread and butter and black pepper.

Chicken Canapés

4 to 6 persons. Time: 20 minutes

2 oz. cooked chicken or
  tongue
2 oz. lean ham
1 oz. Cheddar cheese
  (grated)

2 oz. butter
2 teaspoons anchovy essence
pinch cayenne pepper
chopped parsley

Mince the chicken and ham, put it into a mortar with all the other ingredients and pound until it is the consistency of paste. Spread this mixture on rounds of fried bread—one per person. Put in a hot oven for a few minutes before serving. Garnish with chopped parsley.

Eggs with Foie Gras

6 persons. Time: 15 minutes

3 hardboiled eggs
1 small jar foie gras
1 gill cream

watercress or lettuce
paprika pepper
salt

Shell the eggs, remove the yolks, cut the whites into halves and cut a small piece off the ends to make them stand firmly. Put the yolks into a mortar with about ½ tablespoon of foie gras and pound well. Add the cream, pinch of pepper, and salt to taste. Put the mixture into the egg white cases piling it up in the middle. Serve very cold on a bed of lettuce or watercress.

Eggs with Prawns

6 persons. Time: 20 minutes

3 hardboiled eggs
1 dessertspoon chopped
  capers
1 tablespoon filleted
  anchovies
1 small pickled onion, finely
  chopped

1 teaspoon Worcester
  sauce
cayenne pepper
boiled prawns
watercress

Shell the eggs, cut them in half lengthwise and take out the yolks. Put into a mortar the yolks of eggs, capers, anchovies, sauce and a pinch of pepper and pound well. Add the chopped onion and share out the mixture into the cases of hardboiled eggs. Arrange these on a bed of watercress with the prawns piled up in the middle, or three or four placed on each egg.

Grapefruit Cup

6 persons. Time: 15 minutes

3 grapefruit
small bottle cherries

pinch ground ginger
Maraschino or sherry

Remove the pulp and juice from the grapefruit and put it into a basin. Add the cherries (halves), the ginger and 2 to 3 tablespoons of maraschino or sherry. Mix well and serve very cold.

Langoustine Cocktail

4 to 6 persons. Time: 20 minutes

2 doz. large prawns
1 tablespoon shredded chives
tomato ketchup

1 lemon
castor sugar
paprika pepper

The prawns should be already boiled. Flake out the white meat into cocktail glasses, lightly powder with sugar and squeeze a little lemon juice over. Put a dessertspoon of tomato ketchup on top, shred chives over, add a shake of pepper. Chill before serving.

Liver Pâté

Time: 50 to 60 minutes

1 lb. pig's liver
¾ lb. streaky bacon
1 large egg
1 tablespoon cream

½ teaspoon mixed chopped
   herbs
pepper, salt

Put the liver twice through the mincer, get your butcher to do the first mincing, cut the rind from the bacon and put the rashers through the mincer also. Put the minced liver and bacon into a basin, add the herbs, beaten egg, cream and seasoning to taste. Mix well together, put into a greased mould and cover with foil, then stand the mould in a deep baking tin with enough water to reach half-way up the sides of the mould, cook in the oven for ¾ to 1 hour. When cooked, take out of oven, leave to cool, turn out and wrap in a piece of foil. This pâté will keep for some time in a refrigerator.

Larks' Tongues Pâté

Time: 1 to 1¼ hours

3 doz. larks' tongues
½ lb. truffles
4 oz. pork liver
6 oz. ham

1 or 2 eggs
½ gill cream
1 tablespoon brandy
pepper, salt

Pass the ham and liver twice through a mincer, then rub through a wire sieve. Put the larks' tongues into a mortar, pound well. Add the chopped truffles, cream, beaten egg (or eggs), brandy and seasoning to taste. Put into a greased mould, cover with

grease-proof paper and tie a piece round to reach above the top.
Steam for 1 to 1¼ hours. (I have never made this, neither had the
old cook who gave me the recipe, but she had seen it made far
back in the days when she was a kitchenmaid.)

Marino Patties

Puff pastry cases   1 gill Béchamel sauce
1 lamb or calf's sweetbread   1 gill cream
¼ lb. ham   parsley (chopped)
¼ lb. mushrooms   butter and lemon

Wash the sweetbread, soak in cold water for 1 hour. Rinse, then
blanch by putting the sweetbread into a pan with just enough
water to cover, add a few drops of lemon-juice, slowly bring to
the boil, cook gently for about 5 minutes, strain and put into a
basin of cold water. Remove all fat, veins and membranes; press
between two plates. Peel the mushrooms, fry in a little butter,
chop them, the sweetbread and ham finely. Mix together with the
Béchamel sauce and cream, make hot and put into the warmed
pastry-cases. Just before serving, sprinkle with the parsley.

Melon Cocktail

Time: 15 minutes

canteloup or rock melon   Maraschino or Kirsch
castor sugar

Peel the melon, cut the flesh into dice, put into a bowl and
liberally sprinkle with the sugar and as much Maraschino or
Kirsch as liked. Put the bowl into the refrigerator until very cold.
Serve in individual glasses.

Olives (stuffed)

2 per person. Time: About 20 minutes

1 doz. Spanish olives (large)   1 small jar foie gras
1 hardboiled egg yolk   paprika pepper
1 oz. butter   fried bread

Fry small rounds of bread—about an inch in diameter—in fat and
leave on soft paper to drain. Put into a mortar the foie gras, egg

yolk and a small piece of butter, pound well together, then pass through a sieve. Remove the stones from the olives and fill them with the foie gras mixture; let some of it show at one side. Place an olive in the centre of each round of bread and serve garnished with parsley.

Oyster Cocktail

2 or 3 oysters per person. Time: 10 minutes

oysters   tarragon vinegar
Worcester sauce   lemon juice
tomato ketchup   cayenne pepper

The oysters must be very fresh. Put 2 or 3 into individual glasses. Well mix together in a basin 1 tablespoon of lemon juice, 1 tablespoon of tomato ketchup, ½ tablespoon of tarragon vinegar, ½ teaspoon of Worcester sauce and a pinch of pepper. Put this over the oysters and serve very cold. (As well as being an appetizer, this is a good, 'morning after the night before' pick-me-up; guaranteed to kill or cure.)

Pineapple Pourri

6 to 8 persons. Time: 20 to 30 minutes

1 large tin crushed pineapple   2 tablespoons mayonnaise
2 Cox's apples   (see p. 135)
½ head celery   chervil
1 small truffle (optional)   cayenne pepper

Peel and core the apples, put them into a bowl with the pineapple, the washed and finely cut celery, chopped truffle if used, and a good pinch of cayenne. Add the mayonnaise and mix well together. Keep in the refrigerator until required. Serve in individual glasses sprinkled with the chervil.

5

Soups

From the age of seven and until after I had been in service for some time, the word soup had the same effect on me as did the use of bad language. It reminded me of the time when I knew the real mortification of poverty, when I had to take the family wash-stand jug to the soup kitchen for 'charity' soup—then watery pea soup. But for many years now I have enjoyed both preparing and eating soups.

Today I suppose you can say that there are three ways of making soups. The easiest way, of course, is to buy it in a tin or packet. It is certainly a means of providing a quick meal; present-day ready-made soups are very good indeed, and they can be embellished in lots of ways. For instance, if you're buying a tin of cream of chicken, asparagus, or celery soup, or any of the white soups, they're much enhanced by the addition of a tablespoon of cream or a knob of butter. The same applies to tomato soup. And if you're buying a brown soup, mulliga-tawny or oxtail, then a little Worcestershire sauce adds to the flavour, or mushroom ketchup or anchovy sauce; these things make it something it wasn't when you tipped it out. But if you're going to use any of my recipes you have to start by making stock. The easiest way is, of course, to use stock cubes and, having dissolved these in water, add anything in the way of vegetables—onions, carrots, turnips, swedes; any of these increases the value of the cubes.

If, however, you are prepared to take the trouble, there is only one real way to make soups and that is from stock which you prepare yourself. For most meat soups you need only bones and vegetables as a basis. But if you want to make a consommé or a clear soup, then you have to have meat: shin of beef does very well, so does knuckle of veal, the latter making the gelatine you need for consommé.

I divide soups into five different kinds: the broth type, thick soup, purée, clear, and finally, fish soup. Fish soup is on its own because it has a different stock.

Broth is an easy one. It is the liquid in which you have boiled chicken, rabbit, veal or mutton, anything like that with vegetables and barley or rice added. You don't need to thicken it.

Then we come to thick soups. For these you can use stock of any kind, according to the type of soup that you're making, whether it's white soup, brown or vegetable. If you haven't got enough stock, you can supplement with milk, or milk and water; but I use milk for vegetable soups only by adding it to the vegetable water.

For thick soups I use either flour or arrowroot to give them thickness. For a very rich soup, such as Good Woman's soup (why it was called that I don't know. Perhaps because it was as difficult to make as it was to find a good woman), the thickening would be yolks of eggs and cream. It's a delicate soup and has to be treated very carefully, particularly when adding the yolks of eggs.

Purée you might think comes under the heading of a thick soup, but it's quite a different type. It differs because it is not thickened with flour, arrowroot or cornflour but with peas, lentils or beans which are cooked in the stock, rubbed through a sieve, and put back in the pan, thus making a thick purée.

Clear soup is the most difficult to make, although once you've got the hang of it, it's quite easy. It is a trouble but not an anxiety. You must start with a very good stock. You can't make it with just bones or any old scraps of meat you've got left, or vegetable water. The recipe for the stock I give is among those at the beginning of the collection that follows; it needs to be done in two stages.

When it's clear, you can colour it with caramel to your liking, either having it a very pale brown, golden brown or dark brown, which ever you think helps to set off the other courses. (By the way, never put potato in a clear soup because it clouds immediately.) I used to enjoy dicing the vegetables. We had those fancy cutters which made little stars and crescents and that sort of thing—it appealed to my childish mind. Sometimes we'd add vermicelli or noodles. These were put into the soup about fifteen to twenty minutes before it was ready to be served. One cook I had didn't put them into the soup; they were cooked separately, kept hot and then put into the soup later or the soup poured straight on to them. She said that anything added to a clear soup took away its clearness. She was right, of course, but it is going a bit far.

Some people say that they dislike fish soups because either the flavour is too strong or it tastes of nothing at all; but it doesn't have to be the one or the other, it's just a matter of taking care with the seasonings. I have often bought fish such as whiting, cod or rock salmon, all comparatively cheap, simmered it gently in equal quantities of milk and water—or water only if I had no milk—then carefully lifted out the fish, thickened the liquid with flour or cornflour to serve as soup before the fish. Once the fish is removed, taste the liquid to see if it needs more seasoning, be careful not to over-salt; a teaspoon of Anchovy ketchup will give added flavour if the soup seems insipid.

The thing to remember with soup is that you simply cannot rush it. If the recipe says simmer slowly, and they practically all do say simmer slowly, it's no good thinking you can boil rapidly for half an hour and get the same effect. You won't. It's a case of do as you're told. When you buy fresh bones they need at least five to six hours of slow simmering to get the goodness from them, then take them out, put in the vegetables and simmer slowly. It takes a long time to get a stockpot, but once you've made it you can keep adding to it and, with a refrigerator, you don't have to boil it up every day as we did. Be very careful how you season stock because it's the basis of many sauces, and if it is too highly seasoned it can ruin the flavour of a particular kind of sauce. Seasoning can always be added afterwards. It's the flavour of the bones and vegetables with the salt and the pepper that counts.

Many people have their own idea of what to put in a stockpot. If I have a chicken or a gamebird, the carcase goes in, so do lamb bones or mutton bones. Giblets and bacon rinds are very good indeed; in fact any odd pieces of meat that are left over can be used. The remains of gravy from the Sunday joint often gets thrown down the sink because you don't know what to do with it. Put that in. Any odd root vegetables that are not enough to do anything with can go in, but I never add cooked vegetables to the stockpot because they can soon turn it sour. Also, when all the goodness is extracted from the raw vegetables, don't leave them in either. Strain and throw them away.

Although this book is not intended for vegetarians, it is possible to make a very good soup without using any meat or bone at all. We hear that the French are horrified at the way we throw our vegetable water down the sink, and I suppose they're right when they say there's more nutriment in the water than in what you've cooked, but when I cook I'm not counting the calories and such-like. I cook, as I've said, because I enjoy eating, not because it's going to do me good. I hope it does good as well but that, like the vegetable water, is only incidental.

One further hint: when you're first starting a stockpot and if you've bought bones from the butcher, it's a good idea to leave them in cold water for an hour or two (using the same water that you're going to boil them in), because the cold water draws out the meat juices. If you put the stockpot straight over the heat, this tends to set the bones. Another thing to remember is to keep skimming off the fat as it rises until it is almost boiling. You'll find for the first hour the fat constantly comes to the surface. A good way to help this is to put in a little cold water, perhaps half a cup, and this makes the scum rise and also makes for a good clear stock.

Stock for Clear Soup

Time: 4 to 5 hours

1½ lb. shin of beef
1 lb. knuckle of veal
1 fair-sized onion
1 fair-sized carrot
1 small turnip
1 stick celery

muslin bag of herbs (parsley,
   thyme, bay leaf & mace)
½ doz. peppercorns
3 cloves
½ teaspoon salt

Cut the meat into small pieces and put into a pan with the bones.
(If marrow in the bones, scrape out, otherwise the soup may be
cloudy.) Add the salt, bring to the boil, remove scum. Add half
a cup of cold water to help the scum to rise again, simmer for an
hour, taking care to remove all the scum as it rises. Now add the
peeled vegetables—not cut up—and the herbs, simmer for another
3 hours. The pan must have a tightly-fitted lid. Strain, and when
cold, remove all fat from top.

Clearing the stock

5 to 6 persons. Time: 25 to 30 minutes

4 oz. lean beef
1 small carrot
1 small turnip

2 pts clear soup stock
The whites and shells 2 eggs

Put the stock into a very clean pan. Remove all fat from meat and
put it through a mincer, add it to the stock with the sliced carrot
and turnip. Slightly whisk the egg whites, crush the shells, add
them to the stock, whisk over a fair heat until almost boiling.
Remove whisk, lower heat, let the soup just simmer for 20
minutes. Strain through a clean scalded tea-cloth or fine soup
strainer. Add seasoning if required.

Bone Stock

Time: About 4 hours

Meat bones, cooked or un-
   cooked
2 carrots
2 or 3 sticks celery
bunch herbs

½ doz. peppercorns
salt
1 quart water to each 1 lb.
   bones

Remove the fat from the bones, break them into small pieces and
put into a pan, cover with the cold water and quickly bring to the

boil to make the scum rise. Remove this, add a little more cold water and boil to make the scum rise again, skim off every particle, then add the washed and peeled vegetables, herbs, peppercorns and salt to taste. Bring to the boil again and simmer for 3 hours; strain and leave to get cold then carefully remove all fat from the top.

Game Stock

Time: 4 hours

Trimmings, meat and bones of any kind of game (about 2 lb.)	1 medium onion
	1 sprig each thyme and parsley
1 ham-bone or 4 oz. lean bacon	2 bay leaves
1 lb. shin of beef	1 blade mace
3 medium carrots	½ doz. peppercorns
1 large leek	¼ teaspoon celery salt
	3 quarts water

The game can be cooked or uncooked. Cut the shin of beef into small pieces, put it into a pan with the game, ham-bone or bacon, cover with the water, bring to the boil and skim well. Add the washed, peeled and cut-up vegetables, the herbs, bay leaves, mace, pepper-corns, celery salt and about ½ teaspoon of salt. Bring to the boil again, simmer gently for 4 hours, strain and leave to get cold, then remove every particle of fat from the top.

BROWNING FOR STOCKS AND SOUPS

Put ½ lb. of lump sugar into a pan with ½ gill of cold water. Leave on a low heat until the sugar has dissolved, then boil quickly until it is a very dark brown in colour. Add 1 gill of cold water and keep boiling until it is like a thick syrup. Leave until cold then put into a bottle or jar and cork well. This will keep for some considerable time.

Stock for White Soup

Time: About 4 hours

Bones and remains of poultry, veal-bones or meat (4 lb. in weight)	4 pts water
	2 bay leaves
2 medium onions	4 cloves
2 medium carrots	2 sprigs parsley
2 sticks celery	salt

Put the meat and bones into a pan, cover with all the water, except 1 cupful, bring to the boil and skim well. Add the cupful of cold water, bring to the boil and skim again. Add the washed, peeled and sliced vegetables, bay leaves, cloves, parsley and ½ teaspoon of salt, bring to the boil and simmer for 3 hours, skimming from time to time. Strain through a fine sieve, leave to get cold, then remove every particle of fat from the top.

Fish Stock

Quantity: About 2½ pints. Time: About 1 hour

1½ lb. white fish (cod, ling, plaice)
1 small onion
½ head celery
3 pts water
sprig parsley

3 peppercorns
1 bay leaf
1 blade mace
2 cloves
salt

Clean the fish and cut into pieces, put into a pan with the mace, bay leaf, the onion stuck with cloves, the peppercorns, parsley, washed cut-up celery, ½ teaspoon salt and the water. Bring to the boil, simmer for ¾ to 1 hour, skimming from time to time, then strain and leave until cold; carefully skim off all fat.

Court Bouillon for Boiled Fish

Time: About 1 hour (for Bouillon)

1 pt water
½ pt white wine
1 lemon (juice only)
2 carrots
2 onions (small)
1 doz. peppercorns

2 bay leaves
bunch parsley
sprig basil
1 clove garlic (if liked)
salt

Peel and slice the carrot and onions. Put all the ingredients and a ½ teaspoon of salt into a fish-kettle or large pan, bring to the boil and simmer for 1 hour. Wash the fish and, if no strainer in pan, wrap the fish in muslin, leaving two ends with which to lift the fish when done. The fish must be covered by the water, add more if not enough in pan. Add more salt if needed.

Asparagus Soup

4 to 6 persons. Time: 1½ hours

2 bundles asparagus tips	1 gill cream
1 cabbage lettuce	salt, pepper
2 pts white stock	

Well wash the lettuce, cut into quarters and place at the bottom of a pan. Scrape the asparagus, cut off the points and put them aside, cut the green stalks into small pieces and put on top of the lettuce in the pan. Pour on the stock, bring to the boil and simmer until tender, then rub through a sieve and return to pan. Put the asparagus points in another pan with just enough boiling water to cover, simmer for 10 minutes, strain and put them into the stock. Add the cream and seasoning to taste, make hot but do not boil after adding the cream. A little green colouring may be added to improve the appearance of the soup.

Breton Soup

4 to 6 persons. Time: About 2 hours

1 cos lettuce (medium), failing that Webbs	a little chervil
2 small carrots	2 pts stock
1 leek	1 gill cream
1 medium onion	1 large egg yolk (or 2 small)
1 medium turnip	½ oz. butter
½ head chicory	pepper, salt

Wash and shred all the vegetables, chicory and chervil, put them into a pan with the butter and ½ pint of stock. Let them simmer until tender, stir occasionally to prevent burning. Then pour in the rest of the stock, add a little salt and pepper—paprika if preferred. Bring to the boil, then simmer gently for 1 to 1¼ hours. Mix the yolk of egg with the gill of cream, add to the soup 5 minutes before serving. On no account let it boil after adding the egg and cream.

Cold Consommé (with Prunes)

4 to 6 persons. Time: 1 hour

2 pts clear stock (see p. 33)	white wine
¾ lb. prunes	pepper, salt
1 lump sugar	

36

Soak the prunes overnight in just enough white wine to cover them. Then, put them into a pan and gently simmer until tender, add the lump of sugar and set aside to get cold, then remove the stones. Heat the clear soup, add seasoning and make sure that all fat is skimmed from top, leave to cool, then place in refrigerator for a while. Do not freeze or the soup will turn solid. Just before serving add the prunes and any wine that the prunes have not absorbed. Serve in soup-cups.

Fish Soup

4 persons. Time: 1 hour

1 fresh haddock	1 egg
½ pt picked shrimps	1 blade mace
2 pts fish, or white stock	1 slice bread
½ oz. butter	1 teaspoon chopped parsley
1 dessertspoon flour	pepper, salt

Remove all the bones from a fair-sized haddock, put the flesh into a mortar with the shrimps and pound well, add the parsley and the slice of bread previously steeped in half a pint of milk. Put all into a pan, add the stock and mace, bring to the boil; simmer gently for 30 minutes then rub through a sieve. Return to pan, add the beaten egg, roll the butter into the flour and stir in a morsel at a time. Do not let it boil again.

Good Woman's Soup

4 to 5 persons. Time: 45 minutes

2 pts white stock	1 gill cream
1 cabbage lettuce (medium-sized)	1 oz. butter
1 bunch watercress	½ teaspoon each tarragon, chervil
small piece cucumber	pepper, salt
2 egg yolks	

Well wash and shred the lettuce, peel the cucumber, cut into slices lengthwise and then into strips, wash and pick the stalks from the watercress. Melt the butter in a pan, cook the vegetables for about 5 minutes then add the stock, tarragon, chervil and seasoning to taste. Bring to the boil and simmer for about 15 minutes, or until the lettuce is tender. Lightly beat the eggs, mix with the cream, stir this into the soup and stir until it thickens; it must not boil or the eggs will curdle.

Green Pea Soup

4 to 5 persons. Time: 1½ hours

2 pints white stock
¾ lb. green peas (weighed
after shelling)
½ lb. spinach
1 small onion

1 sprig mint
2 oz. butter
1 oz. flour
1 gill cream
pepper, salt

Remove the stalks from the spinach, wash in 2 or 3 changes of water and drain. Melt 1 oz. of the butter in a pan, put in the peas, mint, spinach, cover with a tightly-fitting lid and cook for about 15 minutes on a low heat. Add the stock and the finely-chopped onion and boil gently until tender, then rub through a fine sieve. Melt the remainder of the butter in the pan, stir in the flour, add the pea soup and bring to the boil, stirring all the time. Just before serving add the cream.

Lobster Soup with Forcemeat Balls

4 persons. Time: 1½ hours

1 fair-sized lobster (boiled)
2 pts water
1 egg
1½ oz. butter
1 oz. flour

3 oz. breadcrumbs
Lemon juice
½ teaspoon anchovy essence
1 teaspoon chopped parsley
paprika, pepper, salt

Pick out the meat from the shell of the lobster, pound this shell and the small claws in a mortar then put them into a pan with the 2 pints water; bring to the boil, simmer for 1 hour, strain and return to pan. Put half of the lobster meat with the butter and flour into the mortar, pound well, rub through a sieve and put into the fish stock in pan. Leave on a low heat for 5 to 10 minutes—do not let it reach boiling point—then add the anchovy essence, 1 teaspoon of lemon juice and seasoning to taste. Mince the other half of the lobster meat and mix with the parsley, breadcrumbs and a little seasoning. Mix with the beaten egg, roll into balls and drop into the soup 5 to 10 minutes before serving.

Minestrone Soup

6 persons. Time: 1¼ hours

1 small cabbage heart
½ lb. green peas (fresh or frozen)
½ lb. French beans (fresh or frozen)
2 leeks
1 carrot
4 medium potatoes
¼ heart celery

3 pts stock or 2 pts stock, 1 pt water
2 medium tomatoes
1 bacon rasher
6 to 8 oz. Patna rice
3 oz. grated cheese
1 clove garlic
2 oz. butter
pepper, salt

Well wash and shred the cabbage and celery, peel the vegetables and slice them, including the French beans. Put through a mincer the rasher and clove of garlic. Melt the butter in a pan, put in all the vegetables, peas also, the bacon and garlic and cook without browning for about 10 minutes. Add the stock—and water if used—the washed Patna rice, the tomatoes sliced and seasoning to taste. Stir until it boils, then simmer until the rice and vegetables are soft, about ½ to ¾ of an hour. Serve with the cheese either sprinkled on the top or handed separately.

Onion Soup

4 persons. Time: 1½ hours

2 pts white stock or bone stock
1 lb. Spanish onions
¼ pt. milk

2 oz. breadcrumbs
1 oz. flour
chopped parsley
cayenne pepper, salt

Peel and slice the onions and put them into a pan with the stock, bring to the boil and simmer for 1 hour. Rub through a sieve, return to pan, add seasoning and sprinkle in the breadcrumbs. Mix the flour with the milk, stir it into the soup and simmer for 3 or 4 minutes. Pour into the tureen and sprinkle with the parsley.

Ox-Tail Soup

6 to 7 persons. Time: 5½ to 6½ hours

1 ox-tail
¼ lb. lean ham
1 large onion
1 medium carrot
1½ oz. butter
1½ oz. flour
1 wineglass port

½ teaspoon each parsley and thyme
1 saltspoon celery powder
3 cloves
2 quarts water
pepper, salt

Wash and cut up the ox-tail and put it into a pan with the butter. Peel and cut up the vegetables and add them, with the thinly-cut ham, the cloves, herbs, celery powder and seasoning to the ox-tail, add ½ pt of water. Stir over a fairly high heat until the meat and vegetables are a good brown colour. Add the rest of the water, bring to the boil, then simmer slowly for 5 hours, strain and leave until cold. Skim off all the fat, put back into pan and reheat on low gas. Mix the flour with a little water, stir into the soup, simmer for 5 minutes. Add pieces of the ox-tail cut up small, and just before serving add the wine.

Palestine Soup

4 persons. Time 1½ hours

1½ lb. Jerusalem artichokes
1 small onion
1 small turnip
½ head celery
2 small potatoes

1½ pt. white stock
¼ pt. milk
1 gill cream
cayenne pepper, salt

Peel and cut up the vegetables and put them into a pan with the stock. Bring to the boil and simmer gently for about 1 hour—or until the vegetables are soft. Rub through a sieve, return to pan, add the milk, cream and seasoning to taste. Do not let it boil after adding cream. Serve with Melba toast.

Potato Soup

4 to 5 persons. Time: About 1½ hours

2 pts. white stock
1½ lb. potatoes
1 small onion
1 leek
¼ head celery

1 oz. butter
1 oz. sago
½ pt. milk
1 gill cream
cayenne pepper, salt

Wash the leek and celery, remove the green parts and leave to drain. Melt the butter in a pan, add the peeled and sliced potatoes, the cut-up onion, leek and celery and stir over a low heat for 5 minutes; do not let it brown. Add the stock and seasoning to taste, bring to the boil and simmer for 1 hour. Rub through a fine sieve, return to pan, add the milk and bring to the boil stirring all the time. Sprinkle in the sago and cook until transparent; add the cream just before serving. Do not boil after adding cream.

Russian Bortsch

5 to 6 persons. Time: About 2 hours

3 beetroots (uncooked, medium-sized)	4 egg yolks
1 small onion	lemon juice
2 sticks celery	1 oz. butter
1 tablespoon red cabbage	pepper, salt
3 pts water	fried croûtons

Wash and peel the beetroot, celery and onion, cut into small pieces. Melt the butter in a pan, add the vegetables and red cabbage and cook for about 5 minutes without browning, add the stock, season to taste, bring to the boil and simmer for 1 hour. Rub through a wire sieve, return to pan, add 1 teaspoon of lemon juice. Lightly beat the eggs, allowing 1 yolk to each $\frac{1}{2}$ pt of liquid, stir them into the soup; keep over a low heat without boiling until the eggs have thickened the soup, stirring all the time. Serve with fried croûtons of bread.

Scotch Broth

4 to 6 persons. Time: About 3 hours

$1\frac{1}{2}$ lb. neck of mutton	1 teacupful barley
2 medium onions	1 teaspoon chopped parsley
2 medium carrots	3 pts cold water
1 turnip	pepper, salt
1 small leek	

Cut the meat from the bones and remove any fat; put the bones, meat and water into a pan, bring to the boil and skim. Wash the barley, add it to the pan with the seasoning and simmer for 1 hour. Peel the vegetables, cut them into dice, add them to the pan and continue cooking for 1 to $1\frac{1}{4}$ hours. Remove the bones and skim again if fat is floating on the top; add the parsley just before serving.

Spinach Soup

4 persons. Time: About 1 hour

2 lb. spinach	$1\frac{1}{2}$ oz. butter
1 small onion	1 oz. flour
$1\frac{1}{2}$ pts white stock	pinch of nutmeg
$\frac{1}{2}$ pt milk	pepper, salt

Wash the spinach in several waters, remove the stalks, put the
spinach into a pan with just enough water to cover the bottom,
add the shredded onion and cook until tender. Drain and rub
through a hair sieve. Melt the butter in a pan, blend in the flour,
add the stock, spinach pulp, milk, nutmeg and seasoning to taste.
Bring to the boil, stirring all the time, simmer for 5 minutes and
serve with croûtons of fried bread.

Tomato Soup

4 to 5 persons. Time: About 1½ hours

2 lb. tomatoes
1 medium carrot
1 medium onion
2 sticks celery
2 oz. lean ham
1 dessertspoon cornflour
1½ oz. butter

1½ pts water
½ pt milk
1 sprig parsley
½ doz. peppercorns
1 gill cream
pepper, salt

Melt the butter in a pan, add the vegetables and ham, sliced, and
cook for 5 minutes—take care it does not burn. Add the sliced
tomatoes, parsley, peppercorns and water, simmer slowly for
45 minutes. Rub through a hair sieve, return soup to pan, add the
half pint of milk, hot. Mix the cornflour with a little cold milk,
add to the soup, stir until it boils, add the seasoning and nutmeg,
simmer for 5 minutes. Just before serving add the cream. On no
account let it boil after adding cream. Serve with fried croûtons.

Vegetable Soup

4 to 5 persons. Time: 4 hours

2 qts. water
2 oz. Carolina rice
2 onions
1 head celery
3 small carrots

1 potato
4 oz. green peas
1 lb. split peas
1 oz. butter
pepper, salt

Wash the rice and put into a pan with the butter, carrots, onions
and split peas—soaked overnight—the celery and the
potato sliced; fry the whole a nice brown, then put into a pan with
the water. Stew very slowly for 4 hours, then strain off the
liquor and rub the vegetables through a sieve. Put the purée back
into the pan with the liquor and reheat. Season to taste. Just
before serving add the boiled green peas.

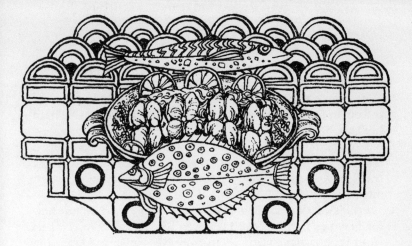

6

Fish

Fish is the most economic of foods because the cheaper kinds are the most nutritious. You can't say that about meat. For example, scrag-end of mutton hasn't the food value of loin, nor does pickled pork compare with leg of pork in the same context. But herrings, like eels or mackerel, have as great a food value as their more expensive confrères, salmon, turbot or Dover sole. For instance, one of the cheapest dishes and one most suitable for invalids is whiting. A lot of people think it's tasteless; that's poppycock. It is not tasteless at all if it's done in the right way; steamed, skinned and served with a sauce. Properly prepared, it's a delicacy. I used to long for it when I was in hospital and not allowed to eat meat. All they served were slabs of Icelandic cod, cooked to the consistency of cottonwool. Apart from the smell, it could have been used for the same purpose.

It sounds nonsense, but the secret of well-cooked fish lies in the buying of it. Fish must be fresh. You used to be able to tell whether fish was fresh or not by the firmness and by the smell of it, because fish that was even a day old became flabby and odorous. With refrigeration it's not so easy to judge because it comes out stiff, odourless and often tasteless.

As I have said earlier in this book, it's a good idea, by trial and error, to find a good fishmonger and stick to him. I've been fobbed off with fish that looked fresh because it had just come out of the refrigerator and smelt all right, but when I got it home it was flaccid and rank. I took it back to the shop but I could have saved myself the journey; the fishmonger wasn't interested.

Fish is a food that should be bought in season. The best time for herrings is from May to November, and they're cheapest from June to September. Sprats from November to March, but cheapest in December when there's a glut. Eels are good from September to November and cheapest in October, and mackerel, even with refrigeration, should be bought in season, from April to July, and they're cheapest in May and June. Of course, when I say cheap, I mean in relation to the price of other fish; when I was a girl they used to come round our street with herrings at forty-eight a shilling—a farthing each! Both for quality and nutrition, it is better and cheaper to buy fish that is in season. Today fishmongers are more obliging than they were, and are prepared to clean fish for you. Even so, they don't remove all the scales, and that should always be done. If you find it difficult, a good tip is to plunge the fish into boiling water for a minute or two, then the scales will rub off easily and you won't need to scrape them.

If you get fish straight from the sea or river and you want to fillet it yourself, it's not difficult. First you must wash, dry and skin the fish, then lay it flat on a board and with the point of a very sharp knife cut right down the backbone from the head to the tail. Then insert the knife into this slit and carefully separate the fish from the bone, keeping the knife lightly pressed against the bone all the time. You need a sharp knife and one that is pointed.

Apart from fish needing to be well cleaned, it needs very slow cooking if you're boiling it. If you try to cook it in a hurry, you'll find that the outside of the fish cracks and not only is it hard to get out of the water, it is also unsightly. Again, once you've boiled your fish and it's ready, don't leave it in the water because, although you may think you're keeping it hot, all the flavour of the fish is going into the liquid, which will be all right to make fish soup with, but that's not the present purpose. So take it out and keep it hot some other way, either by putting it between two plates on top of boiling water or at the bottom of the oven. If you haven't got a fish kettle with a strainer, and these really are ideal things in which to cook fish, a good idea is to wrap any fish for boiling in muslin, making sure that you leave two ends of the material outside the saucepan, so that you can lift it out. Done that way, the fish shouldn't break.

The French boil their fish in court bouillon and I've given a recipe for that on page 35. Like a good sauce, wine does something to fish.

If you bake fish, keep it covered with oiled or buttered paper and baste it occasionally, otherwise it will get very dry. One recipe for baked fish that I particularly remember is to soak it in white wine then coat it with a mixture of chopped mushrooms, shallots, herbs and breadcrumbs. Top this liberally with butter, cover with oiled paper, baste from time to time, and even such fish as cod or hake taste delicious.

If you're frying fish like thick steaks of turbot, halibut or cod, you can use an ordinary frying pan, and it is a good thing to do this because you can turn the fish without breaking it. But with smaller cuts you need a deep pan with a wire basket and enough fat to immerse the fish completely. Whatever method you use, make sure that the fat is hot enough—it must have a faint blueish smoke coming from it. If it isn't the right temperature the fat soaks into the fish; it doesn't seal the outside, and you get a soggy mess that no amount of draining on soft paper or greaseproof paper will alter. If you can't fry all the fish at the same time, you must make sure that the fat is at the correct temperature for each frying.

One cook that I served under, when she grilled fish like salmon, red mullet or turbot, used to sprinkle them with pepper and salt, give a squeeze of lemon juice and then wrap them in thick buttered paper. When the fish were cooked in the paper in this way, none of the juices escaped. I've tried it myself on less expensive fish, cod-steaks and the like, and I must admit that they turned out very well.

I think that fish is coming back into its own again. Real fish, I mean; not that frozen prepacked stuff. Of all the dishes that one serves I think fish benefits most from a sauce. Even salmon or trout are greatly enhanced by serving a sauce with them.

And these two fish, I think, are almost better boiled than cooked in any other way. If you do boil salmon or salmon trout, put them into boiling water. This will ensure that they keep their colour, but with other kinds use warm water because boiling water is inclined to break the skin of a fish. With white fish, put either a tablespoonful of vinegar or the juice of half a lemon in the water. This helps keep the flesh white. And don't throw away the stock that you've made from boiling—it makes a marvellous fish soup—and finally, only use just enough water to cover the fish.

To sum up, the accent is on choosing and buying. Don't go for the more expensive fish; buy the cheaper kind in season when it is the best of its kind. Don't buy salmon when it's cheap because it's likely to be of an inferior quality. When you buy cod or hake go to town on it, give it a good sauce or enhance it with egg. The yolk of an egg added to a sauce makes a deal of difference. There are so many ways of cooking and serving fish and I've given recipes for most of the cheaper kind. A fish pie, for example, can make a delicious meal. One last point— make sure that the skin of fish is fully removed. I've found that the fishmonger may take off the black skin, but he often seems to leave the top one on.

Bouillabaisse

7 to 8 persons. Time: 20 to 30 minutes

several different kinds of fish	2 teaspoons chopped parsley
1 lobster (cooked)	1 bay leaf
½ lb. tomatoes	1 bunch herbs
1 medium onion	1 clove garlic (if liked)
½ gill salad oil	pepper, salt
water	

Oily fish, such as herring and mackerel, are not suitable for this dish. Good fish to use are, fresh haddock, whiting, cod and hake. Wash and clean the fish, remove the heads, tails and fins, cut the fish into slices, remove all the meat from the lobster. Peel the onion and garlic—if used—cut them into slices, also the tomatoes. Put all into a pan with the herbs, bay leaf, parsley, salad oil and seasoning to taste. Add just enough water to cover the fish, bring to the boil, then boil quickly for about 20 minutes. To serve, remove the fish and keep it hot. Put 4 to 5 slices of bread in a tureen and pour over the fish liquor, serve as soup. Follow with the fish garnished with cut lemon and sprigs of parsley.

Bream Stuffed

4 persons. Time: ¾ to 1 hour

1 bream (about 2 lb.)
2 oz. mushrooms
2 oz. breadcrumbs
2 oz. butter

1 egg yolk
melted butter
½ teaspoon mixed herbs
pepper, salt

Wash the bream and wipe with a soft cloth but do not remove the scales. Peel and chop the mushrooms, lightly fry them in 1 oz. of the butter. Put into a basin the breadcrumbs, herbs and seasoning, rub in the other 1 oz. of butter, add the mushrooms and mix with the egg yolk to a firm mixture. Stuff the fish with this, put it into a greased fire-proof dish, pour over a little melted butter and bake in the oven for about 45 minutes. Serve with anchovy sauce (see recipe for white sauce, p. 140).

Gas 5; Electricity 375°

Cod Collops

4 to 6 persons. Time: About ½ hour

1½ lb. filleted cod
1 small onion
3 oz. butter
1½ oz. flour
¼ pt milk
¼ pt water

1 teaspoon Worcester sauce
1 teaspoon mushroom
  ketchup
1 lemon
pepper, salt

Wash and dry the cod, cut into collops about 2 to 3 inches square. Make hot 2 oz. of butter in a pan, flour the collops and lightly fry them in the butter for 2 to 3 minutes. In another pan melt 1 oz. of butter and mix with 1 oz. of flour, add the milk, water, Worcester sauce, mushroom ketchup and seasoning to taste; bring to the boil. Put the cod collops into this and cook on a low heat for 20 to 30 minutes, or until the fish is soft. Just before serving add ¼ teaspoon of lemon juice, put the collops into a hot dish and pour over the sauce.

A collop was originally a slice of meat, or, even further back, an egg fried on bacon. When I was a kitchen-maid, the cook gave us this dish on Collop Monday, which was the day before Shrove Tuesday.

Crab Devilled

3 to 4 persons. Time: About 15 minutes

1 crab (cooked)
1 gill brown sauce (see p. 130)
1 tablespoon breadcrumbs
½ teaspoon French mustard

1 teaspoon each chopped
  gherkin
  Worcester sauce
  chutney
  lemon juice
cayenne pepper, salt

Take out all the meat from the body and claws of the crab. Heat the brown sauce in a pan, add the crab-meat and all the other ingredients, put over a low heat and stir until hot. Wash and dry the large shell of the crab and fill it with the mixture, cover with the breadcrumbs and bake in the oven for about 10 minutes.

Gas 5; Electricity 375°

Eels Fried

4 persons. Time: About ½ hour

2 eels (about 2 lb.)
2 oz. chopped mushrooms
1 egg
breadcrumbs

lemon
frying fat or oil
fried parsley
pepper, salt

If the eels are not already skinned the best way to do this is to cut off head, turn back the skin at the top of the neck and draw it down towards the tail; then open the fish and remove the inside, take care not to break the gall. Clean the fish and take out the backbone, cut the eels into pieces about 3 inches long. Peel the mushrooms, put them through a mincer and mix with the breadcrumbs and a little seasoning. Beat the egg, dip the fish into it and then cover with the breadcrumb mixture. Fry in a deep pan of hot fat until a golden brown colour. Serve with a piquant sauce (see p. 137) and garnish with fried parsley (see p. 142) and cut lemon.

Haddock Stuffed

3 to 4 persons. Time: ¾ to 1 hour

1 fresh haddock (about 2 lb.)
veal forcemeat (see p. 105)
¼ pt fish stock or water

1 oz. butter
brown breadcrumbs
pepper, salt

48

Wash and clean the fish, stuff with the veal forcemeat and either sew up or use very fine skewers. Place in a fire-proof dish, pour on fish-stock or water, add seasoning; dot with the butter, cover and cook for ¾ to 1 hour. When cooked, sprinkle with the brown breadcrumbs and serve with anchovy or white sauce (see p. 140).

Gas 4–5; Electricity 350°–375°

Halibut with Shrimp Sauce

4 to 5 persons. Time: To fry, about 10 minutes

Halibut (about 2 lb.)	fried parsley (see p. 142)
1 egg	pepper, salt
breadcrumbs	1 gill picked shrimps for
1 tablespoon flour	sauce
frying fat or oil	

Wash the fish and cut into slices about ¾ to 1 inch thick. Sprinkle with the seasoning and coat with flour and dip the slices into the beaten egg and cover with the breadcrumbs. Fry in a deep pan of hot fat to a golden brown (about 10 minutes); serve garnished with fried parsley.

For the shrimp sauce, heat ½ pt of white sauce (see p. 140) made with fish stock if possible instead of milk; when hot put in the gill of picked shrimps.

Herrings Soused

4 persons. Time: 1 to 1¼ hours

4 herrings	3 cloves
vinegar	1 bay leaf
peppercorns, ½ doz.	pepper, salt

Well wash the herrings and, if preferred, bone them. Sprinkle each fish with the seasoning and place in a fire-proof dish. Add peppercorns, bay leaf and cloves and cover with a mixture of 3 parts vinegar to 1 part of water—using just enough liquid to cover the fish. Cover with a lid or a piece of grease-proof paper and cook in the oven for 1 hour.

Gas 3–4; Electricity 325°–350°

Kedgeree

3 to 4 persons. Time 20 to 30 minutes

any cooked fish (about 1 lb.)
¼ lb. rice
1 hardboiled egg
3 oz. butter

1 teaspoon chopped parsley
milk
cayenne pepper, salt

Boil the rice until soft, drain well. Flake the fish finely. Melt the butter in a pan, add the rice and fish, stir over a fair heat until hot; use a little milk if it seems too dry. Add seasoning to taste and the sliced white of the egg. Pile the mixture up on a hot dish and garnish with the parsley and the yolk of egg put through a sieve. Dried haddock is particularly good for this dish.

Lobster Croquettes

4 to 6 persons. Time: About 10 minutes to fry

1 lobster (large)
1 egg
1 oz. flour
¼ pt milk
frying fat or oil

½ gill cream
chopped parsley
cayenne pepper
salt

Remove all the meat from the lobster and chop into small pieces. Melt the butter in a pan, blend in the flour, add the milk and bring to the boil, stirring all the time. Remove from heat, stir in the lobster, cream and seasoning to taste; spread out on a plate to get cold. When firm, make into oval shapes, dip them into the beaten egg and coat with breadcrumbs. Fry in a fairly deep pan of hot fat to a golden brown colour; serve on a hot dish, sprinkle with the parsley.

Hand anchovy or shrimp sauce (see recipe for white sauce, p. 140).

Lobster Salad

6 to 7 persons

1 hen lobster (cooked)
1 cos lettuce
1 endive
1 beetroot (cooked)
small piece cucumber

2 hardboiled eggs
box of mustard & cress
½ pt. mayonnaise (see p. 135)
cayenne pepper

The endive must be of the curly kind with greeny-yellow leaves. Wash the lettuce and endive, dry in a clean cloth, shred and put into a salad with the cleaned mustard and cress. Lightly mix in half the chopped beetroot, a few slices of cucumber and half of the meat from the lobster; add seasoning to taste, pour on the mayonnaise, mix well. Finely chop the whites of the eggs, put the yolks through a sieve. Decorate the salad with alternate rows of the rest of the lobster, diced beetroot, thinly-sliced cucumber and the yolks and whites of the eggs.

Lobster Soufflé

3 to 4 persons. Time: 25 to 30 minutes

1 large lobster (cooked)	1 oz. breadcrumbs
2 eggs	1 teaspoon anchovy essence
1 oz. butter	1 gill cream
½ oz. flour	pepper, salt
¼ pt milk or fish stock	

Remove all the meat from the lobster, put into a mortar and pound well. Melt the butter in a pan, add the flour and cook for 1 minute. Add the milk or stock, stir over a gentle heat until it boils, keep stirring for 2 or 3 minutes. Add the pounded lobster, anchovy essence, breadcrumbs, cream and seasoning to taste. Mix well, then beat in the yolks of the eggs. Whip the whites of the eggs until they are stiff, then lightly fold them into the mixture. Put into a greased soufflé dish, tie a piece of greaseproof paper round the outside to come higher than the dish and bake in an oven for 25 to 30 minutes.

Gas 6; Electricity 425°

Mackerel Boiled

4 persons. Time: 15 minutes

2 mackerel	herbs
1 small onion	pepper, salt

Clean and wash the mackerel, cut off the head and fins. Peel and slice the onion and put it into a pan or a fish kettle. Add the herbs and seasoning to taste, put the mackerel on the top, cover with cold water, bring to the boil and simmer gently until the fish is cooked. Lift out of the pan and place on a hot dish. Serve with green gooseberry sauce (see p. 132). Mackerel is put into cold water, as hot water would crack the delicate skin.

Mackerel Grilled

4 persons. Time: 15 to 20 minutes

4 mackerel
2 oz. butter

paprika pepper
salt

Wipe the fish clean and dry it, split down the back and sprinkle
with seasoning. Melt the butter and pour some over the fish.
Place under the grill, turning frequently and pouring on a little
of the butter each time the fish is turned. Cook from 15 to 20
minutes. Serve with parsley sauce (see p. 140).

Red Mullet Baked

4 to 5 persons. Time: 20 minutes

3 red mullet
1½ oz. butter
breadcrumbs

nutmeg
½ lemon
salt and pepper

Clean and lightly scrape the fish. Grease a fire-proof dish. Sprinkle
some breadcrumbs on the bottom, place the fish on this, season,
add a grate of nutmeg on each and the juice of the ½ lemon. Add
enough breadcrumbs to well cover the fish, and dot the butter in
small pieces over it. Bake in a moderate oven for 15 to 20 minutes
or a little longer if not cooked enough. Can be served in the
oven-proof dish. Serve with wine sauce (see p. 140).

Gas 3 to 4; Electricity 350° to 375°

Russian Salad

5 to 6 persons

1 large tin mixed diced
  vegetables (about 1 pt)
1 doz. prawns (cooked)
2 oz. smoked salmon
½ doz. green olives
1 tablespoon mixed chopped
  capers and gherkins

1 small cos lettuce
1 dessertspoon caviare
2 tablespoons salad oil
1 tablespoon tarragon
  vinegar
1 gill mayonnaise (see p. 135)
cayenne pepper, salt

Shell the prawns and slice the salmon into small thin pieces.
Wash the heart of the lettuce, dry in a clean cloth, put at the
bottom of a large salad bowl. Mix together the salad oil and
vinegar, add a little seasoning and mix the vegetables with it; add

the salmon, capers and gherkins, and caviare, put into the salad bowl with the lettuce, pour over the mayonnaise. Arrange the prawns round the edges alternately with the stoned olives cut into halves.

Salmon Maître d'Hôtel

6 to 7 persons. Time: About 20 minutes

2 lb. salmon	1 dessertspoon capers
1 pt good fish stock	a mixed bunch parsley and
1 oz. butter	fennel
1 oz. flour	salt, pepper
white wine, vinegar	

Cut the salmon into slices about an inch thick, remove the bones and sprinkle with vinegar. Chop the parsley and fennel very fine, cover each side of the fish slices with the herbs. Melt the butter in a pan, blend in the flour, add the roughly chopped capers and season to taste, pour in the fish stock, bring to the boil, stirring all the time. Put in the slices of salmon and simmer very gently until tender. Serve with melted butter if desired.

Salmon Steaks with Green Hollandaise Sauce

1 slice per person. Time: 30 to 35 minutes

Scotch salmon	parsley
olive oil	tarragon
1 lemon	watercress
butter	pepper, salt

Well oil a piece of grease-proof paper and lay it in the bottom of a fire-proof dish. Wash the salmon, lay the slices on the oiled paper, dot with butter, add seasoning to taste and sprinkle with a few drops of lemon juice. Cover with another piece of oiled paper and bake in the oven for 30 to 35 minutes, or until the salmon is tender. While it is cooking wash the parsley, tarragon and watercress, put the leaves into boiling water for 5 minutes, dry in a cloth and rub through a wire sieve. Enough is needed to make 1 tablespoon when put through the sieve, this is then stirred into the hollandaise sauce. Serve the fish on a hot dish, and the sauce in a sauce-boat.

Gas 4–5; Electricity 350°–375°

Scallops Baked

4 persons. Time 25 to 30 minutes

1 doz. scallops
2 oz. butter
breadcrumbs

1 lemon
parsley
pepper, salt

Remove the scallops from their shells and beard them. Grease a fire-proof dish and place a layer of breadcrumbs on the bottom —about ¼ inch thick, put the scallops on this, add seasoning, a little lemon juice and a layer of breadcrumbs, not too thick. Dot with the butter and bake in a moderate oven for 25 to 30 minutes. Serve with fried parsley (see p. 142).

Gas 4–5; Electricity 350°–375°

Smelts Fried

2 to 3 persons. Time: About 4 to 5 minutes to fry

1 dozen smelts
1 egg
breadcrumbs

frying fat or oil
parsley
pepper, salt

Wash the smelts, drain and dry them in a clean cloth, then dredge with flour. Beat the egg, dip the fish into it and coat with the breadcrumbs. Have ready a deep pan of hot fat, put the smelts into the wire basket, place it in the pan and fry to a bright brown colour—about 4 minutes. Drain on to soft paper and serve garnished with fried parsley and cut lemon. Serve with plain white sauce or anchovy (see p. 140).

Filleted Sole with Parmesan

3 to 4 persons. Time: About ½ hour

2 soles (filleted)
2 oz. butter
½ oz. flour
2 oz. grated Parmesan cheese
¼ pt milk

½ gill white wine
½ gill cream
½ gill fish stock or water
1 lemon
pepper, salt

Skin the fillets if not already done, place them in a greased fire-proof dish, sprinkle with the juice of ½ lemon and season to taste. Pour over the wine and fish stock—or water—and bake in a moderate oven for about 10 to 15 minutes. Melt 1 oz. of butter in a pan, blend in the flour, add the milk and stir over a low heat until it boils, then add 1 oz. of the cheese and the other 1 oz. of butter a morsel at a time. When the soles are cooked, remove from oven and strain the liquid from the soles into the pan of sauce, add the cream and pour this over the fish. Sprinkle with the rest of the grated cheese and brown under the grill for about 5 minutes.

Gas 3–4; Electricity 325°–350°

Sole Normande with Truffles

3 to 4 persons. Time: ½ hour

1 sole	1 wineglass white wine
1 onion	1 teaspoon each chopped
½ doz. button mushrooms	parsley and thyme
1 oz. butter	paprika pepper
2 fresh truffles, or a small	salt
bottle of	

If using fresh truffles wash 2 or 3 times in lukewarm water and brush them carefully to remove grit; break into very small pieces. Peel the onion, put into a basin and pour over boiling water, leave for 5 minutes, then cut into thin slices. Wash the sole, cut off the head and fins, remove the black skin. Butter a fire-proof dish, lay the onion slices at the bottom and the sole on top of them. Sprinkle with the parsley and thyme, pieces of truffles, seasoning to taste. Pour the white wine over it, dot with butter, cover with greaseproof paper and bake in an oven for 30 minutes.

Gas 4–5; Electricity 350°–375°

Trout Baked with Almonds

4 to 5 persons. Time: 1 hour

2 trout	1 wineglass white wine
1 oz. butter	parsley
2 oz. ground almonds	pepper, salt

Clean the fish in cold salt water and remove the fins, dry, and place in a well-buttered, fire-proof dish with a lid, season to taste and spread the ground almonds over the trout, melt the butter and pour over. Pour the wine round the sides of the dish, cover and bake in an oven for 20 to 30 minutes—according to the size of the fish. Sprinkle with the chopped parsley before serving.

Gas 4–5; Electricity 350°–375°

Trout Grilled

1 per person. Time: 15 minutes

small trout, 1 per person	nutmeg
oiled butter	pepper
lemon	salt
parsley	

Clean the fish and score the skin on both sides. Sprinkle each side with the seasoning and a grate of nutmeg. Brush the trout each side with the oiled butter and grill for 15 minutes, turning once. Garnish with parsley and cut lemon. Serve with Hollandaise or black butter sauce (see pp. 133 and 129).

Fillets of Turbot

6 persons. Time: 5 to 6 minutes to fry

1 small turbot	1 small lobster (cooked)
3 oz. butter—or oil	parsley
flour	pepper, salt
1 lemon	

Get the fishmonger to fillet the turbot, then cut each fillet into 3 portions. Sprinkle each piece with the seasoning and a few drops of lemon juice, then coat with flour. Make the butter or oil hot in a pan, put in as many fillets as the pan will easily hold and fry to a golden brown—turning each piece once. Each panful should take about 5 to 6 minutes to cook. Drain on soft paper and serve garnished with fried parsley. Serve with brown bread and butter and shrimp sauce (see p. 138).

Whitebait Fried

4 persons. Time: About 5 minutes

1 lb. whitebait	1 lemon
flour	pepper, salt
frying fat or oil	

Whitebait must be very fresh and should be kept on ice in a refrigerator until required. For an inexperienced cook they are not an easy dish as great care is needed that they do not clamp together in the frying-pan.

Wash and drain the fish and dry in a clean cloth. Sprinkle flour on another cloth, put some of the whitebait in it, gather up the corners and vigorously move the fish around until all are well-coated with the flour. Put them into a wire frying basket, shake off any surplus flour, then put the basket into a deep pan of hot fat and fry the fish for a few minutes; keep moving the basket around while frying. When cooked drain on to soft paper. Continue in this way until all the whitebait are fried, but be careful not to put in too many at one time or they will stick together. When all are cooked, sprinkle with lemon juice and seasoning. Serve garnished with fried parsley and pieces of cut lemon.

7

Entrées

The entrée when I was a kitchen maid and in my early days as a cook was an important course, but today, when dinners are so much less formal and shorter, it is often served as the meat course. It has been, as the Americans say, phased out. It began happening in my last years in service before the war. In the same way that the three-course lunch had been reduced to two courses, the dinners were reduced to five courses by omitting the hors d'œuvre and entrée. It still included the cheese and dessert, of course. Sometimes the roast, or the remove—which is the same thing—would be left out and the entrée made the main course.

I very much liked preparing an entrée because it gave me a chance to use the skills I had acquired and, unless it was game or poultry, it was interesting to cook and to garnish. Sometimes, if the main meat course were omitted, I would have to make two entrées. First a very light one, quennels of veal, or sweetbreads or vol-au-vents of puff pastry filled with savoury meat of minced poultry or chicken or even pâté. This would be followed by the heavier one of fillet steak or veal or ox-tail or lamb cutlet or sweetbreads.

Both the light and the heavy ones needed to be served attractively. They would have to be decorated and the potatoes done in any one of a dozen ways. We certainly never served them plain boiled. It was the combination of colours that made the dish look so appetizing. For instance, if I served lamb cutlets, the potatoes would always be mashed, whipped with cream and the yolk of an egg added to colour them yellow. The cutlets fried in egg and breadcrumbs were a golden brown and there would be alternative heaps of green peas, baked tomatoes and mushrooms. It looked attractive and appetizing; you couldn't fail to have your appetite stimulated by such design and colours.

People say, and I have earlier in this book echoed them, that hors d'œuvre are to stimulate the appetite. But every course should do the same, not only for what you are eating at the time but for the courses that are to follow: attractively served food and variation in colour are of equal importance with the cooking. Then whether it is a cold or a hot entrée we come back to my hobby-horse, the sauce to be made to accompany it.

It's a well-known fact that in those days (I don't know whether it's so now) practically every entrée that was served—whether hot or cold, the main dish or subsidiary—was given a sauce, and the combination of preparing the entrée and making the sauce was, for me, the high spot in cooking the dinner.

Cooking a roast is a matter largely of time and method, so although I was saved the labour I was rather sorry that in my latter days as a cook the entrée was omitted, and, if I could, I would persuade the mistress of the house to have an entrée as the main course.

Offal (somehow I can't like the word) is used to a certain extent as an entrée. Kidneys in my days of service were sent up as a breakfast dish, but sometimes they were used for the entrée. As a matter of fact, on the occasions when there wasn't a main roast, both kidney and liver lent themselves to a variety of ways of cooking and serving. Stuffed hearts, too, made a substantial dish. Despite its wretched name, offal was never despised by 'them' upstairs but considered rather as a delicacy.

It has been suggested to me that an entrée makes a good meal to eat while watching television. Perhaps it does, but is it worth the time and trouble that the preparation takes? Surely the whole object of a meal, a meal which many skills have gone into preparing, is that people should appreciate it. If it's only a subsidiary to one's eyes and ears being attacked by vision and sound, then I don't think that it matters what people who want to watch television eat because they won't notice. Serve them with corned beef sandwiches until they get their priorities right.

Beef Galatine

7 to 8 persons. Time: About 2½ hours to boil

1½ lb. lean beef	1 tablespoon mixed chopped
½ lb. bacon	herbs
2 eggs	1½ gills stock
6 to 8 oz. breadcrumbs	pepper, salt
glaze	

Remove all skin and sinew from the beef and put it through a mincer—or get your butcher to do this. Cut the rind from the bacon and dice it, or put through the mincer if preferred. Mix it with the beef, herbs, seasoning to taste and 6 oz. of breadcrumbs —add more if a drier mixture is liked. Beat the eggs, add them with the stock to the mixture, mix well together, make into a roly-poly shape and put into a scalded and floured cloth; securely tie the ends. Put into a pan of boiling water, let it boil gently for about 2½ hours. When cooked, remove from pan and untie cloth and re-tie tightly as it generally becomes loose during the cooking. Put the roll between 2 plates with a heavy weight on top to press; leave until cold. Remove the cloth and brush over with glaze (see p. 142). If more than 1 coat of glaze is needed wait until the first coat is dry. Decorate with chopped aspic and maître d'hôtel butter (see p. 144); put through a forcing pipe.

Beef à la Philadelphia

5 to 6 persons. Time: About 20 minutes

2 lb. fillet of beef	breadcrumbs
4 bananas	½ pt Espagnole sauce
1 egg	(see p. 131)
2 oz. lard	creamed potatoes (see p. 117)

Remove all fat and sinew from the beef and cut into rounds or squares. Put the fat into a pan and make hot, put in the beef and cook for 10 minutes, turning them often. Cut the bananas into halves lengthwise, then cut each piece into half. Dip them into

the beaten egg, coat with breadcrumbs and fry in the fat in which
the beef was cooked; drain on to soft paper. Serve the beef on a
bed of creamed potatoes, arrange the bananas on the top and
pour round the Espagnole sauce. Hand maître d'hôtel butter
(see p. 144).

Beef Fillets à la Napoleon
3 to 4 persons. Time: About 10 minutes

1 lb. beef fillet
½ lb. veal forcemeat
   (see p. 105)
1 egg
2 oz. butter
breadcrumbs

½ pt Bordelaise sauce
   (see p. 129)
fried croûtons
creamed spinach (see p. 122)
pepper, salt

Flatten the beef slightly with a rolling pin and cut into small
rounds. Cover each piece with a layer of veal forcemeat—not too
thick—dip the pieces into the beaten egg, coat with the breadcrumbs. Melt the butter in a pan and fry the fillets on both sides
to a golden brown; this takes about 10 minutes, they should be
slightly under-done; drain on soft paper. Serve on a bed of
creamed spinach garnished with the fried croûtons. Hand the
Bordelaise sauce to which has been added a little seasoning.

Beef Tournedos with Creamed Spinach
4 to 5 persons. Time: About ½ hour

1½ lb. fillet of beef
2 oz. lard
1 oz. butter
salad oil

1 dessertspoon chopped
   parsley
creamed spinach (see p. 122)
pepper, salt

Remove all fat and sinew from the beef and cut into rounds about
3 inches in diameter and ¾ inch thick. Flatten them with a rolling
pin, brush each side with salad oil, sprinkle with the parsley and
seasoning. Melt the lard in a pan and when hot put in the beef
rounds and fry for 8 to 10 minutes, turning several times; drain
on soft paper. Serve on a bed of creamed spinach and hand
Italian sauce (see p. 134).

Calves' Brains in Scallops

4 persons. Time: 20 minutes

2 calves' brains
1 dessertspoon vinegar
½ pt white sauce (see p. 140)
breadcrumbs
½ gill cream

1 teaspoon finely-chopped
  parsley
paprika pepper
salt

Wash the brains in salt water, remove the skin and fibres and drain. Simmer them for about 10 minutes or until tender in lightly-salted water to which the vinegar has been added. Remove from the pan, cut each brain in half. Put each in a scallop shell. Heat the white sauce, add the chopped parsley, remove from heat and stir in the cream. Pour enough over the brains to fill the scallop shells, add a pinch of paprika pepper, cover with the breadcrumbs and brown under the grill.

Chicken Kromeskies

5 to 6 persons. Time: 15 to 20 minutes

6 oz. cooked chicken
2 oz. tongue
streaky rashers
batter (see p. 158)

1 gill white sauce (see p. 140)
frying fat or oil
paprika pepper, salt

Mince the chicken and tongue, add a pinch of pepper and salt to taste. Heat the white sauce over a low gas and stir in the minced mixture. Blend well then turn on to a plate to cool and become firm. Cut the rinds from the rashers and cut each one into halves. When the chicken mixture is firm make small pieces about the size and shape of a cork; roll each piece in a half rasher. Dip them into the batter and fry in a fairly deep pan of hot fat until a golden brown colour. Drain on soft paper and serve with fried parsley (see p. 142).

Chicken à la Milanaise

5 to 6 persons. Time: About 15 minutes to fry

1 chicken (cooked)
1 egg
3 oz. Gruyère cheese
breadcrumbs

frying fat
tomato sauce (see p. 139)
4 oz. macaroni
pepper, salt

A boiling fowl does very well for this recipe. Cook the bird
and then leave it until cold. Grate the cheese, mix with the
breadcrumbs and seasoning. Remove the skin from the chicken,
then cut into small joints. It can either be completely boned or
the legs divided into 2 pieces. Dip each piece into the beaten egg,
then coat with the breadcrumb mixture. Fry in the hot fat to a
pale brown colour, turning once. This takes about 15 minutes.
Drain on to soft paper and keep warm. Put the macaroni into
boiling salted water, cook very quickly for 15 to 20 minutes,
drain well. To serve, put the macaroni into a hot dish and pile
the fried chicken on the top. Pour the tomato sauce round.

Hare Jugged

4 to 5 persons. Time: 3 hours

1 hare	1½ pts stock
4 oz. bacon	1 wineglass port wine
2 onions	3 or 4 cloves
1 leek	lemon juice
2 pieces celery	1 bunch herbs
2 oz. dripping	pepper, salt
1 oz. flour	forcemeat balls (see p. 103)

Cut the hare into neat pieces and wash in cold salted water, make
sure all blood clots are washed away, drain and dry. Remove the
rind from the bacon then cut into small pieces. Peel the onions,
wash the celery and leek, shred them finely. Heat the dripping in
a pan, lightly fry the bacon, take out of pan, and then fry the
pieces of hare until they are brown on both sides. Put the bacon
and hare into a pan, add the vegetables, herbs, cloves in a small
muslin bag, dessertspoon of lemon juice, wine and seasoning to
taste. Pour on the stock, bring to boil and simmer gently for 2½
to 3 hours. About half an hour before it is done add the flour
previously mixed with a little cold water; stir this into the pan.
When the hare is cooked remove cloves and drop in about a
dozen forcemeat balls which have been previously fried until
brown. To serve, pile the hare in a hot dish with the forcemeat
balls around. Hand croûtons of fried bread and red-currant jelly.

Indian Pilau

6 to 8 persons. Time: 1 to 1½ hours

1 boiling fowl	3 oz. raisins
1 large onion	3 oz. almonds
3 hardboiled eggs	4 cloves
¾ lb. Carolina rice	cayenne pepper, salt
4 oz. butter	

First cook the bird, but take particular care not to overcook it. As soon as it is done, remove from pan. Well wash the rice and leave to drain. Melt 2 oz. of the butter in a pan, put in the sliced onion and fry, add the rice and cook a little, but do not let it brown. Add the water in which the fowl was boiled, and the cloves, and simmer gently until the rice is soft. If all the water is absorbed before the rice is cooked, add more water. While it is cooking cut the fowl into joints and lightly fry in the other 2 oz. of butter; leave on one side but keep hot. Blanch and split the almonds and bake them in the oven until they are brown. Dish the rice in a heap on a deep hot dish; place the chicken joints round it and the eggs cut into slices, and pile on the top the raisins and almonds.

Lamb Noisettes

4 to 6 persons. Time: 15 to 20 minutes to cook

6 lamb cutlets	1 dessertspoon tarragon
1 small onion (chopped)	vinegar
3 large firm tomatoes	2 teaspoons chopped parsley
1 oz. ham (chopped)	1 teaspoon chopped mint
1 egg	2 dessertspoons salad oil
3 oz. butter	pepper, salt
breadcrumbs	

Cut the meat from the bones of the cutlets in 1 piece—making 6 noisettes. In a deep plate mix the oil, tarragon, parsley, mint and onion, put the noisettes into this, add the seasoning and turn the meat over several times until it is well-coated with the mixture; leave for 3 to 4 hours. Cut the tomatoes into halves, carefully remove the seeds from the insides. Mix the ham with the breadcrumbs, using as many as will be needed to fill the tomato halves. Stand the tomatoes on a greased baking tin and fill them with the ham and breadcrumbs, pour over 1 oz. of the butter (melted), and bake in the oven for 15 to 20 minutes. Remove the meat from the plate, drain, then dip the noisettes into the beaten egg and coat with breadcrumbs. Put the rest of the butter into a pan and when hot put in the meat; cook until brown on both sides, then on a low heat for 10 to 15 minutes. Serve them on croûtons of fried bread and garnish with the tomatoes.

Madras Curry

6 persons. Time: 1½ hours

2 lb. beefsteak	3 gills milk
3 medium-sized onions	1½ tablespoons Madras curry
2 medium cooking apples	powder
6 oz. desiccated coconut	½ lemon
2½ oz. butter	½ lb. Patna rice
1½ oz. flour	pepper, salt

Either buy curry powder or make your own, see recipe below. Pour 1½ gills of boiling water over the coconut and leave for ½ an hour; strain, keeping the water. Remove all fat and sinew from the meat and cut into small squares. Melt the butter in a pan, add the chopped onions and fry until brown, add the curry powder and flour and fry a little, put in the meat and let that also brown a little. Add the chopped apple, seasoning, coconut-water and milk, stir until it boils, cover with a tightly-fitting lid and simmer gently for 50 minutes to 1 hour—or until the meat is tender. Just before serving add the juice of ½ lemon. Serve with Patna rice. A gill of cream improves white curries, but is not an absolute necessity.

To cook the Patna rice: Wash the rice in several waters, to remove the loose starch. Drain and put into a pan of boiling salted water, boil fast for 15 to 20 minutes, or until the rice feels tender if pinched between the finger and thumb. Do not let the rice boil too long or it will become mashy. When ready, pour in some cold water, then strain through a fine colander or sieve, rinse out the pan and return the rice to it. Cover with a clean cloth and keep hot until required.

Madras Curry Powder

¾ oz. cardamom seeds	½ oz. black pepper
2 oz. coriander seeds	¼ oz. cinnamon
¾ oz. caraway seeds	1 oz. turmeric
2 oz. cumin seeds	¼ oz. mace
¾ oz. cayenne pepper	½ oz. cloves

65

Finely powder all the seeds and put into a warm oven to dry, mixing them all thoroughly together. Allow to cool, then put into a glass jar with a tight lid.

(I do not know anybody who ever attempted the exceedingly tedious task of grinding this collection of seeds. None of the cooks that I knew ever made the powder, neither can I see much merit attached to 'home-made'.)

Rabbit Pilau

5 to 6 persons. Time: 1 to 1½ hours

1 rabbit
½ lb. Carolina rice
3 medium-sized onions (sliced)

4 oz. butter
1 to 1½ pts stock
pepper, salt

Wash the rabbit and cut into neat joints. Heat 2 oz. of the butter in a pan, add the onions, cook until lightly brown. Wash the rice, drain, add it to the onions and stir over a low heat for 10 minutes; add the boiling stock and leave to simmer. Carefully fry the rabbit joints in the rest of the butter until they are a good brown colour, then add them and any butter left in the pan to the rice; season. Continue to cook gently for about an hour—or until the rabbit is tender—keeping the lid tightly closed. Add a little stock from time to time, to prevent the rice from sticking to the bottom of the pan. Serve in a hot dish with the rabbit piled on top of the rice.

Rumpsteak and Oyster Pie

5 to 6 persons. Time: 1½ to 2 hours

1 lb. rumpsteak
2 doz. oysters
1 egg
1 tablespoon flour
1 gill stock

½ lb. flaky pastry (see p. 174)
1 dessertspoon walnut ketchup
1 wineglass port wine
pepper, salt

Wash the steak and cut into thin narrow strips. Mix the flour and seasoning on a plate and dip the pieces of meat into it. Beard the oysters, roll each oyster inside a strip of beef. Fill a pie dish with these—any oysters left over can be put on top. Pour in 1 tablespoon of stock. Roll out the pastry, put a strip round the edge of the pie dish, brush over with water then cover with the rest of the pastry, leaving a small hole in the middle. Press the edges together and ornament the top with any odd pieces of pastry cut into leaves. Brush the whole top with the beaten egg. Bake in a hot oven until the paste has risen and set, then lower the heat, cover with greaseproof paper otherwise pastry will be too brown before the meat is done. While the pie is cooking, put the rest of the stock into a pan with the walnut ketchup and port. Make it hot; when the pie is cooked strain this gravy into it through a funnel and hand any left over.

Gas 6–7; Electricity 400°–425°

Shepherd's Pie

4 persons. Time: About ½ hour

1 lb. meat (cooked)	mashed potatoes
1 small onion	1 teaspoon mixed herbs
1 small carrot	1 tablespoon tomato purée
1 oz. butter	½ pt brown stock
1 oz. flour	pepper, salt

Remove any fat or gristle from the meat and put it through the mincer, then mince the carrot. Melt the butter in a pan, add the finely-chopped onion and brown, stir in the flour. Gradually pour in the stock, bring to the boil, simmer for 5 minutes. Mix the meat with the herbs, tomato purée and seasoning to taste, put into a greased pie dish, pour on the thickened stock and mix well; cover with the mashed potatoes and bake in a moderately hot oven for ½ to ¾ of an hour. If the top is not brown enough it can be put under the grill for a few minutes.

Gas 6–7; Electricity 400°–425°

Sweetbread en Ramequins

6 to 7 persons. Time: ½ hour to cook

3 calves' sweetbread	1½ teaspoons chopped sweet
bacon rashers	herbs
2 oz. mushrooms	paprika pepper, salt
breadcrumbs	
1½ tablespoons butter	
(melted)	

Prepare the sweetbreads as in recipe for Marino patties (see p. 27); after they are pressed cut each one into 3 to 4 pieces, put a thin strip of bacon round each piece. Peel the mushrooms and chop finely, put them into basin with the herbs, breadcrumbs and seasoning; pour on the melted butter, mix well. Grease some fire-proof ramequin cases, put a little of the breadcrumb mixture at the bottom, then a piece of sweetbread, then cover with more breadcrumbs. Stand the ramequin cases on a tin in a moderate oven and bake until brown.

Gas 4–5; Electricity 350°–375°

Tongue Cassolettes

4 persons. Time: About ½ hour

½ lb. tongue (cooked)
¼ lb. ham
½ small onion
½ doz. small mushrooms

1 oz. butter
½ lb. shortcrust pastry
1 gill brown sauce (see p. 130)
potatoes

Roll the pastry out very thinly. Grease some small patty pans and line them with the pastry. Lay a piece of greased paper in each one, fill them with uncooked rice and bake in the oven until pale brown. Take out the rice and paper. Put the tongue and ham through a mincer, add the chopped mushrooms. Melt the butter in a pan, add the finely-chopped ½ onion and lightly fry, add the minced mixture and the brown sauce, put over a gentle heat and cook for 3 to 4 minutes; add more seasoning if required. Put this mixture into the pastry cases, cover the top with mashed potatoes and bake in the oven for 10 to 15 minutes. When cooked, carefully remove them from the tins and serve on a hot dish.

Gas 5–6; Electricity 375°–400°

Veal Creamed

4 persons. Time: 1 hour to cook

1 lb. fillet of veal
2 large eggs
½ pt white sauce (see p. 140)

1 gill cream
paprika pepper, salt

Finely mince the veal—or ask your butcher to do this—then put it into a mortar and pound well. Add the yolks of eggs, one at a time, the white sauce, cream and seasoning to taste; mix well together. Beat the whites of eggs to a very stiff froth and fold into the mixture. Grease a round china dish, put the mixture into

it, cover with grease-proof paper and tie a piece round the outside
to come above the top. Steam for 1 hour.

Veal Cutlets

5 to 6 persons. Time: 20 to 25 minutes

2 lb. veal cutlets
4 to 6 oz. ham
1 egg
breadcrumbs
½ pt mushroom sauce
  (see p. 135)

3 oz. frying fat
1 dessertspoon mixed herbs
½ lemon
cayenne pepper, salt

Choose the best end of neck of veal and cut the meat from the
bones, keeping the shape as much as possible. Mix the breadcrumbs with the herbs, grated rind of ½ lemon and the seasoning.
Dip the cutlets into the beaten egg, coat with the seasoned
breadcrumbs. Put the fat into a pan and when hot fry the cutlets
until brown on both sides—turning frequently; cook until tender,
about 15 minutes. Cut the ham into small, thin slices, roll them
up on to a skewer and brown under the grill. Serve the cutlets on
a bed of mashed or creamed potatoes with the ham rolls on top,
pour mushroom sauce round.

Veal Kidney with Red Sauce

2 to 3 persons. Time: About 20 minutes

2 veal kidneys
2 oz. butter
1½ oz. flour
1 small onion

½ pt stock
1 wineglass Madeira
salt

Wash the kidneys and skin them. Put 1 oz. of butter into a pan,
add the finely-chopped onion and fry to a pale brown colour. Cut
the kidneys into thin slices, put them into the pan with the
onions and fry quickly on each side, moving the pan around
while frying, then remove from heat. In another pan melt the
other 1 oz. of butter, blend it with the flour, pour in the stock
and stir over the heat until it thickens. Add the wine and salt to
taste, pour over the kidneys and cook very slowly for 10 to 15
minutes.

8

Poultry and Game

I have put poultry and game together, not because game tastes like poultry but because they are at least birds. Though—and here I go again—when you buy frozen chickens today like lumps of concrete you do begin to wonder. The chickens I used to cook are now what are called free range birds, those that roam around pecking up insects and feeding themselves on a variety of foodstuffs apart from the corn they are given, and these are full of flavour. The frozen ones, while they are not tough or unpleasant to taste, have simply no flavour. But still, even if I think of them as inadequate, at least most people can afford to buy them. Chickens used to be a treat—for working-class people it was a luxury—and even when I was a cook it was the sort of food that was treated with respect. A chicken could be easily ruined in the cooking because the flesh was so succulent and delicate that if it were poorly cooked or incorrectly stuffed you could ruin the flavour. When I cook a chicken now I stuff it with sausage meat one end and veal forcemeat the other end, and everybody wants the stuffing and they couldn't care less about the chicken. It's just a vehicle. Nevertheless, chickens now are a more economical proposition than buying meat. They are an everyday dish instead of being a Christmas treat as they used to be for most people, and turkeys will soon become as popular now that they can produce them in such small sizes. I'm not going to generalize about the cooking of poultry. I give individual recipes which I think speak for themselves.

Game includes a large variety of birds. I suppose a swan is game; I've never cooked one, but my first cook told me that it was often served in her first place as a kitchen maid. She also said swans weren't good eating as they were leathery and oily. Many people, I think, would like to sample them just because they feel that they have missed out. Personally I don't see why people go for swans, saying how marvellous they are and what symbols of purity and grace. For my money they are the most ferocious-looking beasts, with their beady eyes contemptuous and condemning, and they come at you as if they've got a grudge against you, hissing away any beautiful thoughts you might have.

But back to cooking: I suppose the most popular game bird in this country is the pheasant. A hen bird is the best for eating, though not so attractive in appearance as the cock. The cock bird has beautiful feathers, but as you don't eat the feathers it doesn't matter, does it? Pheasants must hang for a while after being shot, and with their feathers on, because the feathers keep the flavour in and the air can't get to the bird. It's difficult to give an exact length of time for hanging a pheasant. So much depends on people's taste and, of course, the weather. They should be hung where a certain amount of draught will blow through, and if the weather is cold and dry you should keep them longer than in muggy weather. It used to be considered that when the tail feathers pulled out easily then they were ready, and this rule applies to most game. Some people say that game is only ready when it is on the point of decomposition. So much depends on the cook and the taste of the people for whom one is cooking. I cooked for people who liked them very high indeed, and this meant that the plucking and drawing of them was a hazardous task.

Next in general popularity are partridges. Why partridges are plumper than other game I don't know; I suppose it's because nature made them like that. I don't think it's anything to do with the food they eat, or the rapidity with which they

71

eat it. It you're buying a partridge always look for yellow legs and a dark bill. This is a sure sign that the bird is good. You used to be able to buy red-legged French partridges, but I'm not just being patriotic when I say they're not nearly as good as our English ones. Whenever you're buying any game bird, the things to look for are very smooth legs and a breast that's firm and hard. If you can press it in easily or if its legs have a ragged appearance, then the shopkeeper has had it too long and it's not worth buying.

Then of course there is grouse. There are two kinds, black and red, although, contrariwise, the black hen bird is a sort of mottled brown. Some people are fascinated to watch birds, they've no desire either to shoot them or to eat them; others can't wait for the Glorious Twelfth so that they can reduce the bird population with all possible speed. There are others who enjoy eating them and, for the gourmet, the woodcock is the best of all game birds—and it is the one that must be hung longest, even allowing for individual taste. I've found from experience that a woodcock is not considered worth eating until it is almost decomposing. The flesh then becomes impregnated by a most delicious flavour.

Small game birds such as quails and ortolans should never be drawn; they are cooked with the entrails inside. All others should be hung, then plucked and drawn, and this drawing the bird, which is almost on the point of decomposing, can never be anything but unpleasant. No bird should ever be subjected to water. Water washes away all the flavour. Wipe out the insides with tissue paper and then with a clean dry piece of muslin. All water birds, like duck, must be eaten as soon as possible because the flesh is oily and very soon becomes rank and very strong-tasting indeed.

With the small game birds that I've mentioned—quails, ortolans, snipe and so on—just draw out the gizzard and they should be eaten fresh, almost within gunshot, you might say, and if possible on the day they're shot. In some countries very small birds—larks, thrushes and turtle-doves—are eaten, but for the Englishman, with his sentimentality for all creatures that don't provide a satisfying meal, these are taboo. So don't cook birds like that if you want to keep your friends.

I have included a recipe for larks' tongues in the hors d'œuvre section, and for doing this I shall be a favourite for the unpopularity stakes, but I've done it as a museum piece. I've never used them myself, but the old cook who was in service where they had swans told me how she had also prepared larks' tongues and she gave me the recipe. They were considered a very great delicacy indeed. And when you think of the size of a larks' tongue, you will understand that twenty-four larks made only enough pâté for two people eating very small portions. The whole idea to my mind is a travesty of nature; I'm not a country lover by any manner of means but I should hate to feel that, as in Keats' *La Belle Dame Sans Merci,* 'the sedge has withered from the lake, and no birds sing'. Larks are not trapped in this country now, but trapping is still done in France and Italy.

When I was in service and there was no such thing as foil to wrap poultry and game in, they were always larded or barded. Barding was simple to do since it just meant covering the bird with fat bacon. To prevent the bacon from curling we would snip it with scissors here and there and tie it on the bird with thin twine—or with large birds like turkeys or chickens, we'd use a very fine skewer.

Larding needed more care. We had larding needles of varying sizes. These we used to thread fat bacon into the birds. The bacon was about a quarter of an inch thick, an eighth of an inch wide and about two inches long. After these strips had been threaded into the larding needles the skin and a little of the flesh of whatever we were larding would be pierced. the strips pulled through leaving two equal lengths at each end.

Since we had no refrigerator we kept the fat bacon, or lardoons as they were called, in the coldest possible place, since the cooler they were the easier they were to thread. I give this explanation as my recipes allow for larding and barding, but since the introduction of tin foil many people may consider these methods to be unnecessary.

Chicken en Casserole

5 to 6 persons. Time: 1¼ to 1½ hours

1 chicken	1½ oz. flour
½ lb. mushrooms	1 pt stock, made from carcase
1 small onion	and giblets
2 tomatoes	1 bunch mixed herbs
2 oz. butter	paprika pepper, salt

Divide the chicken into neat joints, mix the flour with a pinch of paprika pepper and a saltspoon of salt, dip the chicken joints into this. Melt the butter in a pan and when hot fry the peeled and chopped onion and mushrooms to a pale brown, add the sliced tomatoes and fry for 1 minute, add the rest of the seasoned flour, stir well. Gradually pour in the stock and bring to the boil, stirring all the time. Pour this over the chicken, add the bunch of herbs and cook in the oven for 1¼ to 1½ hours.

Gas 5; Electricity 375°

Roast Chicken stuffed with Herbs

4 to 5 persons. Time: 1 to 1¼ hours

1 large chicken	½ pt stock
chicken liver	½ teaspoon each
1 small onion (minced)	thyme, parsley,
1 small carrot (minced)	chervil, tarra- } (chopped)
2 tablespoons breadcrumbs	gon
1½ oz. butter	1 wineglass white wine
1 oz. flour	pepper, salt

Finely chop or mince the chicken liver and mix it with the breadcrumbs, herbs and seasoning, add enough melted butter to moisten the mixture. Stuff this into the crop of the bird, retrussing securely, then put it into a moderately hot oven; cover the breast with grease-proof paper. Put a little fat into the pan and baste frequently. Cook for 1 to 1¼ hours, according to the size of the bird. While the chicken is cooking, melt the butter in a pan, lightly fry the onion and carrot, add the flour and cook to a pale brown colour. Gradually pour in the stock and bring to the boil stirring all the time, pour in the wine and simmer gently for 15 minutes. About 20 minutes before the chicken is ready, remove the grease-proof to allow the breast to brown, then take out of oven, remove the trussing string and place on a dish with a little of the sauce poured round and the remainder handed.

Gas 6–7; Electricity 400°–425°

Chicken stuffed with Oysters

5 to 6 persons. Time: 1 to 1½ hours

1 large chicken	2 oz. fat
1 veal sweetbread	½ teaspoon chopped parsley
1½ doz. oysters	½ lemon
½ doz. mushrooms	nutmeg
2 fat bacon rashers	½ pt mushroom sauce
1 egg yolk	(see p. 135)
1 oz. butter	pepper, salt
½ oz. flour	

Prepare the sweetbread as for Marino patties (see p. 27) then chop it finely. Beard the oysters and roughly chop half of them. Peel and chop the mushrooms and mix them with the parsley, grated rind of ¼ lemon, ¼ of nutmeg grated, the chopped oysters and seasoning to taste. Bind together with the beaten egg yolk, stuff the breast of the chicken with this mixture, and fill the body of the bird with the rest of the oysters. Cover the breast with the fat bacon, put the chicken into a baking tin with 2 oz. of fat and bake in the oven for 1 to 1¼ hours, according to size; baste frequently while cooking. Remove the bacon about 20 minutes before the chicken is ready, sprinkle the breast with flour and pour over a tablespoon of hot butter to brown the breast. When cooked, take out of oven, remove the trussing string, serve on a hot dish with mushroom sauce in a sauce-boat.

Gas 6–7; Electricity 400°–425°

(This recipe and the recipe for turkey stuffed with truffles were given to me by an old cook in domestic service. She was given the recipes by her grandmother who was a cook in 1825.)

Chicken Pilaff

5 to 6 persons. Time: About 1 hour after the stock is made

1 large chicken	1 dessertspoon curry paste
2 Spanish onions	1 teaspoon curry powder
2 small onions	½ doz. peppercorns
1 carrot	1 bayleaf
4 oz. butter	baked tomatoes (see p. 123)
6 oz. Patna rice	pepper, salt
2 pts stock (or water)	

Cut the chicken into pieces small enough for serving, remove the skin and the feet and wings at the first joint. Put the backbone, giblets, bones and trimmings into a pan with a level teaspoon of salt, add the stock—water will do if no stock—the carrot, bayleaf, ½ a Spanish onion and the peppercorns. Bring to the boil, simmer for 2 hours, then strain. Wash the rice, drain well. Heat 2 oz. of butter in a pan, add the 1½ Spanish onions, chopped finely, fry to a light brown colour then add the rice and 1½ pts of the chicken stock; add more seasoning if required and put over a low heat until the rice has absorbed most of the stock. Melt the other 2 oz. of butter in a pan, fry the pieces of chicken to a golden brown. Sprinkle them with the curry powder, then put them into the rice with the curry paste; continue cooking until the chicken and rice are tender, adding more stock if needed. A few minutes before serving, reheat the butter in which the chicken was fried, cut the 2 small onions into thin slices and fry until brown. To serve, heap the pilaff in the centre of a dish, scatter on the fried onion rings and arrange the baked tomatoes round.

Roast Duck

4 to 5 persons. Time: 1 to 1¼ hours (according to size)

1 large duck	½ pt stock
sage and onion	apple or orange sauce
stuffing, or }(see p. 104)	(see pp. 127, 136)
apple stuffing	pepper, salt
fat	

Aylesbury duck is the best for roasting as the flesh is very white. Stuff the body of the bird with the sage and onion or apple stuffing, put it into a baking tin, pour hot fat over the bird— butter or dripping—and cover the breast with grease-proof paper. Roast in a fairly hot oven for 1 to 1¼ hours, or until the duck is tender. About 15 to 20 minutes before the bird is cooked, remove the paper from the breast to allow it to brown; baste frequently while the duck is cooking. When done, place on hot dish and keep warm, drain off nearly all the fat in the tin, sprinkle in a little flour, stir well, then add the stock and keep stirring until it boils, simmer for 2 to 3 minutes. Serve this gravy in a sauce-boat; hand apple or orange sauce.

Gas 6–7; Electricity 400°–425°

Goose à la Provence
4 to 5 persons. Time: About ½ hour after the beans are cooked

cooked goose-remains	1 oz. goose fat
½ lb. ham, or } (cut up)	1 gill tomato purée
½ lb. lean bacon }	1 oz. butter
2 medium onions	breadcrumbs
½ lb. haricot beans	pepper, salt

Soak the beans overnight, then put them in a pan with the water in which they were soaked, add more cold water if needed; bring to the boil and simmer for 1 hour or a little longer if the beans are not soft enough. Cut the remains of the goose into neat pieces. Make the goose fat—or dripping if not fat—hot in a pan and put in the roughly-chopped onions, fry to a light brown, add the tomato purée and about ½ pt of the bean water, simmer for 5 minutes. Strain the beans and add them to the onions and purée. Put half of this mixture into a casserole, put the pieces of goose and ham or bacon on top, then add the rest of the bean mixture. Cover with white breadcrumbs and bake in a moderate oven for 20 to 30 minutes.

Gas 4–5; Electricity 350°–375°

Goose Roast
6 to 10 persons. Time: About 2½ hours for large goose and
1½ hours for small goose

1 goose	sage and onion stuffing (see
fat for basting	p. 104)
½ oz. flour	watercress
½ pt stock	½ oz. butter

Stuff the body of the goose with about ½ lb. (according to size of bird) of sage and onion. Put it into a baking tin with 1 or 2 tablespoons of fat, cover the breast with grease-proof paper and roast for 1½ to 2½ hours, according to size of bird; baste frequently while cooking. About 20 minutes before the bird is ready, remove the grease-proof paper, sprinkle a little flour over the breast and pour on the ½ oz. of hot butter to brown the breast. When cooked, take out of tin, pour off most of the fat from the tin and stir in a small amount of flour, add the stock, bring to the boil and simmer for 5 minutes, pour into sauce-boat. Serve the goose on a dish garnished with parsley and hand apple or cranberry sauce (see p. 131).

Gas 6–7; Electricity 400°–425°

77

Pigeons Roast with Chestnut stuffing

4 persons. Time: About ½ hour

2 pigeons	1 teaspoon chopped parsley
½ lb. fat bacon	½ teaspoon chopped thyme
4 streaky bacon rashers	1 lemon
½ lb. chestnuts	1 pt milk and water
1 oz. butter	pepper, salt
1 gill brown sauce (see p. 130	

Pluck, draw and truss the birds. Make a slit in the chestnuts and boil for 2 to 3 minutes until the outer and inner skins can be easily removed, then cook them in the milk and water until soft. Strain, chop them, then pound in a mortar with the same weight of finely-minced fat bacon; season and stuff the pigeons with this mixture. Cover each bird with the streaky rashers, put a piece of grease-proof paper on top and bake in a fairly hot oven for 20 to 30 minutes, according to size. While they are cooking, boil the pigeon livers for 5 minutes, chop finely, mix with the parsley, thyme, butter, strip of lemon peel and the brown sauce; simmer for 5 minutes then strain. Serve the pigeons on a hot dish, remove the trussing string but leave the rashers on the birds. Hand the sauce.

Gas 6–7; Electricity 400°–425°

Turkey Roast

*Time: 24 lb. bird 3½ to 4 hours; 18 lb. bird 2¾ to 3¼ hours;
12 lb. bird 1¾ to 2 hours*

1 turkey	2 lb. sausage meat, or
3 to 4 slices fat bacon	2½ lb. veal forcemeat
½ pt stock	(see p. 105)
chestnut stuffing (see p. 102)	bread sauce or cranberry
fat for basting	sauce (see pp. 129, 131)

The above times of cooking are for birds bought ready for roasting. Put the chestnut stuffing in the neck end of the bird and the sausage meat or forcemeat in the tail end; retruss the bird securely. Cover the breast with the slices of fat bacon and a piece of grease-proof paper. Put into a baking tin with some fat and roast in a moderately hot oven. When the bird is a good brown the heat can be lowered a degree or two; baste frequently while cooking and about 20 minutes before it is ready take off the grease-proof paper and the bacon to allow the breast to brown.

When done, remove from oven, pull out all trussing strings, put on hot dish. Pour off most of the fat, sprinkle a little flour into the tin, gradually add the stock and simmer for 5 minutes; pour into a sauce-boat. Serve with either cranberry or bread sauce.

Gas 6–7; Electricity 400°–425°

Turkey stuffed with Truffles
Times as given for previous recipe for roast turkey

1 turkey	½ oz. flour
½ lb. fat bacon (chopped)	½ pt Espagnole sauce
½ lb. truffles (chopped)	(see p. 131)
½ lb. chestnuts	1 wineglass sherry
fat for basting	veal forcemeat (see p. 105)

Cut a slit in the chestnuts and boil them for 3 to 4 minutes, remove the outer and inner skin, put them into lightly-salted water and boil gently for about 20 minutes, or until soft, drain, rub through a sieve. If using fresh truffles they must be well washed and brushed. Mix the finely-chopped bacon with the chestnut purée and the truffles, and stuff the body of the bird with this mixture; stuff the crop with the veal forcemeat. Put the bird into a baking tin, cover the breast with grease-proof paper, add some basting fat and roast in a moderately hot oven. Baste frequently while cooking. Shortly before the bird is cooked remove the grease-proof paper and baste the breast well with the hot fat to brown it. Put the Espagnole sauce into a pan and when warm pour in the sherry; make hot but do not let it boil. Serve in a sauce-boat. It is a good idea after stuffing the bird to leave for 12 to 24 hours before cooking; this allows the flavour of the truffles to permeate all over the bird.

Gas 6–7; Electricity 400°–425°

Capercailzie Roast
5 to 6 persons. Time: 1 to 1¼ hours

1 capercailzie	watercress
3 streaky bacon rashers	bread sauce (see p. 129)
3 oz. butter	½ pt game stock or water
½ oz. flour	

Pluck, draw and truss the bird as for roast chicken. Cover the breast with the bacon, then with a piece of greaseproof paper. Put into a baking tin with the butter and bake in a moderate oven for 1 to 1¼ hours according to the age of the bird; baste frequently. About 20 minutes before it is ready, remove paper and bacon, dredge the breast with flour, baste with the fat to brown the breast. When done, remove from the oven, pour most of the fat out of the tin, sprinkle with flour, add the stock, stir until it boils, simmer for five minutes then pour into a sauce-boat. Serve the bird in a hot dish garnished with watercress. Hand bread-sauce and fried breadcrumbs (see p. 141).

Grouse Roast

3 persons. Time: ½ to ¾ hours

1 grouse	1 teaspoon lemon juice
1 fat bacon rasher	watercress
3 oz. butter	pepper, salt
fried breadcrumbs	

Pluck and draw the bird. Mix a little butter with the seasoning and lemon juice and put it inside the bird with the liver. Then truss as for roast chicken. Tie the fat rasher over the breast, put the bird into a tin and roast in a moderately hot oven. Baste often with butter. A few minutes before serving, remove the rasher of bacon and dredge the breast with flour and baste again with butter. The time for roasting depends upon the size and age of the bird. A young bird takes from 25 to 30 minutes and an older one 45 minutes. Put the grouse on a hot dish, remove the trussing strings and skewers if used. Make gravy in the tin as for roast beef, pour a very little around the bird, garnish with watercress. Hand the rest of the gravy separately in a sauce-boat, with chipped potatoes and browned breadcrumbs (see p. 141).

Gas 6–7; Electricity 400°–425°

Grouse Salmi

4 to 5 persons. Time: 30 to 40 minutes

2 grouse	½ pt Espagnole sauce
1 small onion	(see p. 131)
½ lb. mushrooms	1 tablespoon tomato purée
1 doz. green olives	½ wineglass sherry
2 oz. butter	pepper, salt
1 bunch herbs	

Pluck, draw and singe the birds, truss as for roasting. Put them into a baking tin with the butter and cook in a fairly hot oven for about 10 minutes. Remove from oven, untruss and cut into neat joints; put them into a pan. Add the bunch of herbs, the sauce, tomato purée, the peeled and thinly-sliced onion, the peeled mushrooms, stoned olives and the wine, add seasoning to taste and bring to the boil; simmer gently for 20 to 30 minutes. To serve, arrange the joints of grouse on a large croûte of fried bread and pour a little of the sauce over the rest around.

Gas 6–7; Electricity 400°–425°

Larks Roast

3 to 4 persons. Time: About 10 minutes

1 doz. larks	1 teaspoon chopped parsley
1 doz. small bacon pieces	nutmeg
2 oz. butter	fried breadcrumbs
lemon	pepper, salt

Pluck and clean the birds, cut off the heads and feet and pick out the gizzards. Season the birds inside with a little parsley, grate of nutmeg and a very little seasoning; cover each bird with a piece of bacon. Put on to skewers, six on each, place in a baking tin, pour hot melted butter over them and roast in the oven for about 10 minutes. They need constant basting or they will burn. Serve each one on a piece of toast, garnish with the fried breadcrumbs and cut lemon. Hand a rich gravy made with game stock.

Partridges Roast

5 to 6 persons. Time: 40 to 50 minutes

2 partridges	1 oz. ham
2 fat bacon rashers	bread sauce (see p. 129)
2 oz. butter	fried breadcrumbs
½ oz. flour	(see p. 141)
½ oz. cornflour	1 gill stock

Pluck, draw and truss the birds as for roast chicken, lard or bard them with the fat bacon. Place in a baking tin with the butter, put grease-proof paper over the birds and roast in the oven for 40 to 50 minutes, according to the size of the partridges. Baste frequently while cooking. About 10 minutes before they are ready, remove paper and bacon from the breast, sprinkle with flour and baste

81

well to brown. While they are in the oven put the liver and the chopped ham into the stock, bring to the boil and simmer for 20 minutes; strain, thicken with the cornflour for the gravy. Serve the birds on pieces of toast, garnish with the breadcrumbs and hand bread sauce.

Gas 6–7; Electricity 400°–425°

Pheasant Roast

4 to 5 persons. Time: $\frac{3}{4}$ to 1 hour

1 pheasant	1 gill game stock
2 fat bacon rashers	watercress
2 oz. butter	bread sauce (see p. 129)
$\frac{1}{2}$ oz. flour	fried breadcrumbs (see p. 141)

Pluck, draw and truss the bird as for roast chicken. Keep some of the tail feathers to use for decoration when serving. Lard or bard the bird with the bacon (see p. 73), put it into a baking tin with the butter and roast in the oven for $\frac{3}{4}$ to 1 hour—according to the size of the bird. Baste frequently while cooking. About 10 minutes before it is ready, remove the bacon, dredge the breast with flour and baste well to brown. When done, put the pheasant on to a hot dish, drain off any excess fat from the tin, sprinkle in a little flour, gradually pour on the stock; bring to the boil and simmer for 5 minutes, pour into sauce-boat. Serve the pheasant garnished with watercress, .put the tail feathers into place. Hand bread sauce and fried breadcrumbs, chip potatoes.

Gas 6–7; Electricity 400°–425°

Compote of Snipe

4 persons. Time: About 50 minutes

4 snipe	1 gill brown sauce (see p. 130)
2 oz. button mushrooms	$\frac{1}{2}$ gill stock
2 small tomatoes	1 wineglass sherry
1 fat bacon rasher	1 bunch herbs
1 cup vegetable macedoine (see p. 142)	1 oz. butter
1 lb. potatoes (cooked)	pepper, salt

Pluck but do not draw the birds, cover both with the bacon and roast them for 15 minutes in a moderate oven; baste

well with the butter. Remove from oven, allow to cool a little,
then cut into joints; put these into a sauté pan with the peeled
mushrooms. In another pan put the sliced tomatoes, stock, brown
sauce, herbs, wine, the carcases of the birds and a very little
seasoning; bring to the boil and cook gently for 20 to 25 minutes.
Strain this through a fine sieve then pour it over the snipe in
the sauté pan; put on a tightly-fitting lid and cook gently for
about 10 minutes or until the birds are ready. Rub the potatoes
through a sieve and make them hot with a little butter and the
yolk of an egg if liked, make this into a border mould and bake
in the oven until golden brown. To serve, put the potato mould
into a hot dish, arrange the snipe inside and put the heated
macedoine in the centre.

Gas 5-6; Electricity 375°-400°

Poor Man's Game Pie

4 persons. Time: 1½ to 2 hours

4 rooks	½ lb. puff paste (see p. 175)
½ lb. stewing steak	2 oz. margarine
2 hardboiled eggs	pepper, salt
½ pt stock or water	

Do not pluck the birds; skin them by cutting the skin near the
thighs and drawing it over the body and head. Draw the birds
and remove the necks and backs. Great care must be taken when
removing the backs as this is the bitter part and if any is left
behind it will make the bird uneatable. Split the rooks down the
breast, arrange in a deep pie dish, cover with the steak cut into
thin slices, the margarine in small pieces, sliced egg and seasoning
to taste. Pour in enough stock (or water if no stock available)
to three-quarters fill the dish. Cover with the puff paste, leaving
a small hole in the top. Bake for the first ½ hour in a hot oven to
make the pastry rise, then lower the heat and cook for another
1 to 1½ hours or until the birds are tender. When nearly cooked,
brush over with yolk of egg, and just before serving pour in a
little heated stock if available. It is a good idea to cover the
pastry with a piece of grease-proof paper after the first ½ hour to
prevent the pastry browning too much.

Gas 7; Electricity 425° to start

Quail Cutlets

4 persons. Time: About ½ hour

4 quails
½ lb. liver farce (see p. 103)
1 egg
2 oz. butter
breadcrumbs
1 medium tin asparagus tips

½ pt Espagnole sauce
(see p. 131)
1 medium tin petit pois
1 tablespoon chopped parsley
3 oz. frying fat or butter
pepper, salt

Bone the quails, leaving in the leg bones. Cut each bird in half and flatten it with a heavy knife. Melt the 2 oz. of butter in a pan and fry them to a light brown, remove from the pan and put between two plates with a weight on the top one; when cold coat each half with the liver farce, shaping them to look as much like cutlets as possible. Mix the herbs and seasoning with the breadcrumbs, dip the cutlets into the beaten egg, coat them with the breadcrumbs. Put the 3 oz. of fat or butter into a pan and fry the cutlets until they are a pale brown, turning once. Drain on to soft paper. To serve, put the heated asparagus in the centre of a dish, arrange the quail cutlets on top and the heated petit pois round the outside. Hand the Espagnole sauce.

Wild Duck Roast

3 to 4 persons. Time: About 20 to 25 minutes

1 wild duck
2 oz. butter
½ oz. flour
1 wineglass port wine

orange salad
watercress
½ pt brown sauce (see p. 130)
lemon

Pluck, draw and truss the bird for roasting; leave the feet on, twisting them backwards to the thighs. Spread a little of the butter on the breast, cover with grease-proof paper, put into a baking tin with the rest of the butter and the wine. Roast in the oven for about 20 to 25 minutes, according to the size of the bird; baste frequently with the butter and wine in the tin. About 5 minutes before the bird is done, remove the paper, dredge the breast with flour, baste well to brown. While the bird is cooking, peel the orange, remove all skin and pith, cut the orange across in slices. Arrange the fruit in layers in a dish, sprinkling castor sugar and a little brandy between each layer. Serve the duck on a hot dish garnished with watercress and cut lemon. Hand the orange salad and brown sauce to which the port in the baking tin has been added.

Gas 6–7; Electricity 400°–425°

Woodcock Roast

2 persons. Time: 15 to 20 minutes

2 woodcocks	watercress
2 fat bacon rashers	lemon
2 oz. butter	toast
$\frac{1}{2}$ oz. flour	

Pluck and wipe the outside of the birds but do not draw them. Remove the gizzards, skin the heads but do not cut off, remove the eyes. Truss in the usual way, pass the long beak of the bird through the body, like a skewer. Melt the butter, brush some over the birds, then cover with the bacon and a piece of grease-proof paper. Put them into a baking tin, with a piece of toast under each one to catch any drippings from the tail, and roast in the oven for 15 to 20 minutes—less time if liked under-done. Baste frequently while cooking; 2 to 3 minutes before they are ready remove paper and bacon, dredge the breast with flour and baste well to brown. Serve in a hot dish on the pieces of toast and garnish with watercress. Pour off most of the butter from the tin, sprinkle in a little flour to thicken, add $\frac{1}{2}$ gill of stock and boil for 2 to 3 minutes; pour into sauce-boat.

Gas 6–7; Electricity 400°–425°

9
Roasts and Meat Dishes

Whether it's called the roast, the remove or the main course,
it means one and the same thing. It was called the remove when
I was a kitchen maid, but by the time I got to be cook it was
the roast. This course consisted of either roast or braised or
grilled meat and was served after the entrée and always with
vegetables.

Today, of course, the methods of cooking are very different.
All right, we start in the same way by pre-heating the oven for
at least fifteen minutes before putting in a dish and, although
I haven't specified this with all the dishes in the book, I must
here make the point that for everything that is cooked in the
oven, be it fish, meat, sweet or savoury, the oven must be pre-
heated to the required temperature at least fifteen minutes
beforehand. It was after the meat was in the oven that our
methods became more elaborate and laborious than those used
today. Mind you, they were justified by the quality of the meat.
It hadn't been frozen so that the blood had turned to water, as

I'm sure it does now. Otherwise where is the red blood that used to run out of the meat when it was carved? All you get today is a watery substance that makes me feel that the animal was killed just in time to save its life, otherwise it would have died of anaemia.

I can't help feeling that a generation is growing up now that can have no idea of what real food tastes like. I mean young, tender, fresh meat from animals that were reared and fattened on fresh, natural foodstuffs and then killed, hung, cooked and eaten at the appropriate time. Today you can't begin to guess at how long the meat has been killed; it could have been a year before you get it. Therefore methods of cooking must necessarily be far different from what they were in the old days when we cooked in the old laborious ways, but when the meat was very succulent indeed.

I know, of course, that with an ever-increasing population, freezing and factory-farming have to be. At least now people do have enough to eat and the food, such as it is, is within the reach of the pocket of most people. When I was young it was a luxury. We only had a small joint once a week, and if my mother managed to buy pieces of meat, or 'block ornaments' as we used to call them, one other time during the week, we were lucky. But nowadays, with the average family, I don't think a day goes by without them having meat in some form or other.

The recipes that I've given in this book and the methods of cooking are those that I used when I was in service. I was taught that meat, game and poultry must always go into a hot oven to seal the outside and to keep the natural juices inside; nowadays when the juices are unnatural, different methods are in use. After half an hour the oven would be lowered, dripping or other fat put into the pan and the joint or whatever given continual basting. Laborious, yes, but remember that I didn't have to do any housework. In any case, ideas like wrapping in foil weren't known; there was no such thing as foil. We sometimes used to put greaseproof paper over the joint if it was getting brown and I do this myself now, especially if I've bought a very cheap joint of meat, such as flank or brisket.

The method today most constantly in use is to wrap the joint in foil, put it in a low oven and forget all about it. Perhaps there is something in this, because you know the end result is not going to be anything to rave about so you might just as well forget it, certainly the taste won't linger in your memory. I sometimes think that you need to wrap meat in foil if only to find where it is when you open the oven. So much liquid seems to run out of it that if the meat were put in without the foil, all you'd find at the end would be a pool of water at the bottom of the oven. If you can't eat it, drink it! So where I've put the gas heat as 6 or 7 and the equivalent for electricity, it's based on the kind of meat that I cooked years ago. Many of the joints of today, with the indignities they've been subjected to, will need foil wrapping and slow cooking on 2, 3 or 4.

However, some of my early failures were the same as those that can happen today. For instance, in boiling meat, unless the recipe specifically says put into cold water, the meat should always be put into boiling water. This hardens the albumen on the outside and thus prevents the meat juices escaping into the water. But care must be taken not to let the water boil for long after the meat has been put in, for this will harden the meat right through. So once the meat is in and the water boiling again, it must just simmer until cooked, but don't forget to skim every so often. Whatever you do, don't come in late to prepare the meal and think, 'Well, the recipe says two hours' slow boiling, so one hour quick boiling should be the same thing,' because it isn't. This simmering applies even more with a stew where you've got thickened gravy; this needs very long, slow cooking with little liquid. That's why casseroling meat is such a good method because it can be put in the oven with a lower temperature than you can have on a ring, and, of course, with a gas ring, when you turn it very low it may go out altogether.

If you are frying meat, as with frying fish, the fat must be hot, and this refers specifically to deep frying. If it's not hot enough the fat will seep into the meat instead of forming a coating on the outside and you'll find that you've got a sodden lump of fat instead of a golden coating with juicy meat inside. To test the heat, drop a breadcrumb into the fat, and if it starts to bubble straight away, the temperature is correct.

One or two last words on roasts:

I was always taught that a sign of good roasting and of good meat was that in the cooking there was little loss in weight. In fact, more weight is lost through roasting than by any other method. The water evaporates from the meat, and the fat melts.

Often we would use a double baking dish with the bottom filled with water which, as it boiled, prevented the fat in the other from burning. It also kept the oven from becoming too dry, and the cooks told me that if a joint got dry it shrank. This doesn't apply so much to present-day stoves; they're so made that air gets to them and so a certain amount of moisture is always in the oven.

I may seem to have been particularly crotchety and old-fashioned in this section. I don't mean to be. I realize that today there are two types of cook: the one who's prepared to spend her entire time stirring and basting, and the other who leaves things to cook themselves or who prepares what are called instant meals; and this is because there are two types of wife, the one who makes the home her entire life and devotes time to it, and the career wife who wants or has to contribute as much financially towards the home as her husband. So it's up to everyone to apply their own methods and the right way is the way which suits your time, your purse and, above all, your family.

Beef Braised

4 to 5 persons. Time: About 1½ hours

2 lb. silver-side of beef (fresh)	¼ lb. green peas
2 streaky bacon rashers	2 oz. butter
1 medium onion	2 oz. flour
6 small carrots	2 bay leaves
1 lb. small potatoes	1 wineglass Madeira
½ lb. mushrooms	¼ pt stock or water
½ small cauliflower	pepper, salt

Wash and dry the meat, remove the rind from the bacon and dice it. Melt the butter in a pan and lightly fry the bacon; put half of the flour on a plate, coat the meat all over with it and put into the pan with the bacon, fry until just brown on both sides. Wash and peel the vegetables, cut into small pieces the onion, carrot, cauliflower and mushrooms, but leave the potatoes whole. Put half of the vegetables at the bottom of a casserole, lay the meat on top and cover with the rest of the vegetables, with the peas on top; add the bay leaves. Put the rest of the flour into the butter left in the pan, mix well, gradually pour on the stock or water and stir until it boils, then add the wine. Pour this into the casserole, add seasoning to taste, cover with a tightly-fitting lid and cook in the oven for about 1½ hours, or until the beef is tender.

Gas 2–3; Electricity 300°–325°

Beef Pot Roasted

4 to 6 persons. Time: About 2 hours

2 to 2½ lb. topside or rolled ribs	2 oz. dripping
1 shallot	1 gill water
1 small carrot	horseradish sauce (see p. 133)
2 oz. mushrooms	pepper, salt

Wash and wipe the meat and tie or skewer into shape. Melt the dripping in a pan; when hot brown the meat on both sides. Remove the meat and put in the peeled and chopped onion, carrot and mushrooms, lightly brown, then put the meat back in the pan, add the water and seasoning. Cover with a tightly-fitting lid and cook over a low heat until the meat is tender—about 1¾ to 2 hours. Baste frequently with the liquid. This dish must be cooked slowly or the liquid will boil away. Serve on a hot dish with the horseradish in a sauce-boat.

Beef Sirloin Roasted

10 to 12 persons. Time: 15 to 20 minutes to the lb.

6 to 7 lb. sirloin	¾ pt stock or water
4 oz. dripping	grated horseradish
½ oz. flour	pepper, salt
horseradish sauce (see p. 133)	

Wash and wipe the meat and sprinkle over a little seasoning, put into a baking tin with the dripping and cook in the oven, allowing 15 to 20 minutes to the pound. Baste frequently while cooking. When nearly ready dredge a little flour over the meat and baste well to brown. When the meat is done, put on a hot dish and drain most of the fat from the pan; sprinkle in a little flour, mix well, pour in the stock or water and stir until it boils. Garnish the meat with a little grated horseradish, put the sauce and the gravy into sauce-boats.

Gas 6–7; Electricity 400°–425°

Beef Steak and Kidney Pudding

5 to 6 persons. Time: 2½ hours to boil, 3½ hours to steam

1 lb. beef steak	2 tablespoons flour
½ lb. beef kidney	water
¾ lb. suet pastry	pepper, salt

I always use rump steak for this, but skirt or buttock would be all right. Wash the steak and kidney and cut into strips about 2 to 3 inches long and 1 inch wide. Mix seasoning with 1 tablespoon of the flour and coat the meat with it. Grease a pudding basin, and roll out on a well-floured board enough of the suet pastry to line the basin—the paste should be about ½ inch thick. Fill the basin with the meat, add a little more seasoning and enough water to three parts fill the basin, wet the edges of the paste and cover with a lid of suet pastry of the same thickness. Cover with a piece of greased paper, tie on a scalded and floured cloth, make a pleat across to allow the pudding to rise, and either boil for 2½ hours or steam for 3½ hours. Just before serving either cut a hole in the top of the pudding and pour in a little boiling water, or serve a brown gravy separately.

Beef Strogonoff

4 persons. Time: About ½ hour

1½ lb. fillet of beef	1 gill sour cream
1 medium onion	1 dessertspoon Worcester
2 oz. butter	sauce
1 teaspoon flour	chopped parsley
1 gill stock (white)	pepper, salt

Wash the beef, remove all skin and sinew and cut into thin pieces. Mix the flour with the seasoning and coat the meat with it. Melt the butter in a pan, add the peeled and finely-chopped onion and fry to a pale brown, put in the meat and lightly fry, then stir in the stock, Worcester sauce and sour cream. Mix well, bring to almost boiling point and cook until all is a deep yellow-brown; only just simmer or the liquid will dry up. Serve in a deep dish sprinkled with chopped parsley. Fried mushrooms can be added to this dish if liked.

Ham Baked

8 or more persons. Time: Allow 25 minutes to the lb.

1 small ham, or ½ large one	bread raspings, or glaze, or
flour and water paste	demerara sugar

91

Soak the ham for about 12 hours, longer if very salty, cut off any
rusty parts, wipe dry and cover with a fairly thick paste made of
flour and water. Put into a baking tin or fire-proof casserole and
bake in the oven, allowing about 25 minutes to the lb. up to
12 lb.; if larger allow about 15 minutes for each lb. over that
weight. When the ham is done, remove from oven, take off the
paste and carefully pull off the skin. Cover the surface either with
bread raspings, demerara sugar or coat with glaze (see p. 142).

Gas 6; Electricity 400°

Ham Braised with Wine
10 or more persons. Time: About 4 to 5 hours

1 York ham	½ pt sherry or marsala, or 1
½ pt Espagnole sauce	gill of sherry or marsala and
(see p. 131)	1 gill of champagne
1 pt white stock	

Soak the ham for 12 to 24 hours, changing the water once or
twice. Cut off the knuckle bone, put the ham into a pan with just
enough water to cover, bring to the boil, skim and gently simmer
for 3 to 4 hours, according to the size of the ham. When done,
remove from pan and carefully pull off the skin, put the ham into
another pan with the stock and wine and simmer slowly for 30 to
40 minutes. Take out of pan and keep warm, skim all fat from
the stock and wine liquor and boil it to about half quantity, add
the Espagnole sauce, stir and bring to the boil. Serve the ham on
a large dish with a little of the sauce round and the rest in a
sauce-boat.

Hare Roasted in Sour Cream
About 6 persons. Time: 1½ to 2 hours

1 hare	2 oz. lard
2 shallots	2 oz. butter
2 sticks celery	1½ oz. flour
1 pt white wine vinegar	8 peppercorns
1 pt water	3 bay leaves
¼ gill white stock	pepper, salt
1 gill sour cream	

If not already skinned, skin and draw the hare, taking care not to break the gall bladder as you remove the liver. Quickly wash the hare and remove the blood clots. Put into a pan the vinegar, water, onions, celery, peppercorns and bay leaves and boil for 5 minutes; leave to cool, put in the hare and let stand overnight. Then take out of the vinegar and truss by bending the hind legs forward and the front legs backwards, break the sinews to allow the legs to lie close to the body, skewer them into position. Rub the lard over the hare, put into an oblong baking tin and pour over the melted butter; cover with a piece of grease-proof paper and roast in the oven for 1½ to 2 hours, according to the size of the hare; it will need frequent basting as the flesh is inclined to be dry. When done, take out of oven, put on a hot dish and keep warm. Pour most of the fat from the pan, then add to the gravy that is left the stock and cream, boil until it becomes yellow, then strain half of this over the hare and serve the other half in a sauce-boat. Serve also redcurrant jelly.

Gas 6–7; Electricity 400°–425°

Hunters' Steak
4 to 6 persons. Time: About 12 to 15 minutes to grill

2 lb. rump steak	1 teaspoon chopped parsley
¼ lb. ham (cooked)	1 medium onion
6 oz. veal forcemeat	1 bay leaf
(see p. 105)	1 gill white wine
1 truffle	¾ gill salad oil
2 oz. butter	pepper, salt
½ pt Robert sauce (see p. 137)	

The steak should be about 1¼ inches thick. Lay it flat on the table and insert a sharp pointed knife into the centre of the meat as though to slice it in half, cut to within an inch of three sides of the steak so that it forms a sort of pocket. Mix together the oil, wine, parsley, bay leaf, sliced onion and seasoning, put the steak into this and soak it for 2 hours, turning occasionally. While the meat is soaking, chop the ham and truffle, mix it with the force-meat and 1 gill of the Robert sauce, put into a pan and make warm, then remove the meat from the oil mixture and fill the pocket with the sauce mixture; sew up the opening and flatten gently with the hand. Brush with melted butter and grill for about 12 to 15 minutes or until tender; turn once or twice and pour on a little more butter from time to time. When done, carefully remove the sewing twine, place the steak on a hot dish, pour round a little of the other gill of the sauce (heated) and serve the rest separately. (This may be stuffed with oysters blanched for 2 to 3 minutes in boiling water, then bearded and the cavity in the steak filled.)

Lamb, Stewed Leg

6 to 7 persons. Time: Allow 20 minutes to the lb.

small leg of lamb	1 bay leaf
½ lb. streaky bacon	1 sprig parsley
6 small onions	½ pt caper sauce (see white
1 lb. green peas (after shelling)	sauce, p. 140)
¾ pt stock or water	pepper, salt
2 oz. flour	

Wash and wipe dry the lamb, mix the flour with a little seasoning and coat the meat with it. Fry the rashers in a pan until they are crisp, remove from pan and put in the lamb, fry until it is brown all over. Pour away the fat and add the hot stock or water, put back the meat and bacon, bring to the boil and simmer slowly for 1 hour. Then add the onions (they must be very small), the parsley, bay leaf and peas and continue cooking until all is tender. When cooked, place on a hot dish and surround with the peas and onions; serve some of the liquor in a sauce-boat and caper sauce in another.

Lamb, Stuffed Shoulder

6 to 8 persons. Time: 1½ to 1¾ hours

1 small shoulder of lamb	½ doz. pickled mushrooms
1 sweetbread (cooked)	1 pt stock or water
(see p. 27)	½ pt brown sauce (see p. 130)
4 lean bacon rashers	1 bunch herbs
¼ lb. veal forcemeat	1 lemon
(see p. 105)	pepper, salt

Wash and dry the meat. Remove the bones from the underside of the shoulder but leave in the shank bone; fill in the part from which the bones have been removed with the veal forcemeat. Lay two of the rashers at the bottom of the pan, put the shoulder and the other two rashers on top, add the herbs, seasoning to taste, and the stock or water and bring to the boil slowly; stew gently for 1½ to 1¾ hours or until tender. Put the brown sauce into a pan, add the pickled mushrooms and the sweetbread cut into dice, bring to the boil and simmer for 5 minutes. Place the lamb on a dish, pour the sauce around and garnish with cut lemon.

Mutton, Braised Leg

About 8 persons. Time: 2½ to 3 hours

1 small leg of mutton	1 teaspoon chopped parsley
½ lb. pickled pork or bacon	1 oz. butter
2 medium onions	½ doz. cloves
2 carrots	1 bunch herbs
1 small turnip	stock
2 or 3 pieces celery	pepper, salt
½ pt white haricot beans	

Wash the beans and soak them in cold water overnight, then put them into a pan with enough water to well cover, bring to the boil and simmer for 2 hours, or longer if they do not seem soft enough, then strain. Wash and dry the meat, cut the shank bone from the leg. Peel the onions, cut into halves, peel and slice the other vegetables. Line the bottom of a pan with thin slices of the bacon or pork, put the meat on the top, add the onions, stuck with cloves, and all the vegetables. Put the rest of the sliced bacon or pork on the top. Add just enough stock to cover the meat and season to taste. Put on a tightly-fitting lid, bring to the boil, simmer gently for 2½ to 3 hours. When cooked remove from the pan, strain the liquor and boil rapidly to reduce it to a thin glaze. Put the leg on a large dish, pour a little of the gravy over, and around the meat put the haricot beans which have been tossed in butter and chopped parsley.

Mutton, Roast Loin, Boned and Stuffed

6 to 8 persons. Time: About 2½ hours

1 loin mutton	2 teaspoons chopped parsley
2 oz. chopped ham or bacon	1 teaspoon chopped sage
3 tablespoons breadcrumbs	½ lemon
2 tablespoons suet	pepper, salt
1 egg	

Bone the meat or ask your butcher to do this. Wash and dry it, cut off any superfluous fat and flatten meat with rolling pin. Put the breadcrumbs into a basin, add the finely-chopped suet, parsley, sage, ham or bacon, grated rind of ½ lemon and a little seasoning; mix well together. Add the beaten egg, and if not moist enough a little milk. Spread this forcemeat on the inner side of the loin, roll up tightly and bind round with thin twine. Put into a baking tin and roast in a moderately hot oven for 2 to 2½ hours, according to size, basting frequently with hot fat. Make the gravy by straining off most of the fat when the meat is cooked, and pouring in about ½ pt of stock; add a little seasoning. Hand redcurrant jelly and Piquante sauce (see p. 137).

Gas 5–6; Electricity 375°–400°

Mutton, Roast Saddle

12 or more persons. Time: Allow about 15 minutes per lb.

1 saddle of mutton	½ oz. flour
2 sheep's kidneys	½ pt brown stock
2 oz. butter	pepper, salt

Wash and wipe the meat, remove the outer skin from the saddle then fix it over the top with skewers. Roll the flank under the joint, split the tail and curl each half round a kidney. Put the saddle into a baking tin, pour over 1 oz. of the butter, melted, and roast in the oven, allowing 15 minutes to the lb. and 15 minutes over. Baste frequently; if the saddle seems to be browning too quickly, cover with grease-proof paper. About ½ hour before it is done, dredge the top with the flour, pour over the rest of the butter to make the top rather crisp. When cooked, remove from pan, drain off most of the fat, sprinkle in a little flour and mix well, gradually pour in the stock, bring to the boil and simmer for 2 or 3 minutes. Serve this in a sauce-boat, with mint sauce (see p. 135) and redcurrant jelly.

Gas 6; Electricity 400°

Ox-Tongue Boiled

8 to 9 persons. Time: About 2½ hours

1 ox-tongue	lemon
½ pt tomato sauce (see p. 139)	parsley

Choose a tongue with a smooth skin, a rough skin indicates that the tongue is old. If bought fresh from the pickle the tongue requires soaking for 3 to 4 hours. Wash it well, trim the root and skewer into shape; put into lukewarm water just enough to cover, bring to the boil, skim, and simmer for 2½ hours, and continue skimming occasionally. When the tip of the tongue is tender, put it quickly into cold water for a minute or two, this enables the skin to be removed easily. If it is to be eaten hot, cover the tongue with grease-proof paper and reheat in the oven for about ten minutes, then serve with cut lemon and sprigs of parsley. Hand tomato sauce in a sauce-boat.

Pork, Roast Leg with Prunes and Baked Apples
8 to 10 persons. Time: Allow about 25 minutes per lb.

1 leg of pork	½ lb. demerara sugar
large cooking apples (1 per person)	½ wineglass port
1 lb. prunes	2 oz. butter
	salt

Soak the prunes overnight in 1 pt. of cold water.
Wash and wipe the pork, make sure that the rind is well-scored, brush all over with salad oil and sprinkle with salt. Put into a hot oven for the first 20 minutes; then lower the heat slightly, baste frequently and roast, allowing 25 minutes to the lb. and 20 minutes over. While the meat is cooking, put prunes into a casserole with the same water in which they were soaked, add 4 oz. of the sugar and the wine. Put a lid on the casserole and cook in the oven for ¾ to 1 hour, or until soft. Peel and core the apples, place in a fairly deep dish, fill the centres with the rest of the sugar, put a knob of butter on top. Put a tablespoon of water in the bottom of the dish and place in the bottom of the oven to cook—time about 1 hour; be careful not to overcook or the apples will not keep their shape. When the pork is done, remove from tin and put in a large dish, keep hot. Strain most of the fat from the tin, sprinkle in a little flour, pour on about ½ pt of boiling water (or stock if preferred), bring to the boil, simmer for a minute or two, then pour into sauce-boat. Serve the pork with the baked apples arranged round it and the prunes in the casserole.

Gas 6–7; Electricity 400°–425°

Raised Pork Pie
5 to 6 persons. Time: About 2½ hours

1½ lb. lean pork	1 egg
1 lb. raised pie pastry (see p. 176)	½ oz. gelatine
½ pt stock, or water	pepper, salt

Roll out the pastry on a floured board, then line a pork pie mould with it, or any dish as high as a small cake tin would do. Wash the pork and cut into small pieces, fill the mould with it, add seasoning to taste and 2 or 3 tablespoons of the stock or water. Brush the edges of the mould with water, cover with the rest of the pastry, press well together, scallop the edges and leave a small hole in the centre. Bake in the oven for about 2½ to 3 hours; when the pie is about half cooked brush the top with the egg yolk. Dissolve the gelatine in the rest of the boiling stock or water (if the stock is used, slightly less gelatine is needed); when the pie is cold, gradually pour in the gelatine through the hole in the top and leave to set.

Gas 4; Electricity 350°

Roast Suckling Pig

7 to 8 persons. Time: About 2½ hours

1 sucking pig	salad oil
4 oz. butter	lemon
veal forcemeat (see p. 105) or	parsley
chestnut stuffing (see p. 102)	cayenne pepper

The pig should be only about 3 weeks old. When it is cleaned, stuff the body with the veal or chestnut stuffing. Sew it up and truss it the same way as a hare is trussed, with its forelegs skewered back and its hindlegs forwards. Dry well, brush over with the salad oil and cover with two or three thicknesses of grease-proof paper. Put it in a baking tin in the oven for 2 to 2½ hours, according to size. Baste it well with oil or butter while cooking and, shortly before it is done, remove the paper to allow the skin to brown. When it is cooked, cut off the head and split into halves. Divide the pig with a sharp knife down the centre of the back, put the backs together with the ears on each side and the halves of the head at each end of the dish. Season the melted butter with a pinch of cayenne and mix with a little of the gravy from the pig, add a squeeze of lemon juice and pour some of this round the pig—not over or the crisp skin will go soft. Garnish with sprigs of parsley. Serve with tomato or apple sauce (see pp. 137 and 129).

Gas 6; Electricity 400°

Roast Fillet of Veal

5 to 6 persons. Time: 1¾ to 2¼ hours

4 to 5 lb. fillet of veal
1 doz. streaky rashers
sausage forcemeat (see p. 104)

3 oz. dripping or other fat
1 lemon

Wash and wipe the veal, remove the bone and stuff the cavity
with the forcemeat. Tie into a round and skewer, put into a
baking tin with the fat, cover with well-greased paper and roast
in an oven for 1¾ to 2¼ hours or until tender; baste frequently.
Remove the rind from the rashers, roll each one up and put on a
skewer. Put in the oven until crisp. Serve the veal with the bacon
rolls round it and the lemon cut into slices.

Gas 6–7; Electricity 400°–425°

Stewed Veal with Green Peas and Forcemeat Balls

4 to 5 persons. Time: About 2¼ hours

4 lb. breast of veal
4 small onions
1 oz. butter
½ oz. flour
2 oz. dripping or other fat
2 sprigs parsley
2 blades mace

1 glass sherry or white wine
tomato sauce (see p. 137)
mushroom ketchup
½ lemon
1 doz. forcemeat balls
green peas
pepper, salt

Wash and wipe the veal, remove all gristle and superfluous fat.
Melt the dripping or other fat in a pan, put in the veal and brown
it all over. Drain off the fat, then add the parsley, mace, peeled
onions, thinly-peeled rind of half a lemon and the seasoning to
taste. Add enough boiling water to just cover, put on a tightly-
fitting lid and simmer slowly for two hours, then remove from
the pan and strain the liquid. Melt the butter in a pan, blend in
the flour, gradually add 1 pint of the liquid from the veal, bring to
the boil stirring all the time, then add the wine, 3 dessertspoons of
tomato sauce, 3 dessertspoons of mushroom ketchup and the
juice of the ½ lemon, let it simmer slowly for 15 minutes,
skimming occasionally. Serve the veal with a border of boiled
green peas and the forcemeat balls. Pour some of the sauce over,
hand the rest in a sauce-boat.

10

Forcemeats and Stuffings

Forcemeats and stuffings, like sauces, should enhance the dishes they are served with; they shouldn't alter their character. To achieve this requires a certain amount of know-how and care so that no one flavour is so prominent as to disguise the others or that of the main dish. Know-how and care can only be learnt through experience, and experience only comes through trial and error. So when you see a forcemeat or stuffing recipe containing about half a dozen ingredients, you may think to yourself, 'Well, I would prefer a little more of this or a little more of that,' but until you have tried it with the dish you are serving it with, I don't really think you should start deviating from the recipe.

It is also, in a recipe, somewhat difficult to give the precise ingredients as so much depends on the exact consistency required. For instance, if it's wanted for stuffing a bird or rolled veal, it needs to be moister than if you are making forcemeat balls that have to be rolled and then fried. Again, if you were making a mixture for quenelles—a word that frightens some people yet it's a very simple dish—they also need to keep their shape and yet must be light. So, if you're in doubt about the consistency of this mixture, it is a good thing to put a little into boiling water and if the mixture collapses you know it needs more yolk of egg or breadcrumbs added. Remember, too, when making quenelles the water must never go off the boil.

As you read the recipes, it may seem that the stuffing or forcemeats will take longer to prepare than the dish that they are to accompany. Nevertheless, the time and trouble taken will make all the difference, particularly to the plainest of foods.

Finally, if your stuffing or forcemeat is accompanying a cold dish, it is better, if the recipe says suet, to change it to butter. As I began by saying, in this section personal choice and common sense play a very large part in the success of these recipes, which need interpreting in the light of experience.

Bread Panada for Forcemeat, Quenelles, Etc.

½ lb. bread (without crust) ½ gill milk or water
1½ oz. butter   salt

Soak the bread in the milk, or water, for 1 hour, strain and squeeze dry in a cloth. Melt the butter in a pan, add the bread and a pinch of salt, stir over a fairly low heat until it forms a smooth paste and does not adhere to the sides of the pan. Put on a plate to cool and use as required.

Flour Panada for Soufflés and some Forcemeats

¼ lb. flour   salt
1 oz. butter   ½ pt milk or water

Put the butter and milk, or water, into a pan, bring to the boil, sprinkle in the flour and stir vigorously. Using a wooden spoon, keep stirring over a low heat until the mixture thickens and almost forms a ball in the middle of the pan leaving the sides clean.

Apple Stuffing, for Pork or Goose

1 lb. sour apples	1 oz. sugar
2½ oz. Carolina rice	1 oz. butter
1 egg	

Wash the rice, boil until very soft, strain. Peel and core the apples, slice thinly, put them into a pan with just enough water to prevent them burning; simmer until soft. Add the butter, sugar, boiled rice and the beaten egg and mix well; use as required.

Chestnut Stuffing, for small to medium turkey

1 lb. chestnuts (Spanish)	stock or water
2 oz. butter	nutmeg
3 oz. breadcrumbs	pepper, salt
1 large egg	

Make a slit in the chestnuts and roast them for about 20 minutes until the outer and inner skin be easily removed, then put them in a pan with enough stock or water to cover and simmer until soft. Strain, rub the chestnuts through a sieve, add the breadcrumbs, melted butter, beaten egg, a little grated nutmeg and seasoning to taste, mix well together. If it seems too dry, a little milk can be added.

Fish Stuffing

2½ oz. Carolina rice	1 teaspoon curry powder
1 tomato	pepper, salt
lemon rind	

Wash the rice, put into a pan with about ½ to ¾ pt of cold water and a thin strip of lemon rind, simmer until the rice is very soft, strain and leave to cool. Add the peeled and chopped tomato, curry powder and seasoning to taste and use for stuffing fresh haddock or cod.

Forcemeat Balls for Chicken or Turkey

2 oz. lean ham (cooked)
6 oz. breadcrumbs
4 oz. suet
2 eggs
lemon rind

1 heaped teaspoon mixed herbs
1 teaspoon parsley
cayenne pepper, salt

Finely chop the suet and parsley, mix with the breadcrumbs, herbs, chopped ham, grated rind of ½ lemon and seasoning to taste. Beat the eggs and add to the mixture until it has reached a consistency that will easily roll into balls. These may be rolled in flour and fried to a light brown, or, instead of frying, put into the baking tin with the bird shortly before it is done.

Liver Farce or Imitation Foie Gras

½ lb. calf's liver
½ lb. mashed potato
1 small onion
1 oz. fat bacon
2 egg yolks

½ teaspoon mixed herbs
1 bay leaf
½ gill stock
pepper, salt

Wash and dry the liver, cut into thin slices; dice the bacon and fry for a few minutes; add the liver and lightly brown on both sides. Put in the stock, herbs, bay leaf, chopped onion and seasoning to taste and simmer gently until the liver is tender. Pound well in a mortar, add the mashed potatoes and rub all through a sieve, add the yolks of eggs, mix well and use as required.

Mushroom Stuffing for Game

½ lb. mushrooms
6 oz. breadcrumbs
1 oz. butter

1 egg
nutmeg
pepper, salt

Peel the mushrooms, chop finely, melt the butter in a pan, put in the mushrooms and cook over a very low heat for 15 minutes stirring frequently. Remove from heat, add the breadcrumbs, a little grated nutmeg and seasoning to taste. Bind with the beaten egg and use as required.

Prawn or Lobster Stuffing

Make as for roe stuffing but substitute chopped prawns or pieces of lobster instead of the herring roes.

Roe Stuffing

Cod roe	1 level teaspoon chopped
(6 to 8 oz.)	parsley
breadcrumbs	1 oz. butter (melted)
2 egg yolks or	1 oz. suet (chopped)
1 egg	pepper, salt, vinegar

Wash the roe and tie it in a piece of muslin. Put into a pan with enough warm lightly-salted water to cover, add a dessertspoon of vinegar and cook gently until the roe is soft. Remove from pan, pound well in a mortar, mix with the parsley, egg, butter, suet, seasoning and enough breadcrumbs to make the whole into a firm consistency. Use as required for stuffing fish.

Sage and Onion Stuffing

1 lb. onions	1 oz. butter
¼ lb. breadcrumbs	pepper, salt
1 teaspoon crushed sage	

Peel the onions. If large cut them into quarters, put them into boiling water with a little salt; parboil for 15 to 20 minutes. Strain and chop them, add the sage, breadcrumbs, melted butter and seasoning to taste; use as required.

Sausage Forcemeat for Poultry or Veal

½ lb. sausage meat	1 teaspoon each of chopped
¼ lb. breadcrumbs	parsley and sage
1 oz. butter	pepper, salt
1 egg	

Mix the sausage meat with the breadcrumbs, parsley, sage, melted butter and seasoning to taste, bind with the beaten egg and use as required.

Veal Forcemeat No. 1

2 oz. suet	1 level tablespoon chopped
4 oz. breadcrumbs	parsley
1 egg, or milk	1 teaspoon herbs
grated rind of ½ lemon	pepper, salt

Finely chop the suet, add all the dry ingredients and seasoning to taste. Add enough beaten egg, or milk, to moisten, but it must not be too soft.

Veal Forcemeat No. 2 Richer

½ lb. veal	1 dessertspoon chopped
¼ lb. suet	parsley
2 oz. fat bacon	½ small teaspoon mushroom
2 oz. breadcrumbs	ketchup
2 eggs	pepper, salt
½ small shallot	

Put the veal twice through a mincer (ask your butcher to do the first mince), finely chop the suet, dice the bacon. Pound all these in a mortar, then rub through a wire sieve; add the finely-chopped shallot, breadcrumbs, parsley, mushroom ketchup and seasoning to taste. Mix with the beaten eggs to form a fairly moist mixture and use for birds, pork, etc.

II

Vegetables

I find that people talk about vegetables in a tone of voice they wouldn't use when discussing meat, game or soups, as if vegetables are merely an accompaniment for these foods and have little importance in their own right. It's nonsense. Vegetables do accompany other courses, but they're like the bridesmaids to the bride or the best man to the groom, and if they are not dressed as well as the main performers, they spoil the wedding.

I said when I was a cook, and I still say it now, that as much care should be taken in the preparation of vegetables as in the cooking of them. It's essential to remove any damaged or decayed parts. It's false economy to think that good and bad will blend in with the cooking.

Half a pound of good fresh vegetables is better than three-quarters of a pound of second rate. When you're preparing green vegetables, after you've picked off the stalks and any odd bits that don't look quite the same colour, soak them in cold water for at least half an hour before you cook them. Sprinkle with salt, not too much because it tends to harden the fibres of cabbage and cauliflower, and add a little vinegar. The salt has the further advantage that it brings out and kills the insects. The vinegar freshens up the vegetables and, if they are not absolutely fresh, does quite a bit for them. You should use a tablespoon of vinegar to a bowl of water.

It is essential that you wash and clean well, especially with spinach. This needs several washings otherwise it will be gritty. It may look clean and you may not even feel the grit on your fingers, but if you do not use at least three lots of water, you're almost certain to find it unsatisfactory.

There always have been two schools of thought as to whether greens should be cooked with or without a lid on the saucepan and whether you should add a pinch of bicarbonate of soda. Cooking without the lid and the addition of bicarbonate of soda are supposed to keep the greens green. Purists, of course, think that it's a heinous offence to use the bicarbonate. They say it destroys the fine tissue and the nutriment. Personally, I like to have my greens looking attractive even if I go short on nutriment, and I don't think it makes any difference to them whether you cook with the lid on or off.

A point to remember when you're preparing root vegetables, carrots, turnips or swedes, is to do a few extra for your stock-pot. It's no good putting left-overs from a meal in afterwards; they must always be fresh. And, with the exception of old potatoes, you should put all vegetables into boiling water. Naturally this is essential with green vegetables, but I have cooked root vegetables from cold water without any noticeable difference in taste. Here again there are those who say it ruins them, but it's everyone to his choice or from his own experience.

When cooking Brussels sprouts, if they are large, do cut a cross on the bottoms, otherwise you'll find that the top is breaking away while the bottom part isn't cooked. And don't throw away your vegetable water. Use it to top up the stockpot. Be careful when you're cooking root vegetables in particular not to add too much salt, because they absorb water and with it the salt; you may find afterwards that they're over-salty and unpalatable. It's always easy to add salt but you can't take it away, and it's no use, if you think you've overdone the salt, adding more boiling water, because once they are impregnated, it just doesn't work.

Some people don't believe in boiling vegetables, especially those who are concerned about the nutritive value of what they're eating. So they insist that they are steamed. There's no question that, done this way, they do lose their colour; on the other hand, there's no doubt they are more nutritious because some of the goodness does boil into the water, whereas by steaming it's retained. If you are more concerned with food values than looks, steaming is the method to use, but remember that if you're steaming vegetables it will take you twenty to thirty minutes longer. This applies to anything steamed—steamed puddings, for instance, take twice as long as boiled ones.

If you're going to steam vegetables, particularly root vegetables, it's a good idea to put them into boiling water for a minute or two first. This helps to eliminate the rather strong flavour that they have, particularly swedes and turnips. Vegetables can, of course, be cooked in a casserole in the oven. If you do this, I suggest you add a little butter or margarine, about a dessertspoonful, use half a cup of water and have a tightly-fitting lid. Again, this method is going to take longer than does boiling, but you'll find that the vegetables taste excellent.

Although potatoes are generally the most popular and the easiest to cook of vegetables, it's surprising what a sodden mass some people manage to turn out. Either, if they're boiling them, they use too much water or they're boiled so fast that they break up, or they leave them in the water after they're cooked, thinking that they'll keep hot that way; they may do, but this also turns them black and they look and taste foul. Immediately they are cooked they should be drained, for they must be dry and floury. When I was a kitchen maid, and later a cook, whenever we drained potatoes and whatever way we were going to prepare them, we would put a dry clean cloth inside the saucepan after they were drained to absorb all the steam and moisture. That way we got a superb article.

Then there are globe artichokes and asparagus. These are generally served as a course on their own. Globe artichokes have a very delicate flavour and great care must be taken that they are not overcooked. It's rather an acquired taste, I think —dangerous to serve unless you know your guests well, as some people dislike the flavour.

Asparagus requires careful handling and cooking. It should always be bought fresh, but if you need to keep it for a day or two put it into a cool place with the stalks in water. Don't buy asparagus if you find that the heads are drooping and that the white stalks have turned brown; this means they are stale and no amount of care in the cooking or the serving is going to make them anything but stale. If, after you have kept them for a while and they are drooping slightly, I would recommend that they are boiled.

When preparing asparagus, cut the sticks to the same length, scrape them downwards from the green part and tie them in bundles of about eight to ten sticks if they're large, and up to twenty if they are smaller, then soak them in cold water for an hour. They can then be boiled or steamed. In service we had an asparagus cooker. It was a pan with a perforated container which allowed the asparagus to stand upright so that the stalks were boiled in the water but the green tips were only steamed. It was simple and ingenious because the container could be removed and the pan used for other purposes. I'd say without qualification that asparagus is the only vegetable that you can eat either hot, cold or tepid and it's still delicious. We found it an excellent starter for dinner parties because if the guests weren't punctual it didn't matter; it couldn't be ruined and they were pleased to eat it at any heat.

Aubergines, or eggplants as they are sometimes called, are another useful vegetable. I used to wonder why they were called eggplants because they look more like a kind of pestle or a purple-coloured cosh. Then I discovered the rarer kind, the white ones, which do look exactly like a large egg. I imagine they belong to the marrow species. Like marrows, they can either be boiled or baked. I prefer them baked, particularly if they are stuffed with minced ham, tongue or chicken and served with one of the many sauces that go well with them. Again, baked aubergines can be a course on their own.

Although mushrooms are a fungus, since I am not dealing with anything else under this heading, I am considering them as a vegetable. I won't go on about how the mushrooms that grew wild in the fields when I was young, between April and October, had a flavour which the cultivated ones of today don't, because, like chicken, they are now no longer a luxury but are available to everybody. Mushrooms today have an important place in so much of cooking.

Salsify, sometimes called Purple Goat's Beard, was another popular vegetable when I was in service. There are two kinds, white and black. The black tastes strongly of oysters, which is why salsify is called the vegetable oyster. The white, the cheaper salsify, hasn't the same flavour. It looks like a parsnip but is far more expensive.

To some people marrows are an object of derision, and the way they serve them up, I'm not surprised. They boil them as badly as they do potatoes. A marrow, like an aubergine, can be stuffed. If you just peel it and throw it into boiling water, drain in a colander and serve, it's like eating hot water. But a marrow cut into rings, boiled in a very small quantity of water, drained, dried and served with a white parsley or Béchamel sauce, can be delicious.

Celery I prefer raw. I know many people braise celery and it can be steamed or boiled and served with a sauce, but for my money, all you get is the celery flavour. The body of the vegetable has little taste. Boiled onions sounds and is a terrible dish, but braised onions you can go to town on. Is there anything more delicious with some meat courses than braised onions? Lovely round Spanish onions done in a casserole with about a dessertspoonful of water and butter, pepper, salt and a spot of Worcestershire sauce to stimulate the flavour. Boiled onions are dreadful things unless you've got a cold and want to clamp them on your chest. Some people say they draw out fevers; personally I'd sooner have the fever.

Truffles, the *Oxford Dictionary* says, are a subterranean fungus used for seasoning dishes. Well, I've treated mushrooms as a vegetable and I shall apply the same definition to truffles. They grow mainly in France and Italy, but those from France have a distinct edge over the Italian ones. Specially trained dogs or pigs are kept to find truffles, but I understand it's safer to use dogs because pigs are so quick to find them that they've eaten them before the pig-keeper or the truffle-hunter can get to them. Whereas dogs can be trained merely to sniff them out.

I remember when I was cook we were having a dinner party at which one of the guests was a Frenchman and we were serving truffles in some form or other; the butler told me he was making the party laugh with a story about truffle hunting. This Frenchman lived in the Perigord district where truffles are found. He said there was nothing more idyllic than walking through the woods listening to the contented snortings of the pigs and the irate language of the truffle-hunters who couldn't find their beasts!

We used to call them in the kitchen 'black diamonds', and today truffles are almost as expensive as diamonds, but to a cook they are still worth the money, as a very small piece can make a sauce ambrosial. If you put a piece as small as your finger into a box of eggs for a day you would find that every egg would taste of truffles.

I've given a recipe for stuffing a turkey that uses a pound of truffles. I believe that today they cost about £1 an ounce, if not more. It's a recipe Mrs McIlroy, one of the cooks, gave me. She was a down-to-earth Scot, but she said to me that if you could be transported to heaven and presented with a dish prepared by their chief angel chef of nectar, ambrosia and every other flavour they have rolled into one, it wouldn't taste as good as that turkey did. It was the only time I heard her wax poetic.

Aubergines Stuffed

4 persons. Time: About ¾ hour

2 aubergines
1 oz. meat or chicken
  (cooked)
1 oz. ham
1 egg

2 oz. breadcrumbs
1 teaspoon mixed herbs
1 teaspoon chopped parsley
pepper, salt

Wipe the aubergines, remove the stalks, cut them into halves lengthwise. Pick out the seeds, put the pulp into a basin with the minced ham and chicken, or meat. Add the herbs, parsley and seasoning to taste, bind with the beaten egg and fill the aubergine cases with the mixture. Sprinkle with the breadcrumbs and dot with small pieces of butter. Put them into a greased baking tin, cover with grease-proof paper and bake in a moderate oven for ¾ hour, or slightly longer if they do not seem tender. Aubergines can also be stuffed with sausage or veal forcemeat if preferred (see p. 105).

Gas 4–5; Electricity 350°–375°

Artichokes—Globe

1 per person

globe artichokes, 1 per
  person
lemon juice

melted butter
salt

The artichokes must be young and fresh. Cut off the stems and remove the large bottom leaves. Soak the artichokes in cold water and a few drops of vinegar for about ½ hour. Rinse well under the tap and leave to drain for a few minutes. Add a teaspoon of lemon juice to a pan threequarters full of boiling water, put in the artichokes head downwards; add salt to taste and boil rapidly for 10 minutes, then lower the heat and simmer slowly for 30 to 45 minutes—or until the leaves easily come off. Drain and dish in a folded napkin to absorb any excess water. Hand the melted butter separately.

Artichokes—Jerusalem

6 persons

2 lb. Jerusalem artichokes   ½ pt white sauce (see p. 140)
lemon juice   salt
vinegar

Well wash and peel the artichokes, leave to soak in cold water with a tablespoon of vinegar. Put them into boiling salted water, add a tablespoon of lemon juice, bring to the boil and simmer gently for 20 minutes. Do not overcook or they will turn black. Drain, put into a vegetable dish and pour over the white sauce.

Broad Beans and Parsley Sauce

3 to 4 persons. Time: 20 to 40 minutes

1 lb. beans after shelling   1 tablespoon cream
1 lump sugar   1 sprig parsley
½ pt parsley sauce (see p. 140)   salt

Shell the beans and if they are old put them into a basin of boiling water for a few minutes, then remove the skins; this is not necessary if the beans are young. Put them into lightly-salted water, add the sugar and parsley, boil slowly until tender, 20 to 40 minutes, according to age. When cooked, strain them, put into a hot dish and cover with the heated sauce to which a tablespoon of cream has been added.

Carrots as a Garnish

Time: About ½ hour

1 lb. young small carrots   1½ oz. brown sugar
1 oz. butter   brown stock

Remove the tops from the carrots, wash well and put them into a casserole. Add the butter, sugar and just enough stock to cover; cook in a fairly hot oven without a lid on the casserole for about ½ hour, this will allow the liquor to evaporate and reduce the stock to a thick glaze. This may be made in a saucepan if preferred.

Gas 6–7; Electricity 400°–425°

Carrots, New, with Parsley

3 to 4 persons. Time: About 20 minutes

2 lb. carrots
1 oz. butter
½ lemon

1 dessertspoon chopped parsley
pepper, salt

Remove the tops from the carrots, wash well and put into boiling water with a little salt; boil until tender—about 15 to 20 minutes. When soft, strain and return to pan with the butter, parsley and the juice of the ½ lemon; add a pinch of pepper and toss around in the pan for a few minutes before serving.

Cauliflower au Gratin

4 to 5 persons. Time: About 35 minutes

2 small cauliflowers
1 tablespoon Parmesan and
1 tablespoon Cheddar cheese (grated)
lemon juice

½ pt white sauce (see p. 140)
1 oz. butter
½ teacup brown breadcrumbs
paprika pepper, salt

Pick firm and white cauliflowers, cut off the stalk and the outer leaves, leave in salted water for an hour to kill any insects. Then put them into lightly-salted boiling water and cook for about 20 minutes (or less if the cauliflowers are very small); strain and put into a fire-proof dish. Heat the white sauce in a pan, add two-thirds of the cheeses, a pinch of paprika and a few drops of lemon juice; mix well and pour this over the cauliflower. Sprinkle over the rest of the cheese mixed with the breadcrumbs, dot with the butter and bake in a fairly hot oven to a golden brown, 10 to 15 minutes.

Gas 6–7; Electricity 400°–425°

Celeriac

4 to 5 persons. Time: About ½ hour

2 heads celeriac   lemon
½ pt parsley sauce (see p. 140)   salt

Well wash the celeriac and peel off the outside skin, make sure that all discoloured parts are removed. Cut into small pieces and leave in cold water for about ½ hour. Put the pieces into lightly-salted boiling water, add a few drops of lemon juice and cook gently until tender, about 25 to 30 minutes, strain. Make the parsley sauce, using equal quantities of milk and the water in which the celeriacs were boiled; reheat them in this sauce. Cheese or egg sauces may be used instead of parsley (see p. 140).

Celery Braised

3 to 4 persons. Time: About ¾ hour

2 heads celery   1 gill white stock
2 streaky bacon rashers   pepper, salt
1 oz. butter

Pick crisp white-hearted celery, trim and well wash and cut each heart into 2 or 3 portions; put them into a well-greased pan with enough stock to moisten. Remove the rind from the bacon, cut into strips, lightly fry and put on top of the celery, add the butter, cut into small pieces, season to taste, cover with a tightly-fitting lid and cook for about ¾ hour, or until tender.

French Beans

3 to 4 persons. Time: About 20 minutes

1 to 1½ lb. French beans   bicarbonate of soda
½ oz. butter   salt

Cut the ends from the beans and remove the strings from the sides, slice them thinly crosswise and put into cold water for a few minutes. Drain and put the beans in a pan with enough boiling water to cover and a pinch of bicarbonate, boil quickly without a lid for 15 to 20 minutes. When they are cooked they sink to the bottom of the pan; remove the scum before straining, otherwise the beans will discolour. Put into a hot vegetable dish and dot with the butter.

Green Peas with Maître d'Hôtel Butter
5 to 6 persons. Time: 15 to 25 minutes

2 lb. green peas
1 teaspoon demerara sugar
2 oz. maître d'hôtel butter

1 sprig mint
lemon juice
pepper, salt

Shell the peas, put them into a pan of lightly-salted boiling water, add the mint and sugar, boil fairly fast until the peas are tender—about 15 to 25 minutes, according to the age of the peas; leave the lid off. When soft, strain the peas, return to pan, add the maître d'hôtel and reheat.

Leeks Boiled
3 to 4 persons. Time: 30 to 40 minutes

6 to 8 small leeks
½ pt. white sauce (see p. 140)
lemon juice

vinegar
parsley
pepper, salt

Cut off the roots, outer leaves and part of the green tops of the leeks, split them down the middle and soak for ½ hour in cold water; add a few drops of vinegar. Tie them into two bundles, put them into lightly-salted boiling water, add a dessertspoon of lemon juice and boil gently for 30 to 40 minutes. When cooked, strain, put into hot dish, pour over the heated white sauce and sprinkle with chopped parsley.

Marrow Fritters
4 to 5 persons. Time: About 10 to 15 minutes

1 young marrow
1 egg
breadcrumbs

lemon juice
frying fat or oil
paprika pepper, salt

Cut the marrow into slices about ½ inch thick, peel them, put on a plate, sprinkle with a little seasoning and a squeeze of lemon juice, leave for 5 to 10 minutes, turning once. Put the fat or oil into a fairly deep pan, dip the marrow rings into the beaten egg, coat with breadcrumbs; when a faint blue smoke rises from the pan drop in the marrow. Fry to a pale brown, about 10 to 15 minutes, and drain on soft paper. Serve garnished with fried parsley (see p. 142).

Marrow Stuffed

4 to 5 persons. Time: About ¾ hour

1 fair-sized marrow	½ pt tomato sauce (see p. 139)
¼ lb. beef, chicken or ham (minced)	1 level teaspoon mixed herbs
	few drops mushroom ketchup
1 egg	fat
2 tablespoons breadcrumbs	pepper, salt

Peel the marrow, cut a small piece from each end using a long thin spoon, scoop out the seeds. Mix together the minced meat, breadcrumbs, herbs, mushroom ketchup, beaten egg and seasoning and stuff the marrow with this mixture; put back the ends of the marrow, wrap in greased paper, tie round with thin twine. Put it into a greased baking tin with a little dripping or butter, cover this with another tin, and bake in a fairly hot oven for about 1 hour—or longer if not soft enough. When cooked, remove from tin, take off the paper, put the marrow into a hot dish and pour over the heated tomato sauce. Sprinkle with chopped parsley.

Mushrooms Grilled

3 to 4 persons. Time: About 10 minutes

1 doz. large mushrooms	1 lemon
2 tablespoons salad oil	pepper, salt

Remove the stalks, peel the mushrooms and score the under-part, put them into a deep plate, season and pour the oil over each one; leave for about 1 hour. Put them on a greased grill and cook, turning once. Serve on hot buttered toast and squeeze lemon juice over them.

Parsnips Baked

4 to 5 persons. Time: About ¾ hour

2 lb. parsnips	lemon juice
3 to 4 oz. soft brown sugar	pepper, salt
1½ oz. butter	

Peel the parsnips in plenty of cold water as they quickly become discoloured when exposed to the air. Remove any blemished parts and put them into clean cold water with a little lemon juice for

½ hour. If they are large, cut them into quarters lengthwise; if not large cut into halves. Put them into a pan of lightly-salted boiling water, simmer for about ½ hour, then strain. Put them into a fire-proof dish with the sugar, butter and a light sprinkle of pepper; bake in a fairly hot oven, basting frequently with the sugar syrup until the parsnips have acquired a brown colour.

Gas 5–6; Electricity 375°–400°

Potatoes Baked in Jackets

1 per person. Time: 1½ to 2 hours

large evenly-shaped potatoes   pepper
butter   salt

Wash and brush the potatoes in cold water until they are clean; wipe dry and either cut a slit in them or prick all over with a sharp-pronged fork. They can be put in a baking tin or straight on oven shelves and cooked for 1½ to 2 hours according to their size. They are ready when they feel soft if pressed between thumb and finger. To serve, split them into halves, put a liberal amount of butter on each half and a sprinkling of seasoning, close the halves together and serve in a table-napkin on a hot dish. An alternative method is to scoop out the potato into a basin, mix with butter, seasoning and a tablespoon of cream, put back into the potato cases and reheat in the oven for a few minutes.

Gas 4–5; Electricity 350°–375°

Potatoes Creamed

4 to 5 persons. Time: 20 to 30 minutes

1½ lb. potatoes   1 tablespoon cream
½ pt milk   pepper, salt
½ oz. butter

Peel the potatoes, cut into slices ¼ to ½ inch thick, put into a pan with the milk and about ½ saltspoon of salt, bring to the boil, cover with a lid and simmer slowly until soft, about 20 to 30 minutes. When done, pour off the milk, mash well so that there are no lumps, add the butter, cream and a pinch of pepper, beat well.

Potatoes Duchess

5 to 6 persons. Time: 15 to 20 minutes

2 lb. potatoes (cooked)
2 egg yolks
2 oz. butter

1 tablespoon cream
cayenne pepper, salt

Rub the potatoes through a wire sieve. Melt the butter in a pan, put in the potatoes and make warm, add the egg yolks, cream and seasoning to taste; mix well and turn on to a floured board. Divide into a dozen or more squares of the same size, brush over with white of egg, score the top, put them on a greased tin and bake in a fairly hot oven for 15 to 20 minutes, or until a golden brown.

Gas 6–7; Electricity 400°–425°

Potatoes à la Florence

4 to 6 persons. Time: 30 to 40 minutes

½ doz. potatoes (medium-
    sized)
¼ lb. chopped ham
¼ lb. mushrooms

2 oz. butter
2 oz. grated Parmesan cheese
1 tablespoon chopped truffle
pepper, salt

Peel the potatoes and leave in cold water until required. Peel and chop the mushrooms. Cut the potatoes into slices about ¼-inch thick, put a layer at the bottom of a fire-proof dish, then fill the dish with alternate layers of ham, mushrooms, truffle and potatoes; add the seasoning, sprinkle over the cheese; melt the butter and pour over and bake in a moderate oven for 30 to 40 minutes, or until the potatoes are soft.

Gas 5–6; Electricity 375°–400°

Potatoes au Gratin with Cream

1 per person. Time: 1½ to 2 hours

potatoes (medium to large)
2 oz. grated Parmesan cheese
2 oz. butter

1 gill cream
paprika pepper, salt

Pick even-sized potatoes, wash and brush them in cold water, make a slit on one side or prick all over with a sharp-pronged fork. Put them on a shelf in the oven and bake for 1½ to 2 hours, according to the size. When they feel soft if pressed between finger and thumb, remove from oven, cut into halves—separate the halves—scoop out the potato into a basin. Mix with the butter, cream, 1 oz. of the cheese and seasoning to taste. Put back into the cases, sprinkle with the rest of the cheese, and either brown in the oven or under the grill.

Gas 4–5; Electricity 350°–375°

Potatoes Sauté
4 to 5 persons. Time: To sauté, about 5 minutes

½ doz. potatoes
1½ to 2 oz. butter

Chopped parsley
pepper, salt

The non-floury potatoes are best for this dish as they do not break so easily. Peel and boil them until about three-parts done, strain and dry in a clean cloth, then slice them fairly thinly. Heat the butter in a pan, put in the potatoes, season to taste, then toss them in the pan until they acquire a pale brown colour. Put on to a hot dish, sprinkle with parsley and serve as quickly as possible.

Salad Apple and Cucumber
3 to 4 persons

1 cucumber (large)
1 lb apples (eating)
½ lemon

1 gill cream
pepper, salt

Peel and thinly slice the cucumber and apples, sprinkle with the seasoning and juice of ½ lemon; stir in the whipped cream and pile up in a salad bowl.

Salad Banana and Lettuce
5 to 6 persons

½ doz. bananas
1 cos lettuce
1 tomato
3 oz. almonds (chopped)

1 small box mustard and
cress
1 cup mayonnaise (see p. 135)
pepper, salt

119

Well wash the lettuce and shake in a clean cloth, put aside 2 or 3 of the leaves and shred the rest; mix them with the almonds, the peeled bananas cut into rings, sprinkle with the seasoning, put into a salad bowl. Pour over the mayonnaise and arrange the left-over lettuce round the outside alternately with the washed mustard and cress; cut the tomato into rings and garnish the top of the salad.

Salad English

6 persons

2 cos lettuce
1 bunch spring onions
1 small box mustard and cress
4 tomatoes

1 bunch watercress
1 bunch radishes
oil and vinegar
¼ teaspoon castor sugar
pepper, salt

Wash the lettuce and dry in a clean cloth, then shred into a salad bowl. Wash and dry the watercress and mustard and cress, put into the salad bowl with the sliced radishes and onions. Mix 1 tablespoon of oil with 1 of vinegar, add the sugar and seasoning to taste and pour over the salad. Cut the tomatoes into quarters and arrange round the outside.

Salad Green Peas and Eggs

3 to 4 persons

½ lb. green peas (cooked)
3 hardboiled eggs
1 cabbage lettuce

2 oz. cream cheese
½ cup mayonnaise
pepper, salt

Wash and dry the lettuce in a clean cloth, arrange the leaves (not cut up) at the bottom of a salad bowl. Cut the eggs into halves lengthwise and take out the yolks; mix the peas with the mayonnaise and fill the egg cases with them; arrange this on the lettuce leaves. Mix the yolks of eggs with the cream cheese, add a little seasoning, roll into balls and put between the egg cases.

Salad Orange

4 to 5 persons

2 large Jaffa oranges
1 dessertspoon salad oil

1 dessertspoon lemon juice
paprika pepper

Peel the oranges, removing all the white pith; divide into slices, take out all the pips. Mix together the oil and lemon juice, add a little paprika and sprinkle over the oranges.

Salad Surprise

4 to 5 persons

1 cos lettuce
1 endive (curly)
1 tin pineapple slices (about ½ doz.)
½ gill pineapple juice
1 bunch watercress

2 tablespoons salad oil
1 tablespoon lemon juice
1 tablespoon vinegar
¼ teaspoon made mustard
pepper, salt

Well wash the lettuce, endive and watercress, dry in a clean cloth. Shred the lettuce and endive, put them into a salad bowl with the watercress, sprinkle lightly with the seasoning. Cut the pineapple into small pieces and pile on the top, pour over the juice. Mix together the oil, vinegar, lemon juice and mustard and pour this over everything in the bowl. This salad goes well with game.

Salsify White

3 to 4 persons. Time: 30 to 40 minutes

1 lb. salsify
2 oz. butter
½ pt white sauce (see p. 140)

1 lemon
paprika pepper
salt

Wash the salsify, cut off the tops and about 1 inch from the stalks, scrape and rinse it. Tie into bundles with thin twine or tape and leave in cold water with the juice of ½ lemon for 15 to 20 minutes. Then put the salsify into lightly-salted boiling water, just enough to cover; add the butter and juice of the other ½ lemon, simmer until tender—30 to 40 minutes. Strain, put into a hot dish and pour over the heated white sauce and arrange croûtons of fried bread round.

Instead of white sauce a Béchamel sauce can be used (see p. 128). Salsify can also be done in the same way as cauliflower au gratin.

Seakale au Gratin

4 to 5 persons. Time: About ½ hour

1 lb. seakale	1 teaspoon chopped parsley
1 oz. grated Parmesan cheese	1 lemon
1½ oz. butter	pepper, salt
1 oz. breadcrumbs	

Wash the seakale and tie into small bundles, put into a pan of lightly-salted boiling water and cook gently until tender—20 to 25 minutes; strain and put into a fire-proof dish. Mix the cheese with the breadcrumbs, parsley and seasoning, add the juice of ½ lemon and spread over the seakale; melt the butter and pour over, brown in the oven or under the grill.

Spanish Onions Braised

3 to 4 persons. Time: 2 to 2½ hours

4 Spanish onions	1 teaspoon soft brown sugar
2 oz. butter or dripping	1 bay leaf
½ gill brown stock	pepper, salt

Skin the onions, melt the butter or dripping in a pan with the sugar, put in the onions, bay leaf, stock and a very little seasoning. Cover the pan and cook over a very low heat for 2 hours, or longer if the onions are very large. Shake the pan occasionally and turn the onions once or twice; the combination of the butter, sugar and stock will make a kind of brown sauce which will have the effect of glaze on the onions. When the onions are soft, skim as much fat as possible from the liquid and pour the rest of the liquid over the onions.

Spinach Creamed

4 to 5 persons. Time: 15 to 20 minutes

2 lb. spinach	½ gill cream
1½ oz. butter	pepper, salt

Remove the stalks from the spinach and wash in several lots of clean water; leave to soak for about 15 minutes in cold water, add a little salt. Drain and put the spinach into a large pan with no other water but what adheres to the leaves, have the heat low at first until the leaves become moister, then cook until tender—

about 15 minutes. Strain through a colander, pressing out the water, then rub through a wire sieve. Melt the butter in a pan, put in the spinach purée, cream and seasoning to taste. Stir over a low heat for a minute or two, serve in a hot dish garnished with croûtons of fried bread.

Tomatoes Baked and Stuffed

3 to 4 persons. Time: About 20 minutes

½ doz. tomatoes	1½ oz. butter
2 oz. ham (cooked)	2 oz. breadcrumbs
1 oz. mushrooms	½ teaspoon chopped parsley
1 egg	pepper, salt

Pick firm, fairly-large tomatoes, remove the stalks, cut a small piece from the top of each one. Scoop out the soft part from the insides with a spoon, taking care not to break the skin of the tomatoes. Rub this through a sieve, mix it with the minced ham, peeled and finely-chopped mushrooms, parsley, breadcrumbs and seasoning to taste; bind with the beaten egg. Fill the tomato cases with this mixture, sprinkle over a few breadcrumbs, dot with the butter and bake in a moderate oven until tender—about 20 minutes. Care must be taken not to over-cook or the tomatoes will break. Serve each one on a croûton of fried bread slightly larger than the base of the tomato.

Gas 4–5; Electricity 350°–375°

Turnips Mashed

4 to 5 persons. Time: ¾ to 1 hour

2 lb. turnips	cayenne pepper
2 oz. butter	salt
1 tablespoon milk or cream	

Thickly peel the turnips, cut into quarters and put into a pan of boiling water, add salt as needed; boil them until soft—¾ to 1 hour. Strain into a colander, pressing out as much water as possible; rub them through a sieve. Put the sieved turnips into a pan, add a pinch of cayenne, the butter and the milk or cream; stir well and make hot.

12

Sauces and Garnishes

The other day I picked up a book about the kind of clothes people wore and the kind of houses they lived in and what they ate, and I was astonished to read that, before the beginning of the nineteenth century, sauces weren't even known in this country. The book went on to quote a Frenchman who said, 'The English are a nation with only one sauce,' but he didn't specify what that sauce was. It's my bet it was that everlasting white sauce people dish up—liquid interspersed with lumps. It also quoted another Frenchman as saying, 'Anyone can learn to cook, but a good sauce-maker is born, not made.' I don't agree with that at all. I think that if people put their minds to it and have a love of cooking, they can learn to make a sauce. I'm not saying that they can become a famous sauce-maker like Escoffier, but that they can turn out some mighty good ones. But I do agree with another thing the Frenchman said, that sauces are an essential part of cookery—not just knowing how to make them, but knowing which particular dish requires a particular type of sauce. One sauce may go with several dishes, on the other hand it may be right for one particular dish only. It's not only learning how to make them but how to place them.

You've got to start off with a base for any sauce. One of the secrets is that each sauce has got to have a flavour of its own and yet mustn't disguise the flavour of the dish that it's going to go with. Unless of course the dish is so insipid that it hasn't got a flavour, in which case you might as well use any bottled sauce. One of the things I was taught when I started cooking was not to think of making an intricate or elaborate sauce until I became experienced. The cook who taught me went this far with the Frenchman in that she said it's no good thinking that because you can turn out a good roast or meat pudding or can cook vegetables well you can try to prepare the intricate and elaborate sauces. She always said that a good plain sauce well made is infinitely preferable to an elaborate sauce badly made, because there are many things that a good plain sauce will go with while there's nothing that a badly made elaborate sauce will go with.

A successful and intricate elaborate sauce is one which has to have exact quantities; it's the subtlety with which you mix them and the way they're blended that make sauces works of art, and a good sauce is a work of art. It will enhance the plainest dish, and although an elaborate sauce is expensive both in time and money, when you consider what it does for the dish it accompanies it's really well worth them both. Often the dish you're making doesn't cost much or you are using the remains of poultry, game, cold meat or fish, but prepare a good Béchamel sauce, and the dish will be transformed: similarly with cold meat, if you use an Espagnole or a Robert sauce.

Before you begin making your sauces, you have to consider the utensils you're going to use. When I was a cook I always made the sauces well in advance. They're not the kind of things that you can knock up at the last minute just before you are serving, so they've got to be kept hot. A bainmarie is just the right thing to do this. If you haven't got one you can manage quite well if you just stand one or two bowls in an ordinary large saucepan. Incidentally, when you are making sauces of any kind, but particularly thick sauces, it's best to use very heavy-bottomed pans because a lot of stirring is needed and this must be done with a wooden spoon because it makes for the best blending and smoothness. I know nowadays there are these plastic spoons, but I think they tend to scratch the pans, and they don't stir nearly so well as the flat wooden spoons.

Most sauces are all the better for being strained through a fine strainer or a hair sieve, except of course the kind that have got the actual ingredients in them. By that I mean that if you were making an egg sauce or a parsley sauce, obviously you wouldn't strain them. We always used a hair sieve for our most delicate sauces, or a tammy cloth, to work which you need to have two people.

I suppose that, apart from mint sauce or fruit sauces, you can divide sauces into two kinds, white and brown, but within these two main kinds there are certain sub-divisions. There's Béchamel, for instance, the white sauce which is made very slowly and gets its flavour from the ingredients that go into making it; it's the long, slow cooking of Béchamel sauce that gives it its flavour, whereas if you're making an ordinary white sauce, then of course the flavour is derived from what you put into it at the last minute, for instance anchovies, parsley or capers.

It's the same with brown sauces; an Espagnole, which is the basis of a good brown sauce, takes a long time to make and an even longer time to cook. The recipe alone seems to occupy most of a page, and the flour and the other ingredients have to be given a long, slow frying to turn them brown, and it has to simmer for two or three hours; it must be stirred frequently and also constantly skimmed, while an ordinary brown sauce can be made as quickly as a plain white sauce.

A most difficult sauce to make well is one that's not thickened with flour, but with the addition of egg yolk and cream. It's tricky because you've got to add the egg yolk and the cream when the sauce is just below boiling point but, so that the eggs don't taste raw, it has to be stirred over heat; yet it must never come to the boil because if it does the eggs and the cream will curdle and the sauce will be ruined. I don't recommend an inexperienced cook to try it out, not on a party anyway. She should practise on her own at first; when mastered it does make a very lovely sauce indeed.

I find it difficult to give in recipes the exact consistency of any particular sauce because it varies according to its purpose. If you want a sauce thick enough to coat whatever it is to be poured over, then you can reckon roughly an ounce and a half of flour to a pint of liquid. It's better to make it too thick, because it's easy enough to add more stock to thin it down; on the other hand, if you've made it too thin, you've got to start all over again, making another pan of thicker sauce to add to the existing one.

One cause of failure is that the sauces are not cooked long enough. If you make a sauce with flour, for instance, you must cook it for at least five minutes. Some people think that as soon as they've added the flour and brought it to the boil, that's that; but it isn't because the flour is still raw. But don't over-boil the sauce because that will take away its flavour. When you have given the sauce its allotted time, transfer it to the bain-marie.

Another thing to be stressed is stirring. So many people make a lumpy sauce because they think they can leave it on a low gas and do something else. I know it's very difficult when you've got a thousand and one other things to do to stand for five minutes stirring, but you really should, because a sauce will not become smooth and creamy unless you continually stir until it has boiled. Then if you must, you can leave it on a low heat, but remember thick sauces in particular burn very quickly; so always, if you leave it, cover the saucepan so that a thick skin doesn't form.

Again, I must emphasize, don't leave the sauce until it has thickened. Of all the dishes that he or she prepares, sauces require most of the cook's attention. You can put things in the oven or on to steam and forget them, but you can't forget a sauce until it's finished.

Apple Sauce

About ½ pint. Time: 25 to 30 minutes

1 lb. cooking apples	½ gill water
2 oz. sugar (brown or white)	pepper
1 oz. butter	

Peel, core and slice the apples, put them into a pan with the sugar and water and cook until soft. Beat to a pulp—or rub them through a sieve—return to pan, add the butter and a shake of pepper, serve hot.

Béarnaise Sauce

1 gill. Time: About 20 minutes

2 egg yolks
1 shallot
¾ gill tarragon vinegar
2 oz. butter

1 dessertspoon chopped
   tarragon
lemon juice
pepper, salt

Peel and chop the shallot, put it into a pan with the vinegar and chopped tarragon, place over a medium heat and boil until the quantity is reduced to about 1½ tablespoons; strain and return to the pan. In another pan melt the butter but do not let it boil. Add a little of this butter and the egg yolks to the vinegar and whisk over a low heat until it thickens—take care not to let it boil. Draw the pan to one side and slowly add the rest of the butter, whisking all the time. Add a squeeze of lemon juice, pinch of pepper and salt to taste. This sauce needs to be served very soon after making; it goes well with fillets of beef and veal.

Béchamel Sauce

About 1 pint. Time: 1 hour

1 pt white stock
1 small onion
1 medium carrot
½ turnip
1 stick celery
1 oz. flour

1 blade mace
1 bay leaf
½ doz. peppercorns
½ pt milk
pepper, salt

Put the stock into a pan with the washed and cut-up vegetables, mace, bay leaf and peppercorns; add a bunch of sweet herbs and seasoning to taste. Slowly bring to the boil, then let it continue to boil until reduced to about half the quantity, strain. Mix the flour with the milk to a smooth paste, then add it to the stock, stirring all the time. Bring to the boil again and simmer gently for 10 to 15 minutes.

Black Butter Sauce

½ gill. Time: 10 minutes

2 oz. butter
1 tablespoon vinegar

1 dessertspoon chopped
   parsley
pepper, salt

Heat the butter in a pan until it is golden brown in colour, or slightly darker, take care that it does not burn. Let it cool a little, then add the parsley, vinegar and a very small amount of seasoning. Reheat, but do not let it boil. Serve with fish.

Bordelaise Sauce

½ pint. Time: 30 minutes

½ pt Espagnole sauce
   (see p. 131)
1 shallot (chopped)
1 wineglass sherry

pinch brown sugar
½ teaspoon each chopped
   parsley and tarragon
pepper, salt

Put the wine and the shallot into a pan, bring to the boil, simmer for 15 minutes. Add the Espagnole sauce, stir until it boils, simmer gently for 5 minutes; if it seems too thick, add a little stock or water. Put in the parsley, tarragon, sugar and seasoning to taste. This sauce is not strained, and should be thick enough to coat the back of a spoon. If not thick enough, boil quickly for a few minutes with the lid off the pan.

Bread Sauce

½ pint. Time: 20 minutes

2 oz. white breadcrumbs
1 small onion
2 cloves
½ pt milk

½ oz. butter
1 dessertspoon cream
   (optional)
cayenne pepper, salt

Peel the onion and stick the cloves into it, put it into a pan with the milk and slowly bring to the boil; add the breadcrumbs and leave the pan on a very low heat until the sauce thickens and becomes soft. Remove the onion, add the butter and seasoning to taste. If using cream, add just before serving, but do not let the sauce boil after adding the cream.

Brown Sauce

About 1 pint. Time: 1 hour

1 pt stock
1 medium onion
1 small turnip
1 carrot
2 or 3 sticks celery
1 oz. butter
1 oz. flour

1 teaspoon mushroom
   ketchup
1 bunch herbs
1 blade mace
½ doz. peppercorns
pepper, salt

Melt the butter in a pan, add the peeled and sliced onion and stir until brown, then add the flour and brown also. Leave the pan on a very low heat and gradually pour in the stock, stirring all the time. Raise the heat, bring stock to the boil while still stirring, skim, simmer for 5 minutes. Peel and cut up the other vegetables and add them to the stock with the herbs, peppercorns, mace, mushroom ketchup and seasoning to taste. Simmer gently for 30 minutes, then strain and reheat.

Caramel Sauce

½ pint. Time: 20 minutes

2 oz. loaf sugar
2 tablespoons water

½ pt sweet white sauce
  (see p. 140)
vanilla essence

Put the sugar into a small pan over a low heat until it has melted and reached a fairly dark brown colour, stir occasionally. Add the water and bring to the boil. Stir this into the sweet white sauce and reheat. Add a few drops of vanilla, strain and serve.

Chaudfroid Sauce (White)

1 pint. Time: About 15 minutes

½ pt Béchamel sauce
  (see p. 128)
¼ pt aspic jelly

½ oz. gelatine
1 gill cream
1 teaspoon lemon juice

Heat the Béchamel sauce. Dissolve the gelatine in the aspic jelly and add this to the sauce. Stir over a gentle heat until it just reaches boiling point (but do not let it boil), then add the lemon juice. Leave to cool, add the cream. When the sauce is on the point of setting, use to coat cold chicken, turkey, game, etc.

Chocolate Sauce

½ pint. Time: 20 minutes

3 oz. grated chocolate
    Menière
2 oz. castor sugar
¾ oz. cornflour or riceflour
2 gills water

1 tablespoon coffee essence
½ teaspoon vanilla essence
1 tablespoon brandy
    (optional)

Mix the cornflour or riceflour with a little of the water, add the
chocolate, sugar and coffee essence. Boil up the rest of the water,
add the chocolate mixture and boil slowly for 10 minutes,
stirring all the time. Add the vanilla essence and brandy if used.

Cranberry Sauce

½ pint. Time: 30 minutes

1 quart cranberries
4 oz. brown sugar

½ pt water

Wash the fruit, put it into a pan with the water, slowly bring to
the boil and simmer gently until the berries are soft. Rub through
a hair sieve, return to pan, add the sugar and reheat.

Custard Sauce

About 1 pint. Time: 15 minutes

1 pt hot milk
1 oz. sugar

3 eggs
½ wineglass brandy

Put the eggs into a basin and lightly beat; pour on the hot milk
and the brandy, stirring all the time, and put the mixture into an
earthenware jug. Stand this in a pan of boiling water and keep
stirring the contents in the same direction until it reaches the
consistency of thick cream. Take care that it does not boil.

Espagnole Sauce

1 quart. Time: 2½ hours

4 oz. veal
2 oz. ham
1 medium onion
1 small carrot
¼ head celery
2 oz. butter
2 oz. flour
3 pt stock
Remains of game or poultry

1 gill tomato purée
1 bunch herbs
½ doz. peppercorns
1 blade mace
2 oz. mushrooms
½ gill claret
½ wineglass sherry
pepper, salt

131

Peel and cut up the vegetables, cut the veal and ham into small pieces. Melt 1 oz. of the butter in a pan and fry all the vegetables, except the mushrooms, to a pale brown. Add the veal, ham, herbs, mace, peppercorns and the remains of game or poultry, if any; stir well over a low heat until all is light brown in colour. Pour off any fat, then add the stock, tomato purée, roughly-chopped mushrooms and the wine; bring to the boil, simmer for about 1 hour. In another pan melt the rest of the butter and blend in the flour. Add the contents of the stock pan to this flour mixture very gradually, stirring all the time until it boils. Simmer gently for 1 hour, occasionally stirring and skimming, then strain through a fine hair sieve or tammy cloth.

This sauce will keep for some time if put into a jar and kept in the refrigerator. It can be used as a basis for other sauces.

Fennel Sauce
½ pint. Time: 15 minutes

½ pt Béchamel sauce   paprika pepper
(see p. 128)   salt
1 tablespoon chopped fennel

Pick the fennel from the stalks, wash it and cook in boiling water until tender; drain well and chop finely. Heat the Béchamel sauce, add the fennel, a pinch of pepper and a little salt if required. This sauce goes well with mackerel.

German Sauce
1 gill. Time: About 10 minutes

2 egg yolks   1 gill Madeira
2 oz. castor sugar

Put the egg yolks, sugar and wine into a basin and stand it in a pan of boiling water. Keep over a low heat and whisk until thick and frothy, but do not let it boil or the eggs will curdle. Serve as soon as it is ready.

Green Gooseberry Sauce
(For Boiled Mackerel)
1 gill. Time: 30 minutes

½ pt green gooseberries   1 oz. butter
2 oz. sugar   1 gill water
Green sorrel (1 tablespoon   pepper
of juice)

Well wash some green sorrel, put it into a clean piece of muslin and press out the juice. Put the gooseberries and water into a pan and cook until soft enough to rub through a wire sieve. Put the pulp into a pan, add a tablespoon of sorrel juice, the sugar, butter and a shake of pepper. Make very hot before serving.

Hard Sauce—Brandy Butter
(For Christmas Pudding)

Time: 10 minutes

4 oz. castor sugar
2 oz. butter

½ wineglass brandy

Beat well together the butter and sugar until it is a soft froth, then gradually beat in the brandy. Leave in a refrigerator for a time to harden.

Hollandaise Sauce

About ½ pint. Time: 25 minutes

2 egg yolks
½ pt milk
1 oz. butter
1 oz. flour

1 dessertspoon lemon juice
cayenne pepper
salt

Melt the butter in a pan, blend in the flour, add the milk and bring to the boil over a low heat, stirring all the time. Remove from the heat, add the lemon juice and stir in the yolks, one at a time. Reheat over a very low heat and stir until thick, but it must not be allowed to boil. If it seems too thick add a little more milk, but it must be brought to near boiling point again.

Horseradish Sauce

1 gill. Time: 10 minutes

2 oz. grated horseradish
1 gill cream
1 tablespoon vinegar (white wine vinegar is best)

½ teaspoon castor sugar
1 level saltspoon of made mustard
salt

Finely grate the horseradish and mix with the cream. Add the vinegar, sugar, mustard and a pinch of salt; put in a cold place for an hour before serving.

133

Italian Sauce

½ *pint. Time: 30 minutes*

1 small onion
2 large mushrooms
1 oz. butter
1 oz. flour
½ pt stock

sprig of thyme
1 bay leaf
3 peppercorns
1 wineglass sherry
pepper, salt

Melt the butter, add the finely-chopped onion and fry to a pale brown, add the flour and brown also. Add the chopped mushrooms, bay leaf, thyme, peppercorns, stock and sherry; bring to the boil, simmer gently for 20 minutes; season to taste, then strain and reheat.

Jam Sauce

½ *pint. Time: 15 minutes*

3 tablespoons jam (raspberry is good)
1 dessertspoon sugar

juice ½ lemon
½ pt water

Mix the cornflour with a little of the water. Put the rest of the water into a pan with the jam, put over a medium heat and bring to the boil, then pour it on to the cornflour, stirring all the time. Return this to the pan, add the sugar and simmer for 6 to 8 minutes; add the juice of ½ lemon and strain before serving.

Maître d'Hôtel Sauce

½ *pint. Time: 20 minutes*

½ pt white stock
1½ oz. butter
1 oz. flour
1 tablespoon cream

1 teaspoon chopped parsley
juice of ½ lemon
cayenne pepper
salt

Melt the butter in a pan, add the flour and stir over a low heat for 1 minute, gradually add the stock, stirring all the time. Simmer gently for 5 minutes, skimming if necessary. Add the parsley, pinch of cayenne, strained lemon juice, cream and salt to taste. Reheat but do not let the sauce boil again.

Mayonnaise Sauce

½ pint. Time: 20 to 30 minutes

2 egg yolks
1 dessertspoon tarragon
  vinegar
1 dessertspoon malt vinegar

½ pt (or just over) best salad
  oil
cayenne pepper

Put the egg yolks into a basin with a pinch of pepper, stir them with a wooden spoon. Add the oil, drop by drop, until at least half is used; after that, the rest can be added at a quicker rate. At intervals while stirring, add the vinegars. In hot weather it helps to stand the basin on a bed of crushed ice while stirring. Should the sauce curdle, put another yolk of egg into another basin and very slowly stir the sauce into it.

Mint Sauce

1 gill. Time: 15 minutes

2 tablespoons mint (finely
  chopped)
1 oz. brown sugar

1 gill malt or white wine
  vinegar
1 tablespoon water

Mix together the sugar, vinegar and water and pour it on to the mint. Stir well, cover and leave for at least an hour before serving.

Mushroom Sauce

½ pint. Time: 25 minutes

1 lb. button mushrooms
½ pt brown stock
1 oz. butter
1 oz. flour

1 saltspoon celery powder
1 teaspoon lemon juice
pepper, salt

Peel the mushrooms and cut them into pieces, then put them into a pan with the stock, celery powder and seasoning to taste and simmer until tender. Melt the butter in another pan, blend in the flour, let it brown a little, remove from heat and gradually pour in the mushroom mixture, stirring all the time; add the lemon juice and simmer for 5 minutes.

Mustard Sauce

½ pint. Time: 20 minutes

1 oz. butter
¾ oz. cornflour
1 gill white stock
1 level dessertspoon of
French mustard

½ gill milk
1 tablespoon lemon juice
pepper, salt

Melt the butter in a pan, stir in the cornflour, add the stock and stir over a medium heat until it boils. Mix the lemon juice with the mustard, stir it into the sauce, add the milk and season to taste. Bring to the boil stirring all the time. Serve with herrings and mackerel.

Onion Sauce

About ½ pint. Time: 1 to 1¼ hours

½ to ¾ lb. onions
1 oz. butter
1 oz. flour

½ pt milk
½ gill cream
pepper, salt

Peel the onions (if large cut in halves), put them into a pan with enough boiling water to cover, add ½ teaspoon of salt. Cook until soft—¾ to 1 hour, strain and chop fairly coarsely. Melt the butter in a pan, blend in the flour, add the milk and stir until it boils; add the onions and season to taste. Just before serving, stir in the cream, but do not let it boil again.

Orange Sauce for Ducklings

½ pint. Time: 15 minutes

½ pt Espagnole sauce
(see p. 131)
½ orange
1 teaspoon lemon juice

1 level teaspoon castor sugar
1 gill claret
cayenne pepper

Put the Espagnole sauce into a pan with the sugar and the thinly-cut rind of ½ orange, let it simmer for 10 minutes. Strain, add the juice of ½ orange, the lemon juice, claret and a pinch of cayenne.

Piquante Sauce

½ pint. Time: 20 to 30 minutes

½ pt Espagnole sauce
(see p. 131)
1 small onion (chopped)
1 dessertspoon chopped
capers

1 bay leaf
2 chopped gherkins
1 gill vinegar

Put the onion, bay leaf and vinegar into a pan, boil gently until
reduced to 2 tablespoons. Strain this into another pan, add the
Espagnole sauce, capers and gherkins, simmer for about 5 minutes,
add seasoning if liked. Can be served with roast pork.

Remoulade Sauce

About 1½ gills. Time: 20 minutes

2 egg yolks (hardboiled)
1 gill salad oil
1 tablespoon vinegar
1 saltspoon made mustard

½ teaspoon each chopped
chives, tarragon, chervil
1 teaspoon chopped parsley
pepper, salt

Finely chop the herbs, put them into a clean piece of muslin and
dip into boiling water for 2 or 3 minutes, then squeeze dry. Put
them into a mortar with the egg yolks and pound well; add the
mustard, pinch of pepper and salt. Put all into a basin and add the
salad oil very gradually—as though making mayonnaise—adding
the vinegar at intervals while stirring. This is a very good sauce
for fish.

Robert Sauce

½ pint. Time: 30 minutes

½ pt Espagnole sauce
(see p. 131)
1 small onion
½ oz. butter

2 tablespoons vinegar
1 teaspoon anchovy essence
½ teaspoon French mustard
pepper, salt

Finely chop the onion and fry it in the butter to a pale brown.
Add the vinegar, mustard and seasoning; put over a medium heat
until reduced to half the quantity. Add the Espagnole sauce and
anchovy essence, simmer for 8 to 10 minutes; strain and serve.

Salad Dressings

(1) French Salad Dressing

3 tablespoons salad oil	½ teaspoon made mustard
1 dessertspoon tarragon vinegar	2 dessertspoons malt vinegar
	pepper, salt

Put the mustard and seasoning into a basin, gradually stir in the oil, then add the vinegar. If preferred, 1 dessertspoon of lemon juice can be used with 1 dessertspoon of malt vinegar.

(2) Cream Salad Dressing

4 tablespoons thick cream	½ teaspoon castor sugar
1 tablespoon white vinegar	½ saltspoon salt
½ teaspoon made mustard	pepper

Mix together in a basin the mustard, sugar and salt; stir in the cream, add a shake of pepper and mix in the vinegar drop by drop.

(3) Salad Dressing

2 egg yolks (hardboiled)	2 tablespoons vinegar
4 tablespoons best salad oil	½ teaspoon made mustard
2 tablespoons Worcester sauce	½ saltspoon salt
	pepper

Rub the egg yolks through a sieve, mix with the mustard and seasoning. Stir in the salad oil, gradually add the vinegar and Worcester sauce alternately until all is thoroughly mixed.

Thick, sour cream makes a good salad dressing; just stir the cream until smooth, add salt and a pinch of paprika pepper and it is ready for use.

Shrimp Sauce

½ *pint. Time: 20 minutes*

¼ pt shrimps	1 teaspoon anchovy essence
½ pt white sauce (see p. 140)	paprika pepper
lemon juice	

Wash and pick the shrimps, put them into a bowl, sprinkle with a few drops of lemon juice, leave for 5 to 10 minutes. Heat the white sauce in a pan, add the shrimps, anchovy essence, pinch of paprika and salt if needed. Do not let boil after adding the shrimps.

Supreme Sauce

About 1 pint. Time: 30 to 40 minutes

1 pt white stock or, boiled   lemon juice
   chicken stock   1 small onion
2 oz. butter   1 bay leaf
1½ oz. flour   2 cloves
1 egg yolk   1 tablespoon cream

Melt 1 oz. butter in a pan, blend in the flour and cook for 1 to 2 minutes. Add the stock, onion stuck with the cloves and the bay leaf. Bring to the boil, stirring all the time; simmer for 20 minutes. Remove from the heat, stir in the rest of the butter, the egg yolk and the cream. Pass through a fine hair sieve or a tammy cloth and reheat; do not let it boil again. Serve with boiled chicken, veal or white entrées.

Tartare Sauce

½ *pint. Time: 10 minutes*

½ pt Mayonnaise sauce   1 teaspoon chopped parsley
  (see p. 135)   1 dessertspoon chopped
1 tablespoon chopped   capers
  gherkins   1 teaspoon chopped chervil

Put the mayonnaise into a basin and slowly stir in the chopped ingredients. Put in the refrigerator for 1 hour before serving.

Tomato Sauce

About ¾ pint. Time: 30 to 40 minutes

1 lb. tomatoes   1 oz. butter
2 oz. lean ham   1 oz. cornflour
1 small onion   1 bay leaf
1½ tablespoons vinegar   cayenne, salt

Slice the tomatoes and dice the ham, put them into a pan with the butter, cut up onion, bay leaf and seasoning. Stir over a medium heat for 5 minutes, then add the vinegar and simmer until all is soft. Rub through a sieve and return to pan. Mix the cornflour with a little cold water, add it to the sauce, stir over a low heat until it boils; simmer gently for 3 minutes and serve.

White Sauce (or Melted Butter Sauce)

½ *pint. Time: 15 minutes*

1½ oz. butter	lemon juice
1 oz. flour	cayenne pepper
½ pt milk	salt

Melt the butter in a pan, blend in the flour; add milk and stir over a medium heat until it boils and is smooth and thick; simmer very slowly for 4 to 5 minutes; if too thick add a little more milk and bring to the boil again. Add a few drops of lemon juice, a pinch of cayenne and salt to taste. This sauce is improved by the addition of ½ gill of cream, but do not let it boil after adding.

This sauce is the basis for several kinds of sauce, such as:

Anchovy sauce, add 2 teaspoons anchovy essence to ½ pt white sauce.

Parsley sauce, add 2 teaspoons chopped parsley to ½ pt white sauce.

Caper sauce, add 1 tablespoon chopped or whole capers to ½ pt white sauce.

Egg sauce, add 2 chopped hardboiled eggs to ½ pt white sauce.

White Sauce Sweet

½ *pint. Time: 20 minutes*

½ pt milk	lemon rind
1 level dessertspoon corn-flour	1 oz. sugar
½ oz. butter	1 dessertspoon cream

Mix the cornflour with a little of the milk and put the rest into a pan with 2 or 3 thin strips of lemon peel; place over a low heat and simmer for 10 minutes Remove from heat, stir in the blended cornflour and the sugar, bring to the boil again and simmer for 5 minutes. Remove the rind, add the cream, but do not let it boil again.

Other flavourings can be used, such as: brandy, rum or coffee. If using these, omit the lemon rind.

White Wine Sauce
(For Dressed Fish)

½ *pint. Time: 30 minutes*

½ pt fish stock (see p. 35)	1 gill white wine
2 oz. butter	lemon juice
1 oz. flour	pepper, salt

Melt 1 oz. of the butter over a low heat, blend in the flour, stir in gradually the stock and wine; bring to the boil, simmer for 15 minutes. Add the remainder of the butter, a morsel at a time. A few drops of lemon juice and seasoning to taste. Strain through a fine sieve, reheat by standing the pan in a larger pan of hot water.

Wine Sauce Sweet

1 gill. Time: 15 minutes

2 tablespoons raspberry jam
1 tablespoon castor sugar
1 gill water

lemon juice
1 wineglass sherry

Put all the ingredients, except the lemon juice, into a pan and stir until boiling, keep simmering until the sauce is thick and syrupy. Add a few drops of lemon juice, strain and serve.

Breadcrumbs to Fry

4 oz. white breadcrumbs
2 oz. butter

pepper
salt

Melt the butter in a pan, put in the breadcrumbs and a little seasoning. Fry until well-browned, moving the breadcrumbs around while cooking. Drain on to soft paper.

Egg Balls
(For Soup or Fish)

4 hardboiled eggs
1 egg
½ oz. flour

cayenne pepper
salt

Put the yolks of the hardboiled eggs into a mortar, pound until smooth. Add a little seasoning and the yolk of the raw egg, mix well together; put the mixture on a floured board, roll into small balls and drop into boiling water for 3 to 4 minutes.

Glaze for Galantines

Boil some strong clear, brown stock over a quick heat until it reaches the consistency of cream; skim, stir constantly until it sticks like jelly to the spoon; care is needed to prevent the stock from burning while it is thickening. When ready, put into a pot until required, then dissolve by placing the pot in hot water. Brush over the galantine with 2 or 3 coats of glaze, but let each coat dry before adding the next.

Macedoine of Vegetables for Garnishing

carrots	cucumber
french beans	peas
turnips	salt

These can be cut into any shape, diced, strips, or made into small balls with a vegetables scoop. Put into lightly-salted boiling water and cook until soft.

Parsley to Fry

Wash the parsley, remove the stalks, dry in a clean cloth. After frying the meat or fish, turn off the heat from under the pan, leave for a minute then toss in the parsley. Let it sizzle a moment, take out and drain on soft paper. The parsley should still be bright green but crisp; if the fat is too hot it will turn the parsley brown.

QUENELLES FOR GARNISHING

Chicken Quenelles

Time: 15 to 20 minutes to cook

½ lb. chicken (uncooked)	½ gill white stock (chicken if
1 oz. butter	possible
1 oz. flour	pepper, salt
1 egg	

Put the butter into a pan with the stock, bring to the boil, sprinkle in the flour and stir vigorously until the mixture leaves the sides of the pan, let cool a little. Remove any skin from the chicken, cut up very small, or mince, put into a mortar, pound well, gradually add the flour mixture, the lightly-beaten egg and seasoning to taste. Pound together, rub through a sieve. Shape into quenelles and poach in boiling water for 15 to 20 minutes. These can be served as a garnish to entrées, or in soup.

Veal Quenelles

¾ lb. veal (lean)	2 egg yolks
½ lb. bread panada (see p. 101)	1 white of egg
2 oz. butter	pepper, salt
1 gill white sauce (see p. 140)	

Put the veal twice through a mincer, pound it in a mortar, rub through a wire sieve, put back in the mortar. Pound it with the butter, bread panada and seasoning to taste, gradually stir in the yolks and the white of egg and the white sauce; pound all well together and cook as for chicken quenelles.

To shape Quenelles: Dip 2 dessertspoons into hot water, fill one with the mixture and smooth it into the shape of an egg (use a knife for this); dip the other spoon into hot water again and remove the quenelle from the spoon, slip it into a well-buttered pan, pour on enough boiling water to half cover the quenelles and poach until firm.

BUTTERS

Anchovy Butter

4 anchovies (whole)	3 oz. butter

Wash the anchovies in warm water, dry, remove the skin and bones. Pound in a mortar with the butter, add a pinch of cayenne pepper if liked, then rub through a sieve. Make the butter into one round or square; alternatively, make into small rolls and put into the refrigerator to get very cold.

Curry Butter

3 oz. butter	black pepper
1 teaspoon curry powder	cayenne pepper

Put the butter on to a plate and with a broad-bladed knife work in the curry powder, 1 level saltspoon of black pepper and a pinch of cayenne. Mix well and put into the refrigerator to get very cold.

Lobster Butter

lobster coral (cooked) paprika pepper
butter salt

Wash the coral, dry in a cool oven, weigh and use double the weight in butter. Put into a mortar, pound well, add seasoning to taste, rub through a hair sieve. Put into the refrigerator until required.

Maître d'Hôtel Butter

2 oz. butter 2 teaspoons lemon juice
2 teaspoons finely-chopped pepper, salt
  parsley

Put the butter on to a plate and with a broad-bladed knife, work in the parsley, lemon juice and seasoning to taste. Mix well and put into a cold place until required.

Watercress or Green Butter

1 bunch watercress pepper
butter salt

Wash and pick the stalks from the watercress, dry in a cloth. Chop or mince it finely, allow 1 tablespoon to each 2 oz. of butter. Pound together in a mortar, add seasoning to taste, put on a plate and leave in the refrigerator until required.

13

Puddings

Puddings can be divided into six kinds: milk puddings, suet puddings, batter puddings, soufflés, sponge puddings and the cold mousse and jelly.

When I was in domestic service, suet puddings were made only for the servants, because they were filling and inexpensive, but 'them' upstairs didn't require them in a six- or seven-course meal. Now back to my hobby horse. Suet puddings and dumplings were of a finer texture than they are now and certainly lighter in colour because the flour was whiter. Today things get added to the flour and it gets darker and darker. Recently, for example, I baked what is known as a snow cake, which I used to cook to the colour of snow in the old days, but it came out cream colour. Again, we didn't use self-raising flour; I don't think there was such a thing. We used plain flour and added baking powder as required. So the recipes that I have given for puddings are all made with plain flour, but as the flour isn't as light in texture today, it is often advisable to add just a little baking powder even if the recipe doesn't specify its use.

When you're making a suet pudding, the suet should be

chopped very finely—the finer the suet the lighter the pudding, and if the board is well floured and the knife dipped into the flour occasionally, chopping suet is not too laborious a process. However, if it bores you, buy it in a packet. Perhaps no one will notice the difference.

When mixing pudding dough, some people tend to make it too firm; it should be soft enough when mixed to drop from the spoon but too soft to handle as pastry. If a lighter pudding is required, reduce the flour by a quarter and make up the weight with white breadcrumbs, which is why people make Christmas puddings with half flour and half breadcrumbs.

Always grease the basin well, and the mixture must reach the top of the basin if you are boiling a pudding, otherwise the water will get in. If you haven't got enough mixture you can fill up the gap with a crust of bread, but remember, of course, to remove this before serving! Then put grease-proof paper over or a scalded floured pudding cloth; you don't need grease-proof paper if you use a floured pudding cloth. And when putting a pudding cloth on don't forget to make a pleat across the middle otherwise when the pudding rises it has no room to expand.

With a rich fruit pudding like a Christmas pudding it's a good idea to make a paste of flour and water and put it over the top of the fruit mixture. This prevents any steam or water from seeping in, but if after cooking the pudding is to be kept for some time, remove the cloth, throw the paste away, rinse and dry the cloth and put it back on the basin. However, when you're reheating it, remember to make another paste to put on the top, otherwise the benefit will be lost. At one place where I was in service, we used to make our Christmas puddings at least three months in advance. We didn't stand them on shelves, we used to suspend them from hooks in the ceiling. The cook had the idea that if the air got all round, it preserved them longer. To my mind, this idea derives from the old way of making Christmas puddings in cloths not basins. Then, of course, the air could get all round.

Steamed puddings need more careful handling than suet. The basin should never be filled when you're making a sponge type of steamed pudding because you must leave room for the pudding to rise. If it is covered with grease-proof paper, make sure that the ends of the paper don't hang in the water otherwise they will soak it up and it will make the pudding wet. Foil paper makes a very good cover for a steamed pudding because it clings closely to the sides of the basin.

If you don't have a steamer, and it really is worth investing in one, use an ordinary saucepan, but make sure that it's large enough to leave a space all round the basin, otherwise you'll find great difficulty in adding to the water, which will reduce as the pudding is steaming. It's a good idea to put an inverted saucer in the pan to raise the bottom of the basin from the water, and the pan must have enough water in it to reach about half-way up the basin. Keep it boiling on a very low gas because if it boils too fiercely the water will get into the pudding and this is disastrous when you're steaming a sponge. Again, if you let it boil too hard, it may boil dry. If you find that the water's getting very low, add boiling water, and remember that steamed puddings take at least half to three-quarters of an hour longer than boiled puddings. If you are steaming a delicate mixture like a soufflé, it must be very gently steamed with the water barely bubbling, but it must never go off the boil; if it does, no adding of boiling water will help. It will be ruined.

When making a milk pudding such as rice, tapioca or macaroni, you can either put it straight into the oven with the milk over the cereal, or you can partly cook it first in a double saucepan. This latter method is best if you are in a hurry—it takes about two hours' cooking in the oven and it simply can't be rushed; if it is, you'll find that the grains, and this applies particularly to rice, won't swell at all and there's nothing more likely to put you off your appetite than a dish full of milk with rice grains floating around in it. On the other hand, you don't want too much cereal for the amount of milk, otherwise you get a pudding of congealed rubber. A good idea if you want to make a richer milk pudding—and despite its reputation, it can be very palatable indeed, not just something for the children or for invalids but a dish worthy of any occasion—add the yolk of a couple of eggs, and if you feel really venturesome, add both eggs and cream. It's really worth going to town on.

It astonishes me how, even today, people look upon cream as a very special thing, to be poured over fruit or used in cakes; but for a great many dishes even one tablespoonful will make all the difference, particularly with milk puddings. But remember, and this doesn't just apply to milk puddings, when you're adding the cream and eggs, wait until the pudding is almost cooked, it must not boil; it must be on the verge of boiling. When the pudding is almost done, lift the golden-coloured skin carefully, then stir in the well-beaten egg yolks and cream—double cream if you can afford it—put the skin back and leave it for about another half an hour and you'll find that, although the pudding doesn't reach boiling point again, the heat will cook both the eggs and the cream.

When you make Yorkshire puddings, pancakes or fritters they must always be made with plain flour. There is no exception to this. Some people think that self-raising flour makes a batter lighter but it doesn't. You'll never get a Yorkshire pudding to rise up and shoot the top off the oven if you've made it with self-raising flour. Mind you, there are people, and my husband is one, who hate Yorkshire pudding that has risen. He likes it on the stodgy side, so for a treat for him sometimes I do make it with self-raising flour, but as I tell him, it isn't really a Yorkshire pudding at all.

When you make batter for fritters, it must be thick enough to coat whatever you're frying in it, but it mustn't be stodgy. Take banana fritters, for example, the batter mustn't be so thin that when you have cooked them you can see the banana; on the other hand it mustn't be so thick that it comes out in one great wodge. One cause of failure is that people don't use a deep enough pan so that there is insufficient fat to cover the fritters, or else the fat is not hot enough. A good way to test the heat is to drop about half a teaspoon of the batter into the fat; if it immediately rises to the surface and frizzles then the temperature is right, but if there's no frizzling and it tends to sink, it isn't. Don't forget that if you can't do all the fritters in one go, then you've got to heat your fat again before beginning with the others. If you haven't a deep enough pan to cover the fritters, then you must turn them over once at least to brown them on both sides, and lift them out with a slicer or a perforated spoon, and remember to drain them on soft paper. I don't recommend trying to make any kind of fritters for a dinner party if it's your first attempt.

Pancake batter must be thinner than fritter batter as it hasn't got to be used as a coating, and if you want a very light pancake, use more eggs. Don't put a lot of fat in the pan, and if you don't feel you're capable of tossing pancakes—and it isn't as easy as it looks—don't bother. Use a very large, wide, palette knife and turn the pancake over with that, but lift it gently first and make sure that the side you're going to turn over is a golden brown because you don't want to turn it over more than once. Pancakes must be served immediately. They're unsociable things to give at a dinner party because you can really only serve one person at a time. When I do them for the family I start off with my husband and work round the children, cooking while they eat, but this is not the sort of thing that you can do when you're entertaining. I'm always left till last unfortunately, hoping that there's going to be enough batter left for me.

Many people are frightened of making soufflés. They seem to think that they are too delicate a thing to attempt, but they are not nearly as difficult as they believe. The main thing is that, subjected to a sudden change in temperature, soufflés are apt to sag, but if you haven't far to take them from the oven to the table, there's no reason at all why this should happen. With the baked ones you serve them in the same dish they are cooked in, so the only change of temperature is on the surface. But whether they are steamed or baked, they do need care in the cooking. The time of serving is also a vital factor as they need to be eaten immediately they're cooked, so they're not for unexpected guests or an unpunctual family.

The foundation of a soufflé is the panada mixture, and although I have given the recipe for this, I'll add a little more here. The yolks and the whites of eggs are beaten separately and then added to the other ingredients or flavouring. The yolks of eggs of course can be beaten quite vigorously when added, but as with all dishes when adding whipped whites of eggs, they are not beaten but folded in. I'll explain what I mean since some people don't know the difference. Beating is the vigorous application of the spoon against the sides of the basin so that air can penetrate the mixture. Folding in is putting the eggs on the top of the mixture and then gently turning it over and over until the two are amalgamated. Slowly and gently the movement must be because the whites of eggs lose the value of being added separately if beaten in.

Directly the mixture is completed, it must be put in the oven. So if, just as you're about to do this, the telephone or the doorbell rings, ignore it completely; you're out. Far better to let them ring again than spoil what should be a work of art. You will also have made sure that the oven is the right temperature, or the water boiling if you are steaming. With a steamed soufflé, put an inverted saucer in the bottom of the pan as I suggested for sponge puddings, making very sure that the water is boiling. Then pour the mixture into a tin or dish that has straight sides and is well greased with melted butter. Around this tie a double thickness of grease-proof paper so that it is at least three or four inches above the top of the tin or dish. Grease this also as you put it round and then grease another piece to cover the top. In serving a steamed soufflé you must turn it out and pour round it the sauce you are serving with it.

With a baked soufflé use a china or earthenware dish. I prefer earthenware as it retains the heat more and, as I have said, the soufflé must be served in the dish in which it's cooked. Use the same method of tying paper round as for the steamed soufflé, but omit the paper from the top because you want this to cook to a pale brown colour, and don't open the oven door unless it's absolutely necessary; should you have to, open it the merest crack, as a rush of air will cause your soufflé to sink and nothing will make it rise again.

One of the reasons for the failure of soufflés is that the eggs are not beaten enough. The whites must be beaten to such a firm texture that if you tip the basin upside down they won't fall out; then they must be folded into the mixture very lightly indeed. The yolks, of course, are added after every other ingredient except the whites. Another cause of failure, particularly with baked soufflés, is a too-rapid cooking, because whether you're making a savoury or a sweet, if you cook it too rapidly it will rise before the middle is firm and when you remove it from the oven the middle sinks; and of course the last cause of failure is that it's not served quickly enough. A well-made soufflé is a pride and joy—the pride of the cook and the joy of those who eat it.

STEAMED PUDDINGS

Brown Betty Pudding

4 to 5 persons. Time: 3 hours

1 lb. apples	brown bread
2 oz. chopped candied peel	½ lemon
4 oz. suet	nutmeg
6 oz. brown breadcrumbs	¼ teaspoon cinnamon
3 oz. castor sugar	vanilla essence

Peel and chop the apples, finely chop the peel. Mix the suet with the breadcrumbs, apples, peel, sugar, a little grated nutmeg, grated rind of ½ lemon, the beaten eggs and a few drops of vanilla essence. If the mixture seems too dry, add a little milk. Grease a basin large enough to take the mixture, put a round of brown bread at the bottom, and line the sides with fingers of brown bread. Put in the mixture, cover with buttered paper and a scalded, floured cloth—or foil if preferred—and boil for 3 hours. Serve with a sweet white sauce to which brandy has been added (see p. 140).

Cabinet Pudding

4 persons. Time: 1 to 1¼ hours

4 oz. sponge cakes	1½ oz. castor sugar
½ doz. ratafias	1 pt milk
4 egg yolks	2 oz. glacé cherries
2 whites of eggs	almond flavouring

Beat the yolks and whites together in a basin. Bring the milk almost to boiling point, stir quickly into the eggs; add the sponge cakes, sugar, ratafias and almond essence, mix well together. Butter a basin or china soufflé-dish and decorate it with the cherries, pour in the mixture, cover with grease-proof paper or foil and steam gently for 1 to 1¼ hours. Take care that water does not get into the dish. When done, carefully turn out on to a hot dish. Serve with a jam sauce (see p. 134).

Canary Pudding

4 to 5 persons. Time: 1 to 1¼ hours

4 oz. flour	½ teaspoon baking powder
3 oz. butter	milk
2 eggs	grated lemon rind
3 oz. castor sugar	

Cream the butter and sugar together until thick and smooth, add the eggs one at a time with a dessertspoon of flour for each egg; beat well. Mix the baking powder with the rest of the flour, add the grated rind of half the lemon. Stir this into the butter mixture as lightly as possible, add sufficient milk to allow the mixture to drop easily from the spoon, cover with buttered paper, steam for 1 to 1¼ hours, turn out and serve with a sweet melted-butter sauce flavoured with lemon (see p. 140).

Caramel Custard

4 to 5 persons. Time: 50 minutes to 1 hour

6 egg yolks	3 oz. castor sugar
2 whites of eggs	1½ pt milk
6 oz. loaf sugar	1½ gill water

Dip the lumps of sugar into the water, put them into a pan and let them brown, take care that they do not burn. Add the water, stir until the sugar is melted, and then boil until the sugar is thick and like syrup. Warm a soufflé mould and pour in the syrup, turning it round so that the mould becomes coated, leave to cool. Beat the yolks and whites of eggs with the castor sugar, bring the milk almost to boiling point and pour over the eggs, stirring all the time. Pour this into the coated mould, cover with grease-proof paper, and steam very gently for 50 minutes to 1 hour.

If to be served hot, when cooked, turn out carefully on to a dish—the caramel will form a sauce round the custard. If to be served cold, leave in soufflé dish until completely cold.

Christmas Pudding

Time: 6 hours

¾ lb. breadcrumbs	1 cooking apple (chopped)
½ lb. flour	6 eggs (large)
¾ lb. suet (chopped)	½ nutmeg (grated)
1 lb. raisins	½ teaspoon cinnamon
½ lb. sultanas	brandy or sherry—1 wine-
½ lb. currants	glass or more if liked
½ lb. mixed candied peel	salt
4 oz. glacé cherries	

If the fruit is not bought already cleaned, wash and dry it in a cool oven; buy 'seeded' raisins not 'seedless'. Cut or pull the raisins into halves, finely chop the peel, cut the cherries into quarters. Put into a large mixing bowl all the dry ingredients, add cinnamon, nutmeg and a pinch of salt. Mix all well together, beat up the eggs and stir them into the mixture with the brandy or sherry. Make sure that all the ingredients are mixed well. Cover the bowl and leave overnight. The next day stir again then divide into 3 or 4 basins according to the size you require. Make enough dough of flour and water to roll out and cover each basin to prevent the water getting in, cover with grease-proof paper, tie on scalded floured cloths—making a pleat across the middle to allow the pudding to rise. Put the basins into boiling water and boil for

6 hours. When done remove the cloths and the dough from the puddings. Cover with greaseproof paper and dry cloths and keep in a dry place until required. When wanted, put another round of flour and water paste on top, replace the cloth and boil or steam for another 2 to 3 hours. Serve with hard sauce (see p. 133) and cream if liked.

Treacle Layer Pudding

4 persons. Time: 2 hours

½ lb. flour
3 to 4 oz. suet
soft brown sugar
1 small teaspoon baking
    powder

water or milk to mix
1 lemon
golden syrup
pinch salt

Sieve together the flour, salt and baking powder, add the finely chopped suet, mix to a stiff paste with the milk or water. Line a greased basin with the sugar. Roll out a little less than half the paste, put a layer at the bottom of the basin, cover with a layer of treacle and a few drops of lemon juice, fill the basin with alternate layers of suet paste, treacle and a sprinkling of lemon juice, damping the top layer to seal on firmly. Cover with buttered paper and steam for 2 hours. Turn out into a fairly deep dish.

BAKED PUDDINGS

Apple Amber

4 to 5 persons. Time: About 20 to 30 minutes to bake

1½ lb. cooking apples
3 oz. brown sugar
2 egg yolks
3 whites of eggs
1 oz. butter

½ doz. glacé cherries
½ lemon
small amount short pastry
1½ oz. castor sugar

Peel, core and cut up the apples, put them into a pan with the sugar, thinly-cut lemon rind, butter and tablespoon of water; stew over a low heat until the apples are soft, then rub through a sieve; add the yolks one at a time and beat well. Line and decorate the edges and sides of a greased pie-dish with the pastry and put the apple mixture into it. Bake in a rather hot oven for 20 to 30 minutes to cook the pastry. Whisk the whites of eggs to a stiff froth, lightly fold in the castor sugar and pile this roughly on top of the apple. Cut the cherries into halves and place here and there on top, put into a cool oven until the meringue has hardened and acquired a pale brown colour.

Gas 6–7; Electricity 400°–425°

Apples Baked

1 per person. Time: About 1 hour

large cooking apples
soft brown sugar or honey

butter
lemon juice

Wash and wipe the apples, core them and make a shallow cut in the skin all round. Fill the centres with the sugar or honey and squeeze a little lemon juice over the fillings. Place in a baking tin with a little water round the apples, put a knob of butter on each and bake in the oven for ¾ to 1 hour according to the size of the apples. Do not over-cook or the apples will not keep their shape.

Gas 5–6; Electricity 375°–400°

Apple Charlotte

5 to 6 persons. Time: About ¾ to 1 hour

2 lb. cooking apples
4 oz. brown sugar
butter (melted)

1 lemon
½ pt cream

Peel, core and thinly slice the apples. Grease a pie-dish or round mould and line with thin slices of bread dipped in the butter; fill the dish or mould with alternate layers of apple, sugar and slices of bread dipped in the butter, finish with a layer of bread. Pour over 1 tablespoon of water and the same amount of lemon juice and bake in the oven for ¾ to 1 hour, or until the apples are soft. This can be served in the dish or turned out; serve with the cream.

Gas 5–6; Electricity 375°–400°

Bakewell Pudding

4 persons. Time: About 1 hour

6 oz. breadcrumbs
3 oz. ground almonds
2 oz. castor sugar
2 oz. glacé cherries
almond essence

2 large eggs
½ pt milk
3 to 4 tablespoons raspberry
  jam

Put the breadcrumbs and almonds into a basin, add the chopped cherries. Beat the eggs with the milk, add to the breadcrumbs with the sugar and a few drops of almond essence. Butter a fairly-deep round dish, put in a layer of jam, then half the mixture, another layer of jam and the rest of the mixture. Bake in a moderate oven for ¾ to 1 hour.

Gas 5–6; Electricity 375°–400°

Empress Pudding

4 to 5 persons. Time: About ½ hour

3 oz. Carolina rice
2 oz. castor sugar
2 eggs
1 oz. butter

1 pt milk
2 tablespoons apricot jam
½ doz. glacé cherries
1 lemon

Wash the rice and cook it in the milk until soft, stir in the butter, 1 oz. sugar and the grated rind of ½ lemon. Allow to cool slightly, then beat in the yolks of the eggs. Put the jam in the bottom of a greased pie-dish, place the rice on the top; beat the whites of eggs to a stiff froth, fold in the other 1 oz. of sugar and pile on top of the pudding. Cut the cherries into halves, put on top of the meringue and bake in the oven on a low heat for about ½ hour.

Gas 3–4; Electricity 325°–350°

Exeter Pudding

4 to 5 persons. Time: About 1 hour to bake

4 sponge cakes
4 oz. breadcrumbs
1 oz. ratafias
3 oz. butter
1 oz. flour
3 eggs

3 oz. castor sugar
½ gill cream
1 lemon
1 wineglass rum (optional)
apricot jam

Mix the breadcrumbs, flour, sugar and grated rind of ½ lemon, rub in the butter. Well-grease a basin or mould and lightly coat with breadcrumbs; cover the bottom with ratafias. Put a layer of the mixture on top, cover with slices of sponge cake thickly spread with jam, add a few ratafias. Continue with these layers until all the ingredients are used; the top layer must be the mixture, pour over the rum if used. Bake in a moderate oven for about 1 hour, serve with a sweet wine sauce (see p. 141).

Gas 4–5; Electricity 350°–375°

French Pancakes

Makes 5 to 6. Time: 15 to 20 minutes

2 oz. flour
2 oz. butter
2 oz. castor sugar

2 eggs
½ pt milk
4 tablespoons raspberry jam

Cream the butter and sugar, add the eggs one at a time with a dessertspoon of the flour, beat well, stir in the rest of the flour and the milk. Put the mixture into well-greased saucers and bake in a fairly hot oven for 15 to 20 minutes. When done, turn out on to grease-proof paper coated with castor sugar, place a teaspoon of hot jam on each, fold over and serve on a hot dish.

Gas 5–6; Electricity 375°–400°

Friar's Omelet

4 persons. Time: About ½ hour

1½ lb. cooking apples
3 oz. breadcrumbs
2 oz. demerara sugar, or 2
   tablespoons golden syrup

1½ oz. butter
1 large or 2 small eggs
lemon

Peel, core and slice the apples, stew them with the sugar or syrup and the grated rind of ½ lemon. When soft, add the butter and the well-beaten egg or eggs. Well-grease a pie dish, put half the breadcrumbs at the bottom, pour on the apple mixture and cover with the rest of the breadcrumbs. Dot with small pieces of butter and bake in a moderate oven for about ½ hour.

Gas 5–6; Electricity 375°–400°

Ground Rice Pudding

3 to 4 persons. Time: ½ to ¾ hour

3 oz. ground rice	1 pt milk
1 egg	1 oz. butter
1 to 2 oz. castor sugar	vanilla essence

Put the milk into a pan, bring to the boil, sprinkle in the ground rice, stir well and simmer for about 20 minutes. Add the sugar and butter, beat in the egg, add a few drops of vanilla essence. Put into a well-greased pie dish and bake in the oven for ½ to ¾ hour.

Gas 2; Electricity 300°

Lemon or Orange Pudding

4 to 5 persons

4 oz. cake crumbs (sponge or madeira)	3 oz. castor sugar
3 egg yolks	1 gill milk
2 whites of eggs	2 lemons or 2 oranges
	1 tablespoon cream (optional)

Cream the yolks of eggs with the sugar, add the grated rind of the lemons or oranges, cake-crumbs, milk and the cream if used. Whisk the whites to a stiff froth, gently fold them into the other ingredients, pour into a buttered dish and bake in a moderate oven for ½ to ¾ hour, or until the mixture is set.

Gas 5; Electricity 375°

Rice Pudding

3 to 4 persons. Time: 2 to 2½ hours

1½ oz. Carolina rice	1 pt milk
1 oz. sugar	nutmeg
½ gill cream (optional)	

Wash the rice, put it into a pie-dish with the sugar and milk, grate a little nutmeg over the top. Bake in a slow oven for about 2 to 2½ hours. If using cream: about 15 minutes before the pudding is ready, remove from oven, carefully turn back the skin from the top, stir in the cream, replace the skin and leave in the oven to finish setting.

Gas 1–2; Electricity 275°–300°

Tapioca Pudding

5 to 6 persons. Time: About 1 hour altogether

2 oz. seed tapioca	1 large egg or 2 small
1½ pts milk	grated lemon rind, or vanilla
2 oz. sugar	essence

Put the milk into a pan, bring to the boil, sprinkle in the tapioca, stir well and simmer until the tapioca becomes clear, stirring occasionally. Remove from heat, allow to cool a little, add the sugar, flavouring, beat in the egg. Put into a buttered pie-dish and bake in a slow oven for ½ to ¾ hour.

Gas 2–3; Electricity 300°–325°

BATTERS AND FRITTERS

Fritter Batter

½ lb. plain flour	½ pt water
2 tablespoons salad oil	salt
2 whites of eggs	

Sieve the flour into a basin, add a pinch of salt; have the chill off the water and stir the salad oil into it. Gradually stir this into the flour and beat until smooth, leave for ½ hour. Just before the batter is required, fold in the stiffly-whipped whites of eggs and use as required.

Apple Fritters

5 to 6 persons. Time: About 10 minutes

3 large apples	lard or oil
castor sugar	1 lemon
fritter batter (see above)	

Peel and core the apples without breaking them, cut into rings about ⅛th inch thick, sprinkle with sugar and lemon juice. Use a deep frying pan, make the lard or oil hot enough so that a faint blue smoke rises. Dip the apple rings into the batter, lift out with a fork and drop into the hot fat, fry for about 6 to 10 minutes; lower the heat slightly after the first minute to allow the apple to cook through—remember to heat up again for the next batch. Drain on soft paper and serve with castor sugar sifted over.

Banana Fritters

4 persons. Time: About 6 minutes to fry

3 to 4 bananas	frying fat or oil
fritter batter (see p. 158)	lemon
castor sugar	

Peel the bananas, cut into halves lengthwise and cut each half into 2 pieces. Put on a plate, sprinkle with lemon juice, cover and leave for 5 minutes. Make the fat hot as for apple fritters, dip each piece of banana into the batter, lift out with a fork and drop into the hot fat. Fry to a golden brown, drain onto soft paper and serve sprinkled with castor sugar.

Pancake Batter

4 oz. plain flour	½ pt milk
2 eggs	salt

Sieve the flour into a basin, add a pinch of salt. Make a well in the centre, break in the eggs, add a little of the milk and beat well. Gradually add the rest of the milk, beating all the time until the batter is smooth; it should run easily off a spoon. If a richer batter is needed, add 1 oz. of melted butter just before using. Let the batter stand for ½ hour, then use as required.

Pancakes with Truffles

About 4 persons. Time: About 5 minutes to fry

pancake batter (see above)	1 gill cream
½ doz. truffles	breadcrumbs
2 oz. butter	frying fat or oil
2 oz. flour	paprika pepper
1 egg	salt
1 gill milk	

Melt 1 oz. of the butter in a pan, blend in the flour, stir over a medium heat until it thickens, gradually pour in the cream and continue stirring over the heat until it almost reaches boiling point—do not let it boil. If the truffles are fresh, carefully wash and brush them, chop finely and lightly fry in the other 1 oz. of butter; stir them into the flour mixture and leave until cold. Make as many pancakes as required, spread a layer of truffle mixture on each one with a little seasoning and fold into a little cushion by first bringing across the opposite edges, then folding across to the other two. Dip these into the beaten egg, coat with bread-crumbs and fry in deep, hot fat or oil for about 5 minutes, or until a golden brown.

Pancakes Savoury

4 persons

pancake batter
tin asparagus tips
parmesan cheese

paprika pepper
salt

Put the asparagus tips into a pan, make hot over a low heat, strain and keep hot. Add 2 oz. of parmesan cheese to the batter and a pinch of paprika; make as many pancakes as required, but make them small. As each one is cooked, put a few asparagus tips in the centre and roll up; place in the oven to keep hot until all are done.

Yorkshire Pudding

4 persons. Time: About 30 to 35 minutes

4 oz. plain flour
1 pt milk or, ½ pt milk, ½ pt water

2 eggs
2 oz. lard or dripping
salt

Sieve the flour with a pinch of salt into a basin, make a well in the centre, break in the eggs, pour in a little of the milk and beat well. Gradually add the rest of the milk or milk and water and beat to a smooth batter—it should not be too thick—cover and leave for ½ to 1 hour. Put the lard or dripping into a baking tin, when very hot pour in the batter and bake in the oven for 30 to 35 minutes.

Gas 7; Electricity 425°

SOUFFLÉS

Apricot Soufflé

4 to 5 persons. Time: 25 to 30 minutes

tin apricots (medium size)
1½ oz. butter
1 oz. flour

4 eggs
1 gill milk
1 oz. castor sugar

160

Drain the syrup from the apricots, cut them into small pieces and pack closely together in the bottom of a buttered soufflé dish. Melt the butter in a pan, blend in the flour, add the milk and stir over a medium heat until it thickens and leaves the sides of the pan; stir in the sugar and let cool a little. Beat in the yolks of the eggs, one at a time, then whisk the whites to a stiff froth and carefully fold into the mixture. Put on to the apricots in the soufflé dish and bake in the oven for 25 to 30 minutes. Serve as quickly as possible.

Gas 6; Electricity 400°

Chocolate Soufflé

4 persons. Time: 50 minutes to 1 hour

3 oz. plain chocolate	1 oz. butter
3 egg yolks	1 oz. flour
4 whites of eggs	1 gill milk
1 oz. castor sugar	vanilla essence

Melt the butter in a pan and blend in the flour. Finely grate the chocolate, warm the milk, add these to the blended flour, stir over a medium heat until the mixture boils and thickens enough to leave the sides of the pan; keep stirring and beating the whole time. Remove from heat and allow to cool slightly, then beat in the yolks of eggs, one at a time. Whisk the whites to a stiff froth, lightly fold them into the mixture. Put into a buttered soufflé mould, tie a band of buttered paper round the outside to come above the top of the mould, cover the top with grease-proof paper. Have ready a pan of boiling water, place an upturned saucer in the bottom and stand the soufflé on it. Make sure that the water reaches not more than half-way up the sides of the mould. Steam for 50 minutes to 1 hour. When done, carefully turn out on to a hot dish and serve with a sweet white sauce (see p. 140) flavoured with vanilla, or boiled custard.

Lemon Soufflé

4 persons. Time: ¾ to 1 hour

3 egg yolks	1 oz. flour
4 whites of eggs	1 gill milk
1 oz. castor sugar	1 lemon
1 oz. butter	

Melt the butter in a pan, blend in the flour, add the milk and stir over a medium heat until the mixture thickens and leaves the sides of the pan. Remove from heat, add the grated lemon rind and 1 teaspoon of the juice, beat in the yolks of eggs one at a time, whisk the whites of eggs to a stiff froth and fold into the mixture. Put into a buttered soufflé dish, cover and steam as for chocolate soufflé.

This may also be baked in the oven if liked for 25 to 30 minutes.

Gas 6; Electricity 400°

Strawberry Soufflé

3 to 4 persons. Time: 25 to 30 minutes

¾ lb. strawberries	1 oz. butter
2 oz. castor sugar	½ gill milk
1 oz. flour	cochineal colouring
2 eggs	

Put half of the strawberries through a hair sieve and sweeten the pulp with 1 oz. of the sugar. Melt the butter in a pan, blend in the flour, add the milk, stir until it boils and thickens, add the other 1 oz. of sugar and the strawberry pulp. Beat in the yolks of the eggs one at a time, add a drop or two of cochineal to give colour, fold in the stiffly-whisked whites of eggs and the rest of the strawberries cut into thin slices. Put into a buttered soufflé mould and bake in the oven for 25 to 30 minutes.

Gas 6–7; Electricity 400°–425°

Vanilla Soufflé

4 to 5 persons. Time: 1 to 1¼ hours

4 eggs (large)	1 pt milk
4 oz. butter	vanilla essence
4 oz. flour	glacé cherries
2 oz. castor sugar	

Melt the butter in a pan, blend in the flour, add the milk and bring to the boil, stirring all the time; keep stirring until the mixture begins to leave the sides of the pan. Remove from heat, cool a little, add the yolks of the eggs one at a time, fold in the stiffly-whipped whites of eggs. Butter a soufflé mould, decorate the bottom with halved glacé cherries, put in the soufflé mixture, cover and steam as for chocolate soufflé but allow 1 to 1¼ hours. Serve with a wine sauce (see p. 141).

COLD SWEETS

Charlotte Russe

4 to 6 persons

Savoy fingers	½ pt cream
glacé cherries	1 oz. castor sugar
jelly	angelica
½ oz. powdered gelatine	½ wineglass sherry

Decorate the bottom of the mould with the halved cherries, some small pieces of angelica and some of the jelly. Cut off the ends of the Savoy fingers and fit them closely in the mould until it is completely lined. Dissolve the gelatine in the warmed water and add the sugar. Stiffly whip the cream, add the vanilla and pour on the strained and cooled gelatine, add the sherry, mix carefully together, put into a mould, place in the refrigerator. When required, trim off the fingers if they are higher than the mould, turn out and decorate the dish with the rest of the jelly broken up.

Chocolate Mousse

3 to 4 persons

¼ lb. plain chocolate	½ gill water
1 oz. castor sugar	1½ gills cream
1 gill milk	vanilla essence
½ oz. gelatine	pistachio nuts
2 whites of eggs	

Put the milk and sugar into a pan, add the grated chocolate, stir over a low heat until the chocolate is melted and the mixture smooth. Melt the gelatine in the water and strain into the chocolate, add about a dozen drops of vanilla essence and leave to cool. Stiffly beat the egg whites and the cream—separately—and lightly fold them into the chocolate mixture. Put into individual dishes and stand in a cool place to set. When set, sprinkle over chopped pistachio nuts.

Crème en Surprise

3 to 4 persons. 30 to 40 minutes to bake

2 eggs	2 oz. walnuts (chopped)
4 oz. castor sugar	3 oz. glacé cherries (chopped)
2 oz. self-raising flour	1 wineglass sherry
1 oz. cornflour	vanilla essence
1 gill cream	lemon
½ oz. butter	¾ gill water
6 oz. apricot jam	

Coat a fire-proof dish with the melted butter and sprinkle with flour. Cream the yolks of the eggs with 2 oz. of the sugar, add a few drops of vanilla essence. Sieve the flour with the cornflour, stiffly whip the whites of eggs, add the flour and whites alternately to the yolks, mixing very lightly; put into a dish and bake in a moderate oven for 30 to 40 minutes. When done remove from the oven, allow to get cold then cut off the top and scoop out the middle, fill the centre with the whipped cream mixed with the walnuts and the cherries and a dessertspoon of castor sugar, replace the top and put into a deep glass dish. Put the jam and 2 oz. of sugar into a pan with the water and boil quickly until thick, let cool, add the juice of ½ lemon and the sherry. When quite cold, coat the pudding with this sauce and decorate with pistachio nuts and a few cherries.

Gas 5; Electricity 375°

Custard (Boiled)

3 egg yolks	2 tablespoons thick cream
1 oz. castor sugar	vanilla essence
½ pt milk	

Put the milk into a pan with the sugar and a few drops of vanilla essence. When hot, but not boiling, pour on to the egg yolks, stirring all the time. Stand the basin in a pan of boiling water and stir until the custard thickens, it should be thick enough to coat the spoon. Care must be taken not to let the mixture boil or it will curdle. Add the cream and stir for a few minutes longer; leave to cool, stirring from time to time.

Gooseberry Fool

4 to 5 persons

2 lb. gooseberries
½ lb. granulated sugar

1 gill water
½ pt cream (thick)

Wash the gooseberries, top and tail them and put them into a pan with the sugar and water. Cook gently until soft, rub through a hair sieve, leave until cool. Stir in the cream and serve in individual glass dishes.

Any fruit can be used for this dish. If strawberries or raspberries, hull them, sprinkle with castor sugar and leave overnight; they can be rubbed through a hair sieve without cooking. Blackcurrants and blackberries should be cooked as the gooseberries.

Honeycomb Mould

4 persons

1½ pt milk
1½ oz. castor sugar
4 eggs
1 oz. gelatine

1 bay leaf
lemon
½ gill water

Boil the milk with the bay leaf, cream the yolks of eggs with the sugar. Let milk cool slightly, remove bay leaf and pour milk over yolks; stir well, put back in pan and stir over gentle heat until it thickens but do not let it boil; put into a basin to cool. Melt the gelatine in the warmed water, add the grated rind of 1 lemon and a teaspoon of the juice, pour into the egg mixture and stir from time to time until nearly cold. Stiffly whip the whites of eggs and fold them into the mixture, put into wetted mould and place in the refrigerator to set. When firm, turn out on to a dish.

Ice Pudding (Baked)

6 persons

1 large block of vanilla ice-cream
4 eggs and 4 whites of egg

6 oz. castor sugar
4 oz. potato flour
1 oz. butter

The ice-cream should be bought before the sponge is made and put into the freezing compartment of the refrigerator to get extremely firm. Beat 4 egg yolks with 4 oz. of the sugar until it is almost white in colour; add the butter (melted) and the potato flour, mix well. Stiffly beat the whites of 4 eggs and fold into the mixture, pour into a shallow greased tin and bake in the oven for 40 to 50 minutes; when done, leave to cool slightly, then turn out on to sugared paper. When the sponge is quite cold, whip the 4 remaining egg whites to a stiff froth and fold in the rest of the sugar. Place the sponge on a fire-proof plate, cut the ice-cream into slices to fit the top of the cake, and on top of this pile the meringue—it should completely cover the ice-cream. Put it in the oven for about 10 minutes, turning it round all the time—the meringue should be slightly brown. Serve very quickly.

Chocolate Ice-cream

6 persons

1 pt custard	2 tablespoons milk
6 oz. plain chocolate	1 pt cream
2 oz. castor sugar	vanilla essence

Make the custard with custard powder. Put the milk into a pan, add the sugar and the grated chocolate and dissolve over low heat. Add the melted chocolate to the custard with a few drops of vanilla essence. Leave until quite cold then stir in the lightly-whipped cream. Freeze in the usual way.

Fruit Ice-cream

6 persons

1 pt apricot, peach or any fruit purée	1 pt cream
2 oz. castor sugar	1 lemon

Rub the fruit (cooked or tinned) through a hair sieve, add a little of the syrup; the purée should not be too thick. Add the juice of the lemon and the whipped cream and mix well, add sugar to taste and a few drops of colouring if liked. Put into the refrigerator for an hour, then stir it once more and place in the freezing compartment.

Lemon Water Ice

6 persons

2 whites of eggs	rind 2 lemons
$\frac{1}{2}$ lb. castor sugar	1 pt water
$\frac{3}{4}$ gill lemon juice	

Cut the rind of the lemons very thin, then put with the sugar and
water into a pan; stir until boiling, then boil quickly, skimming
well, without stirring, for 8 to 10 minutes. Strain into a basin, add
the lemon juice, and when cold freeze. When almost frozen stir
in the stiffly beaten whites of eggs, and continue to freeze until
very firm.

Lemon Meringue

4 to 6 persons

1 lemon	2 eggs
1 oz. flour	1 oz. butter
2 oz. castor sugar	¼ pt water
2 oz. castor sugar (for meringue)	

Prepare the flan case as for fleur pastry (see p. 175). Beat together
the egg yolks, sugar and flour; put the butter and water into a
pan, bring to the boil, add the yolks to this, stirring all the time,
cook until thick, cool, add the lemon juice and grated rind. Turn
the mixture into the flan case. Whip the whites of the eggs until
quite stiff, add a third of the sugar and whip until the mixture
is stiff again. Fold in the remainder of the sugar and pile the
meringue over the lemon mixture. Bake for ½ hour in a cool oven
to brown the meringue.

Gas 1; Electricity 275°

Meringues

4 to 5 persons

4 whites of eggs	lemon or vanilla essence
¾ lb. castor sugar	salt
olive oil	

Put the whites of eggs into a basin with a pinch of salt, whip to
a very stiff froth. Sieve about 10 oz. of the sugar, and fold into
the whites with a metal spoon; add a few drops of flavouring.
Have a large flat board or tin, oil it, then cover with a sheet of
oiled paper. To shape the meringues, have 2 dessertspoons, a
palette knife and cold water. Wet one spoon, take up a spoonful
of the meringue and shape it with the palette knife, pointing the
ends and piling it high in the centre. Wet the second spoon and

use it to take the meringue from the first spoon and place on the prepared board or tin. Continue in this way until all the meringue is used, leaving a space between each one. Sprinkle them thickly with castor sugar and put into a cool oven until crisp and a pale cream colour. The oven must be just hot enough when the meringues are put in to keep them from spreading, but must be lowered later on. Remove any soft inside with the handle of a teaspoon and put back in a cool oven, hollow side up to dry; handle very carefully. Fill the insides with whipped or ice-cream. The cases will keep for a long time in a tin.

Gas 1; Electricity 275° for the first ½ hour.
When replaced: Gas ½; Electricity 250° for the second ½ hour.

Princess Pudding

4 persons

1 gill fruit purée (any fruit will do)	2 oz. castor sugar
	½ oz. gelatine
3 eggs	lemon juice
1 gill milk	

Lightly beat the yolks of the eggs, pour on the almost boiling milk, add the gelatine and the sugar and stir over a low heat until it thickens but do not let it boil. Remove from heat, add the fruit purée, 1 teaspoon of lemon juice and, if liked, a few drops of colouring. Leave until cold, then fold in the stiffly-whipped whites of eggs. Put into a mould and place in the refrigerator to set.

Queen Mab Pudding

4 to 5 persons

6 egg yolks	1 gill water
1 pt milk	2 oz. glacé cherries
4 oz. castor sugar	2 oz. crystallized fruits
½ pt cream	lemon
1 oz. gelatine	vanilla essence

Put the milk into a pan with the thinly-peeled rind of the lemon, bring to the boil, cool for a few minutes, remove the rind and pour the milk on to the lightly beaten yolks. Stir over a low heat until a thick custard is formed—do not let it boil. Dissolve the gelatine in the warmed water and add the custard, when both are cold; add the chopped cherries and crystallized fruits. When quite cold, fold in the whipped cream, put into a wetted mould and place in the refrigerator to set.

Ratafia Trifle

5 to 6 persons

6 to 8 sponge cakes
1 doz. ratafias
1 pt custard (boiled) (see p. 164)
raspberry jam

1 wineglass sherry (or more if liked)
glacé cherries
angelica
½ pt cream

Make the custard and leave to cool. Split the sponge cakes, spread fairly thickly with the jam, put together and place in a glass dish. Crush the ratafias and sprinkle over the sponge cakes. Pour the sherry over the sponge cakes and leave to soak for an hour. When the custard has cooled, pour it over the sponges, pile the stiffly-whipped cream all over and decorate with the cherries and angelica.

Summer Pudding

4 to 6 persons

1½ lb. blackcurrants or raspberries and redcurrants
sugar

slices bread and butter
cream as required

Stew the fruit but do not make it too sweet; cut some thin slices of bread and butter, place around the bottom of the basin, then line the basin with more of the slices, butter side in (they must fit closely together). Put in the fruit to reach half-way up the basin, put a layer of bread and butter on top, then fill with the rest of the fruit, cover with another layer of bread and butter; stand the basin in a deep plate, cover with a plate to fit the top, put a weight on top and leave to get cold. Turn out when cold; if there is any fruit juice in the plate pour it round the pudding, whip the cream and pile on top.

JELLIES

Apple Jelly

Time: About ¾ to 1 hour

1½ lb. apples
¾ oz. gelatine
4½ oz. white sugar

3 gills water
1 lemon

Wash the apples, cut them up without peeling, put them into a pan with the water, sugar and the thinly-cut rind of the lemon. Boil gently until the apples are soft, rub through a hair sieve. Dissolve the gelatine in about 2 tablespoons of warm water, add to the apple pulp, stir well. Put into a cold place to set, stirring occasionally until almost firm. Green colouring can be added if liked. If the apples are extra juicy, slightly more gelatine may be needed.

Cranberry Jelly

Time: ½ to ¾ hour

¾ pt cranberries
½ lb. white sugar

1½ pts water
1½ oz. gelatine

Wash the cranberries, put into a pan with 1¼ pts of the water and simmer until soft—about 20 to 30 minutes. Dissolve the gelatine in the other ¼ pt water. When the cranberries are soft, add the sugar and gelatine, stir until the sugar has dissolved but do not let it boil. Strain through a jelly-bag or piece of muslin, put into wetted mould and leave in a cold place to set.

Lemon Sponge Jelly

Time: About ½ hour

4 eggs
5 oz. castor sugar
3 lemons

½ oz. gelatine
½ pt water

Put the sugar into a basin, grate the lemon rinds on to it, add the yolks of the eggs and cream together. Dissolve the gelatine in the warmed water and add to the creamed yolks with the lemon juice; put into a cold place until nearly setting, stirring from time to time. Whisk the whites to a stiff froth and when the mixture is nearly set fold the stiffly-whipped whites into it. Put into a wetted mould and leave in a cool place to set. In hot weather slightly more gelatine may be needed.

Orange Jelly

Time: About ½ hour

2 oranges
1 gill orange juice
4 oz. white sugar

1½ oz. gelatine
1½ pts water

Thinly-peel the oranges, put the rind into a pan with the sugar and water, stir over a low heat until the sugar has dissolved, simmer for 15 minutes. Dissolve the gelatine in 2 tablespoons of warm water, add the orange juice, pour this into the hot water and orange rind. Strain through a jelly-bag or piece of muslin, put into a wetted mould, leave in a cold place to set.

Port Wine Jelly

Time: About ¾ to 1 hour

¼ pt port wine
2 oz. white sugar
½ oz. gelatine

½ pt water
cochineal

Put the water, sugar and gelatine into a pan, stir over a low heat until all has dissolved, do not let boil. Add the port wine and a few drops of colouring, strain through a jelly-bag or piece of muslin. Put into a wetted mould and leave in a cold place to set.

Quick Jelly

Time: About ½ hour

1 packet jelly (strawberry or raspberry)

2 whites of eggs
1 oz. of glacé fruits (optional)

Put the jelly into a basin, pour on enough almost-boiling water to make 1 pint when the jelly has dissolved. Pour a little of this into the bottom of a wetted mould, leave to set. When the rest of the jelly is cold, but not set, add the stiffly-whipped whites of eggs and continue whisking until the mixture gets thick and almost setting. Add the glacé fruits—if using—and put into the mould, leave in a cold place to set.

14

Pastry

Of all branches of cooking, pastry-making is the one most people seem to fall down on. I admit it does require practice, but pastry is easy to make if you follow instructions. Some people say, 'I can't make pastry, I'm too heavy-handed.' That's nonsense. What do they mean by too heavy-handed! After all, pastry should be handled as little as possible. If it's the kind of pastry where the fat has to be rubbed in you do it with the tips of your fingers and then use a knife to mix in the water; and for all other kinds you use the knife all the time for the mixing. So I don't see where hands, let alone heavy hands, come into it.

It is important in pastry-making that everything should be as cool as possible, and that's where pieces of marble slab are useful. I've got a piece that was once the top of an old-fashioned wash-stand. This wash-stand was given to me by my grand-mother when we were married. When we decided to get rid of it, the second-hand dealer wouldn't give us any money for it but made out he would be doing us a great favour if he took it away. I was so incensed by this that I got my husband cracking on it and he made a very handsome bedside cupboard from the wood. The marble top, well, it just stood in the back yard for months; we didn't know what to do with it. It seemed too good to break up, but one very windy day that problem was solved because it blew over and broke into several pieces, the largest of which is now my pastry board; and very good it is too.

But now about making pastry. One of the reasons for failure in pastry-making is that the amounts of fat to flour are not correct. The ingredients must be weighed carefully. I know it's a great temptation when you make it often to think that, through experience, you can judge amounts, but as with soufflés or sponges, a fractional difference in weight can mean the difference between success and failure. Another reason can be the wrong oven temperature; particularly this applies to puff pastry, where the ratio of fat to flour is higher. If the oven is not sufficiently hot the butter or fat will run out before the starch in the flour has absorbed it. So the oven must be hot to begin with, particularly, as I say, with puff pastry, and then lowered when the pastry has risen. It can be lowered to whatever temperature you think it will require. For instance, if you're making a meat or a fruit pie that needs a fairly long time in the oven, once the pastry has risen and begins to brown, put a piece of grease-proof paper on top; this prevents the pastry from burning, and allows the contents of the pie to cook.

When you're making pastry, don't turn it over when you're rolling it; it isn't necessary. Just lift it occasionally, sift the flour underneath and roll it in quick light strokes away from you, not as if you were running a steamroller up and down an asphalt roadway. If you have to handle it, as when you're making shortcrust, or if you're kneading it a little, do so as lightly and quickly as possible and don't rub the bits from your hands back into the pastry; wash them off into cold water. If you're making a pie in a dish, fill it as high as possible. This helps to keep the pastry up. If it doesn't fill the dish, use a pie funnel, because if you don't, particularly with fruit, the pastry will sink and spoil the whole appearance. In any case, always leave a small hole in the middle of the pie, otherwise the pastry will be mushy underneath. When you've put the pie crust on, brush it with beaten egg, or if you're out of eggs you can use milk. It won't be such a good colour but at least the top will be shining, and when you're making a pie with double edges (and most people do line the edge and then put the lid on), be careful not to stick these together with the egg yolk or they won't rise.

So the main things to remember are: be light-fingered, keep everything as cold as possible, always roll away from you and don't be afraid of the pastry; pick it up and sprinkle the board, but don't keep turning it over—just turn your board if you want to roll it another way.

Choux Pastry

4 oz. flour	water
2 oz. butter	vanilla essence
2 eggs	salt

Pass the flour and a pinch of salt through a sieve on to grease-proof paper. Put the butter and about ½ pint of water into a pan and bring to the boil, remove from heat and add the flour, stirring all the time. Return to heat and stir vigorously until the mixture forms a ball in the centre of the pan, leaving the sides clean. Allow to cool slightly, then add the eggs one at a time; beat well and add about a ¼ teaspoon of vanilla essence. This paste must not be too soft or it will not keep in shape, neither must it be too stiff or it does not rise well; if it does seem too stiff, add the yolk of another egg. This pastry is used for éclairs, cream buns, etc.

Flaky Pastry

½ lb. flour	cold water
4 to 6 oz. butter or half	lemon
butter, half lard	salt

Put the fat in a refrigerator to get cold, then divide into three parts. Sieve the flour and a pinch of salt into a basin, rub in one third of the fat. Make a well in the centre, put in a squeeze of lemon juice and, using a knife, add enough cold water to mix into a smooth, but not too moist, paste. Put on to a floured board and roll out to a long thin strip, take another third of the fat and dot in small pieces over the pastry; flour, and fold as for rough puff pastry. Roll again to a long strip, and dot the remaining third of the fat over, flour and fold again. Roll out once more and it is ready for use.

Fleur Pastry

6 oz. flour
1 oz. sugar
3½ oz. butter

1 egg yolk
1 teaspoon lemon juice
pinch salt

Pass the flour and salt through a sieve, rub in the fat, add the sugar, mix with the yolk of egg and the lemon, knead together to form a pliable dough; if it seems too stiff, add just a little water. Roll out as required. This pastry is used for making open tarts which when cold are filled with fresh or cooked fruit and covered with syrup or jelly.

Puff Pastry

½ lb. flour
½ lb. butter
¼ pt cold water

lemon
pinch of salt

Make sure that the flour is very dry, the butter cool and the water very cold. Sieve the flour and the salt together in a basin, make a well in the centre, add a squeeze of lemon juice and enough water to mix to a soft dough; use a knife for the mixing. Put the dough on to a floured board or marble slab and work the dough until quite smooth; leave in a cold place for 10 to 15 minutes. Put the butter into one end of a clean floured cloth, press out as much moisture as possible, then shape into an oblong and put into a cold place until needed. Now roll the dough out to a long strip about six inches wide, place the butter in the centre and turn the ends of the dough over, making a fold of three, the last fold with the edges towards you. Now turn the pastry round with the fold to the left-hand side and press the edges a little with the rolling-pin; be careful that the fat does not break through. Sprinkle the board and the roller with flour and roll out in short, quick strokes away from you—do not turn the pastry over. Fold into three again and leave in a cold place for 15 minutes; in hot weather it can be put in the refrigerator. Repeat this rolling and folding twice more with 15 minutes between until, in all, seven rollings have taken place. After the last rolling leave for a few hours in a cold place before using.

Rough Puff Pastry

1 lb. flour	water
¼ lb. lard	lemon
¼ lb. butter	salt

Have the fats cold and the water very cold. Sieve the flour and a pinch of salt on to a board, or preferably a marble slab, cut the fat into small pieces and mix with the flour. Make a well in the centre, add a squeeze of lemon juice and a little water and, using a knife, stir in the flour from the sides until it is mixed into a dough; it must be mixed very lightly without breaking the pieces of fats. When made into a dough lift from the board. Flour board and rolling-pin, and roll into a long thin strip about 6 inches wide, in the same way as for puff pastry; do not press too heavily or the fat will break through. Now roll and fold as for puff pastry, but twice instead of three times and without the 15 minutes in between. Leave in a cold place for a short while and use as required.

Raised Pie Pastry

1 lb. flour	water
8 oz. lard	salt

Put the lard and about ½ pint of water in a pan and bring to the boil. Sieve the flour and about a level saltspoon of salt into a basin, make a well in the centre, pour in the hot liquid and, using a knife, mix as quickly as possible until all the flour is absorbed. Then knead with the hands until the paste is free from cracks, but do not let it get cold. This paste must be used as hot as possible, so that if you are putting a piece on to one side to make a lid for a pie, then wrap the piece in grease-proof paper and keep warm on a plate over a pan of hot water.

Rich Short Pastry

½ lb. flour	cold water
5 oz. butter	salt

Pass the flour and a pinch of salt through a wire sieve into a basin, lightly rub the butter into the flour until the whole is as fine as breadcrumbs. Gradually pour in enough water to form the pastry into a flexible dough, using a knife. Use as little water as possible or the pastry will be tough. Flour the board and the roller and roll the pastry to the required thickness; do not turn the pastry over when rolling and always move the pin in the same direction. A richer pastry can be made by adding a yolk of egg to the mixing water. If preferred, half butter and half lard can be used.

Flan Case

Any kind of pastry can be used for flans, but a short-crust, not too thick, is best. Grease a plain or fluted flan ring and stand it on a greased baking tin. Roll out the pastry about a $\frac{1}{4}$ inch thick and line the ring and tin with it, pressing the pastry well down to the bottom and against the sides of the tin to make a good shape. Leave about $\frac{1}{4}$ inch of pastry above the ring to allow for shrinking; cut above that with scissors. Prick the bottom of the pastry and fill as required, bake in a fairly hot oven for about $\frac{1}{2}$ hour. If the flan is to be baked before the filling, then line with grease-proof paper and fill with haricot beans or crusts of bread and bake as usual; after 20 minutes remove the filling and bake for another 10 minutes.

Gas 6; Electricity 400°

Vol-au-Vent Cases

Evenly roll out some puff pastry to about $\frac{3}{4}$ inch thick and cut into rounds the required size. Place on a baking tin, brush with a beaten egg, then cut the top with a smaller round cutter; this is lifted off afterwards to form a lid. Put them into a hot oven and bake for 20 to 25 minutes. If the top becomes too brown before they are cooked, cover with a piece of grease-proof paper. When cooked remove the small top, scoop out any soft part inside, being careful not to break the cases.

Gas 8; Electricity 450°

Apple and Cranberry Tart

4 persons. Time: About ½ hour to bake

1 lb. cooking apples
½ lb. cranberries
4 to 5 oz. brown sugar

8 to 10 oz. short-crust pastry
(see p. 176)
1 lemon

Wash the cranberries, put them into a pan with the thinly-peeled rind of ½ lemon, half of the sugar and 1 gill of water; cook slowly until soft. Peel and core the apples, chop finely—or put through a mincer. Roll out pastry, divide into halves, line a deep greased plate with one half. Cover with the apples, cranberries, a sprinkle of lemon juice and the rest of the sugar, damp the edges and cover with the other half of the pastry. Brush with yolk or white of egg, prick with a fork and bake in the oven for ½ hour.

Gas 6–7; Electricity 400°–425°

Apricot Flan

4 to 5 persons. Time: ½ hour

1 tin apricots
2 whites of eggs
4 oz. castor sugar

½ lb. rich short-crust or fleur
pastry (see p. 175)
almond essence

Bake the flan as directed on p. 177, leave to cool. Drain the syrup from the apricots and arrange the fruit over the bottom of the flan. Mix a few drops of almond essence with 1 dessertspoon of the juice and sprinkle over the apricots. Whisk the whites of eggs to a stiff froth, fold in 3 oz. of the sugar, spread this over the fruit, sprinkle with the rest of the sugar and bake in a cool oven for 20 minutes. This flan can be served hot or cold, but the meringue will not stay crisp for very long.

To cook meringue: Gas ½; Electricity 225°

Bakewell Tart

5 to 6 persons. Time: 30 to 40 minutes

½ lb. short-crust pastry
(see p. 176)
2 oz. ground almonds
2 oz. castor sugar

2 oz. butter
1 egg
apricot or raspberry jam
almond essence

Line a flat, round tin with the pastry and cover with a fairly thick layer of jam. Cream the butter and sugar, beat in the egg, add the ground almonds and a few drops of essence; mix well together. Spread this mixture on top of the jam, cover with narrow, thin strips of the pastry and bake in a fairly hot oven for 30 to 40 minutes.

Gas 5–6; Electricity 375°–400°

Blackcurrant Tart

4 to 5 persons. Time: About ½ to ¾ hour

½ lb. flaky pastry (see p. 174)   6 to 8 oz. brown sugar
   (or slightly more)   1 tablespoon water
1 lb. blackcurrants

Wash the blackcurrants, put them into a pie dish with the sugar and water. Wet the edge of the dish and put a strip of pastry round it, brush over with water, cover with the rest of the pastry rolled to about ⅛ inch thickness. Scallop the edges with a knife, brush over with egg and bake in a fairly hot oven for ½ to ¾ hour. When cooked, sprinkle the top with castor sugar. Pile as much fruit as possible into the dish before cooking as the fruit sinks with the heat and the pastry may get soggy.

Gas 6–7; Electricity 400°–425°

Eccles Cakes

8 to 9 cakes. Time: 15 to 20 minutes

1 lb. flaky pastry (see p. 174)   4 oz. castor sugar
¾ lb. currants   1 egg
2 oz. chopped peel   ground cinnamon
2 oz. butter   nutmeg

Roll out the pastry and cut into rounds about 4 inches in diameter. Melt the butter and mix with the currants, peel, sugar, a quarter of grated nutmeg, and a quarter teaspoon of cinnamon. Place a little of this mixture in the centre of each pastry round, slightly wet the edges and draw them together at the top. Turn the cakes over so that the join is underneath and shape them into a round; press lightly with a rolling-pin, brush with beaten egg and bake in a hot oven for 15 to 20 minutes.

Gas 7; Electricity 450°

Lemon-Cheese Cakes

Time: 15 to 20 minutes

1 lb. flaky pastry (see p. 174)   lemon-cheese (see p. 181)
1 doz. chopped almonds

Line as many tins as required with the pastry, lay a small piece of
grease-proof paper in each, and fill with uncooked rice or haricot
beans—they can be used over and over again for this purpose.
Bake the pastry in a fairly hot oven for 15 to 20 minutes; lightly
brown the almonds at the same time. When the pastry is cooked,
remove the beans or rice and fill the cases with the lemon-cheese.
Sprinkle with chopped almonds.

Gas 6–7; Electricity 400°–425°

Macaroon Cheese Cakes

Time: 30 minutes

fleur pastry (see p. 175)   2 whites of egg
2 oz. ground almonds   raspberry jam
1 teaspoon ground rice   almond essence or vanilla
2 oz. castor sugar   essence

Line a dozen patty tins with the fleur pastry. Put a very little jam
in each tartlet. Stiffly whip the whites of eggs, add the flavouring
and all the rest of the ingredients, mix well together. Stir lightly
and put a good teaspoonful into each tartlet, completely covering
the jam. Bake for ½ hour in the oven.

Gas 4–5; Electricity 350°–375°

Mince Pies

Makes about a dozen. Time: 25 to 30 minutes

1 lb. puff pastry (see p. 175)   egg
mincemeat

Roll the pastry out to the required thickness, about ¼ inch or just
under, line a dozen patty tins with it. Fill them with the mincemeat, wet the edges and cover with another round of pastry. Press
the edges firmly down, brush over with the egg, prick with a
fork and bake in a hot oven for 25 to 30 minutes.

Gas 8; Electricity 450°—slightly lower for short-crust

Treacle Tart

4 to 5 persons. Time: 20 to 30 minutes

½ lb. short-crust pastry
(see p. 176)
2 heaped tablespoons golden
syrup

2 tablespoons breadcrumbs
1 lemon

Put the syrup into a pan with the breadcrumbs, grated lemon rind and the juice, put over a low heat to mix well. Line a tart tin with the pastry, prick the bottom, put in the syrup mixture and cover with cross pieces of the pastry. Bake in a hot oven for 20 to 30 minutes.

Gas 6; Electricity 400°

FILLINGS

Lemon Cheese or Curd

2 oz. butter
½ lb. lump sugar
3 eggs

grated rind 1 lemon
juice 1½ lemons

Put the butter, sugar, lemon juice and the grated rind into a pan over a low heat until the sugar has dissolved. Remove from heat and whisk in the eggs, one at a time, put over a low heat and stir until it thickens like honey. Care must be taken to make sure that the mixture does not quite reach boiling point.

Mincemeat

1 lb. apples
½ lb. sultanas
1 lb. seeded raisins
1 lb. currants
1 lb. beef suet, or 1 lb. butter
(melted)
½ lb. sugar (demerara or soft
brown)

6 oz. mixed peel
½ oz. mixed spice
¼ oz. ground cloves
1 lemon
1 orange
½ to 1 gill brandy
salt

If using suet, chop finely, if using butter, melt over a low heat. Peel and core the apples, put them through a mincer, chop the peel and raisins or mince them also. Put all these ingredients into a large basin, add the currants, sultanas, sugar, spice, cloves,

grated rind of the orange and lemon and the juice of half of each.
Add the suet or melted butter, mix well together, put in the
brandy and mix again. Cover the basin with a cloth, put into a
dry place and stir once every day for a week, then put into jars
and seal down. This mincemeat improves if made a few weeks
before required.

Pastry Custard

2 oz. sugar	½ pt milk
1 oz. potato flour	vanilla essence
1 large egg	salt
1 egg yolk	

Melt the butter in a pan, blend in the flour, cook for 1 minute
but do not brown. Gradually stir in the milk, bring to the boil,
simmer for 5 minutes until smooth, put in the sugar, simmer for
another minute or two while stirring. Add the slightly-beaten egg
and egg yolk, vanilla essence and a pinch of salt, beat well and
stir over a low heat until it thickens, but do not let it boil or the
eggs will curdle. Leave to get cold and use as required.

15

Savouries

The savoury is the last course on the menu, and when I was in service it was a course that was seldom omitted. On some occasions, unless there was a dinner party, the sweet course would be left out, but never the savoury; this was because most men prefer a savoury to a sweet. It is a course which lends itself to endless variety and almost any ingredient can be used. It can be hot or cold, using fish or meat, egg or cheese, so long as it doesn't contain an ingredient that has formed any of the other courses of the meal. For instance, if you had oysters as an hors d'œuvre you certainly would not serve Angels on Horseback as a savoury. The savoury should be small and light, though it can be more substantial if the sweet course is omitted.

Anchovies, caviare or cheese in some form are always popular, and most savouries, even hot ones, have the added merit that they can be prepared well beforehand. The cook in my first place always said that the sign of a good cook was her ability to produce a perfect savoury out of the most unlikely ingredients, and she certainly could. She would say to me, 'Go to the larder, Margaret, and have a look and see what I can use for a savoury.' I used to go in there; I'd gaze around looking at this and that and I'd simply no ideas at all. Then she'd come in, pick out a few bits and pieces which she'd transform into the most delicious course. An ounce or two of smoked salmon, stewed prunes, a few mushrooms, a piece of game or even a scrap of ham. Eventually I got the idea and I'd bring out the most unlikely things almost as a challenge to her. Watching what she did eventually served me in good stead when, as it were, I was in her shoes. I learned to be inventive. There isn't much that needs generalizing about savouries, but to make my point about invention I will repeat a story I have told in my book *Below Stairs*.

It was when I was working as cook to some Jewish people. I know that, along with Scottish people, they are supposed to be close. I didn't find them so, but they did have to be very careful indeed because they were living beyond their means. So food was watched. Mrs Bernard, the mistress of the house, suffered from some obscure complaint of the legs; they swelled up like balloons. She kept to her bed. I noticed that her complaint never affected her appetite for chocolates. She always had her breakfast in bed and I never liked keeping food that came out of a bedroom, and when I knew that the breakfast tray stood on the night commode, I was even less keen. One morning I cooked a kipper for her breakfast. She didn't eat it, so when it came down I slung it straight into the pig bucket. Mr Bernard came down that morning to give the orders for the day, and when he came to the savoury he said, 'Madam says that she would like that kipper she didn't eat for her breakfast made into a savoury.' Well, my heart sank like a stone. I didn't dare tell him I'd thrown it away because it would have ruined their day for them both. So I said, 'Yes, sir,' and as soon as he was gone I flew to the pig bucket and picked it out. It was sprinkled with tea leaves and eggshells and goodness knows what, so I washed it under the tap. Unfortunately, in my anxiety I dropped it into a bowl of soap suds that I was washing up in. I fished it out again and I thought whatever can I do to disguise the flavour of soda and soft soap. I looked in the larder and there was that good old standby, Escoffier sauce. I boned the kipper, put it into the mortar with a few spots of Escoffier sauce, a little paprika pepper, pounded it well and that night I served it on hot buttered toast. Well, all I hoped was that there wouldn't be any adverse reaction, so you can imagine my astonishment when the parlour maid came down and said, 'Madam's compliments, that was the best kipper savoury that she has ever tasted.'

So although I wouldn't advocate throwing things into the pig bucket first and then dousing them in soap and soda, never give up hope; the most unlikely things can satisfy even in an emergency. You may buy a cookery book for general ideas and knowledge, but there's much more fun in experimenting and going one better.

Anchovies on Toast

About 6 persons. Time: ½ hour

½ doz. anchovies (whole)   ½ teaspoon chopped parsley
1 egg yolk   cayenne pepper
2 oz. butter   toast
1 small shallot

Bone and roughly chop the anchovies. Melt ½ oz. of butter in a pan, finely chop the shallot and fry to a pale brown colour; add the anchovies, parsley, yolk of egg, season with the cayenne, stir over a low heat until the mixture thickens. Serve on fingers of previously prepared buttered toast. This savoury should be served very hot.

Angels on Horseback

1 or 2 per person. Time: About 8 to 10 minutes

oysters   lard or frying oil
thin bacon rashers   cayenne pepper
fritter batter (see p. 158)   fried parsley (see p. 142)
1 lemon

Beard the oysters, sprinkle them with lemon juice and a pinch of cayenne. Cut the rind from the bacon, divide each rasher into halves, wrap each oyster in half a rasher. Make the lard or oil hot enough for a faint blue smoke to rise from the pan, dip the oysters into the batter, drop them into the hot fat and fry to a pale brown colour. Serve on croûtons of fried bread and garnish with the parsley.

Cheese Soufflé

5 to 6 persons. Time: 25 to 30 minutes to cook

3 oz. Parmesan cheese	1 gill milk
2 egg yolks	1 oz. flour
3 whites of eggs	paprika pepper
1 oz. butter	salt

Well grease a soufflé mould and tie round it a double thickness of greased paper high enough to be well above the level of the mould. Melt the butter in a pan, blend in the flour, add the milk and bring to the boil, stirring all the time. Remove from heat, add the yolks of eggs one at a time, stir in the cheese, season to taste. Whisk the whites to a stiff froth, fold into the mixture and put into the prepared mould. Bake in a hot oven for 25 to 30 minutes. Serve in the mould and as quickly as possible. It is a good idea to wrap a hot cloth round it as soon as the soufflé leaves the oven.

Gas 6; Electricity 400°

Cheese Straws

5 to 6 persons. Time: About 20 minutes

3 oz. Parmesan cheese	1 egg yolk
2 oz. butter	cayenne pepper
4 oz. flour	parsley

Sieve the flour into a basin, add a pinch of cayenne, rub in the butter, add the grated cheese. Mix the yolk of egg with 1 tablespoon of cold water, add this to the flour mixture and mix to a stiff paste, knead a little. Roll out on to a floured board and cut into thin strips about 3 inches long and ⅛ inch wide and some rings about 1½ inches in diameter. Put these strips and rings on to a greased baking tin and cook in a slow oven until they are just turning a pale brown colour. When cooked, put some of the straws through the rings, serve garnished with parsley. Care must be taken when handling the straws as they are fragile.

Gas 4; Electricity 350°

Croûtons à la Espagnol

5 to 6 persons

½ doz. anchovy fillets	½ doz. small rounds of fried
½ doz. olives (Spanish)	bread
thick Tartare sauce (see p. 139)	parsley

Stone the olives and stuff with a little of the sauce. Put 1 olive on each croûton of bread and arrange an anchovy fillet round it. Garnish with parsley.

Croûtons à la Gruyère

5 to 6 persons. Time: 5 to 10 minutes

4 oz. gruyère cheese	fried croûtons
1½ oz. butter	cayenne pepper
2 eggs (hard-boiled)	chopped parsley

Grate the cheese, pound in a mortar with the butter and the yolks of the eggs, add seasoning to taste. Thickly spread this mixture on croûtons of fried bread and brown under the grill. Serve in a hot dish, sprinkled with parsley, or if preferred, the whites of the eggs rubbed through a sieve.

Croûtons with Pâté de Foie Gras

1 per person

toasted rounds of bread	paprika pepper
pâté de foie gras	salt

Toast small rounds of bread; slice the foie gras into rounds the same size as the toast, put on to a plate, cover with another and heat over a pan of hot water. When sufficiently heated, put a slice of foie gras on each round of toast, season to taste and serve as quickly as possible.

Herring Roes Devilled

1 per person. Time: About 15 minutes

½ doz. hard roes	1 saltspoon made mustard
1½ oz. butter	cayenne pepper
fried croûtons	salt

Melt the butter in a pan, put in the roes and cook for 5 to 10 minutes, drain on soft paper. Put into a mortar with the mustard and a little of the butter they were fried in; pound well, put into a pan, add seasoning to taste and serve on croûtons of fried bread.

Herring Roes Baked

6 persons. Time: About 5 minutes to bake

8 soft roes	lemon
1 shallot	3 tablespoons thick brown
2 mushrooms	sauce (see p. 130)
1½ oz. butter	anchovy essence
breadcrumbs	½ teaspoon chopped parsley

Peel the mushrooms and shallot, chop finely, melt the butter in a pan and lightly fry them; drain off the butter into a sauté-pan. Add the brown sauce, a few drops of anchovy essence and 1 tablespoon of lemon juice to mushrooms and shallot, season to taste, stir over a low heat, add parsley; when hot put a teaspoon into 7 or 8 well-buttered small ramekin cases. Heat the butter in the sauté-pan, put in the herring roes and cook until lightly browned. Put a roe into each ramekin case, cover with the rest of the brown sauce mixture, sprinkle with lightly-browned breadcrumbs, put on a morsel of butter and bake in a hot oven for a few minutes.

Gas 6–7; Electricity 400°–425°

Madras Olives

4 to 6 persons

½ doz. Spanish olives	1 egg (hardboiled)
2 tablespoons chutney	1 teaspoon French mustard
2 small tomatoes	brown bread
1½ oz. butter	

Pour boiling water on the tomatoes, leave for a minute or two, remove the skins. Pound in a mortar the chutney, butter, mustard and yolk of the egg, rub through a wire sieve; stone the olives and fill them with this mixture. Cut the brown bread into rounds slightly larger than the tomatoes, put a slice of tomato on each round add a ring of the hard-boiled white of egg. Place a stuffed olive in the centre of each round, serve on a bed of salad or garnish with watercress.

Mushrooms au Parmesan

4 to 5 persons. Time: 15 to 20 minutes

½ lb. mushrooms
¼ lb. Parmesan cheese
1 shallot
butter

breadcrumbs
1 teaspoon chopped parsley
pepper, salt

Peel the mushrooms, chop roughly, place in the bottom of a fire-proof dish; add the grated cheese, finely-chopped shallot, parsley and seasoning to taste. Cover thickly with breadcrumbs, dot with small pieces of butter and bake in a hot oven for 15 to 20 minutes. Serve in the same dish.

Gas 6–7; Electricity 400°–425°

Prunes Devilled

4 to 5 persons. Time: About ½ hour to stew prunes

1½ doz. prunes (best quality)
1½ tablespoons mayonnaise
  (see p. 135)
lettuce

1 dessertspoon chutney
chopped parsley
cayenne pepper, salt

Soak the prunes overnight and gently stew them in the same water; do not overcook as they must not be broken, leave until cold, remove the stones. Have the mayonnaise very thick, mix with the chutney, a pinch of salt and enough cayenne to make spicy; fill the prunes with this mixture. Arrange 3 to 4 prunes on a lettuce leaf on individual plates and sprinkle with the parsley.

Sardines à la Bombay

4 to 6 persons. Time: About 5 minutes to fry

½ doz. sardines (boned)
1 beaten egg
2 egg yolks
½ oz. butter

breadcrumbs
1 level teaspoon chutney
cayenne pepper
frying fat or oil

Melt the butter in a pan, add the yolks, stir over a low heat until fairly thick, add the chutney, season to taste and turn out on to a plate. Remove the centre bone from the sardines, put them together again, cover each one with some of the egg mixture and roll in the breadcrumbs. Dip each one into the beaten egg and recoat with breadcrumbs. Put the fat or oil into a fairly deep pan; when hot enough for a faint blue smoke to rise, drop in the sardines and fry to a pale brown. Serve on thin strips of buttered toast, garnish with parsley.

Sardine Ramequins
5 to 6 persons. Time: About 10 to 15 minutes to bake

½ doz. sardines (chopped)
2 whites of eggs
1 egg yolk
½ oz. butter

½ oz. flour
1 gill milk
½ teaspoon tomato ketchup
paprika pepper

Melt the butter in a pan, blend in the flour, add the milk and stir over medium heat until thick; leave to cool, then add sardines, egg yolk, ketchup and pinch of the paprika; mix well. Stiffly-whip the whites of eggs, fold into the mixture and divide between 6 to 7 small buttered ramequin cases. Bake in a hot oven for 10 to 15 minutes and serve at once.

Gas 6; Electricity 400°

Scotch Woodcock
About 6 persons. Time: 10 to 15 minutes

2 egg yolks
½ gill cream
½ gill milk
butter

½ doz. anchovy fillets or,
anchovy paste
cayenne pepper
salt

Toast enough bread to make 6 to 8 small squares—about 2 inches. Butter them well, spread with either the fillets pounded in a mortar, or with anchovy paste. Heat the cream and milk in a pan, add the lightly-beaten yolks of eggs, season to taste; stir over a low heat until they thicken, then pour over the squares of toast and serve as quickly as possible.

Shrimp Toast
About 6 persons. Time: 15 to 20 minutes

¼ lb. picked shrimps
1 egg
½ oz. butter
toast

1 teaspoon anchovy essence
1 tablespoon milk
cayenne pepper

Make 6 to 8 small squares of toast—about 2 inches—butter well.
Melt the butter in a pan, add the shrimps, leave over the heat
for few minutes. Lightly beat together the egg and milk, add to
the shrimps with the anchovy essence and seasoning to taste;
stir over a low heat until it thickens. Divide among the squares
of toast, serve as hot as possible.

Vol-au-Vent Sweetbreads

6 persons. Time: 5 to 10 minutes to warm

6 to 8 vol-au-vent cases	½ gill cream
about 4 oz. cooked sweet-bread (see p. 27)	1 teaspoon mushroom ketchup
1 oz. cooked ham	½ teaspoon chopped parsley
½ gill white sauce (see p. 140)	paprika pepper, salt

Chop the sweetbread and ham and put into a pan with the white
sauce. Add the cream, parsley, ketchup and seasoning to taste,
stir over a low heat until just on the boil. Fill the warmed vol-
au-vent cases with this mixture, put back the lids and warm in
the oven for 5 to 10 minutes.

16

Bread, Scones and Cakes

I never stop wondering why people don't make and bake their own bread. Even when I was in service home-made bread tasted far better than bought bread, but now what is delivered unto us is an indignity to the name of bread. Today bread is baked in steam ovens and tastes like dish water, and as for wrapped bread, it can only be compared with the Icelandic cod that we got during the war, which even then, when I was glad to get anything, I thought tasted like cotton wool. People say today's bread is cleaner and, as it's wrapped, it keeps moist. It only keeps moist because it's permanently soggy since it's excluded from the air.

Many people seem nervous of baking their own. They think of the kneading and pulling and having to go and buy baker's yeast. It seems a long and tedious operation, but it isn't once you get into the swing of it. You may think at first that you could use your time better than waiting for the dough to rise, but once you've made two or three bakings you know just how long it needs to rise before you begin again. And if ever home cooking is way above the bought article, it is with bread. The smell alone of newly-baked bread almost justifies the work it entails, and when you cut your golden crusty surface, you will realize for the first time why it is called the staff of life.

Let us go through the motions of bread making. Always, if it's possible, buy the best quality flour whether you're getting brown or white. It must be very dry and, if it's been stored for a long time, put it in a low oven until it has dried out. If you use baker's yeast make sure that it's fresh, sweet and has a pleasant smell. It crumbles easily when it's fresh and it is easy to cream when you mix it with milk.

When I was a cook in service there was only baker's yeast or brewer's yeast. Brewer's yeast was liquid and was inclined to be bitter. Today you can buy dried yeast in tins, so that when you come to the recipes that I've given using baker's yeast you'll know these are my earlier ones and the dried yeast recipes are the more modern. It's important that the yeast should be mixed with lukewarm milk or water as this causes it to grow. Yeast is a kind of plant, and once it starts activating it grows. This, of course, is the reason why the bread swells and aerates the dough. Don't use hot water since that stops the growth. The bread dough must also be kept in a warm place while it is rising. If it gets cold the yeast stops activating and the bread will be heavy and leaden, just like the bread that you buy in the shops. One reason for failure is in using yeast that is not fresh. It's not the kind of thing that you can expect to get immediately from a baker's shop because they don't keep it on the premises. You have to order it. My baker requires two days' notice. However, if I forget to order, or the bread runs out before I thought it would, I use dried yeast.

Another reason for failure is that the oven is too hot when the bread is put in. This causes the bread to rise too much and to be full of holes. You can't bake bread too quickly and there are no short cuts. Remember also that if you've cooked the loaves in a tin, you must turn them out immediately to allow the steam to escape and evaporate, otherwise they can get soggy. For some loaves you don't need a special tin. If you're making a cottage loaf or a Coburg shape, you just put them on a greased baking tin, but if you are making a milk or a sandwich loaf, these will need a bread tin. This should be lightly greased and sprinkled with a little flour, which prevents the bread from sticking. When it's baked you should just have to give the tin a light tap on the bottom for the loaf to come out.

I do recommend people who have never made their own bread and don't like the kind that you get in the shops to try it sometimes. It isn't really any more trouble than making and baking a cake. It will surprise and delight your family and friends, and the beauty of it is that it keeps so well. The crust doesn't go soggy, the bread inside doesn't go dry, and when it does go a bit stale you'll find that you can make breadcrumbs with it, which is more than you can do with bought bread.

When you make cakes there are one or two rules which are worth knowing and following. Always prepare the tins before you begin, whether it's a sponge, a fruit cake or small cakes. If you're making a fruit cake, and especially if it's a very heavily fruited cake, the tins should be lined with greased paper. When I make sponges in tins I always cut a round of paper and lay it on the bottom, buttering or oiling it. I know many recipes say only grease and flour the tins, but I find that if you lay a round of greased paper on the bottom, when you come to tip the sponge out you have no bother at all, it comes away easily; and sponges, because they are made without fat of any kind, just flour, sugar and eggs, are far more inclined to stick than any mixture that's got butter or margarine in it. With small cakes you need only grease the tins and lightly dust them with flour. When I was in service and had to make large cakes in a kitchen range, I always put several thicknesses of paper, often news-paper, round the outside of the tin to prevent the cakes from burning. I also used to stand them on a layer of sand in the baking tin because, when cooking on a kitchen range, you are subjected to rather erratic heat. So by doing this the heat was retained at a constant temperature. But with modern ovens these precautions should not be necessary. Again, when you line your tins with paper, make sure that the paper is a couple of inches higher than the top of the tin to prevent the cake burning when it rises.

When you're making cakes, the materials should always be weighed. With everyday cooking this becomes unnecessary, but with cakes, and certainly sponges, the best results come from absolutely accurate amounts of the ingredients. If you're a bit slapdash and just throw in even an ounce too much flour or an ounce too little sugar, it will certainly make a difference to the finished result. Another rule is to make sure that the oven is the right temperature. Always light it fifteen minutes before the cakes go in, and don't if you can help it open the oven door just to see how the cakes are getting on. Even with a large fruit cake, a blast of cold air won't do it any good, and with sponges it can be absolutely disastrous. We sometimes had to do it when we were cooking in the kitchen range ovens, but today, with pre-set heat, it's quite unnecessary.

Always sieve the flour; it may not look lumpy, but sieving is not just to get any lumps out, it is to allow the flour to become thoroughly aerated, and this helps towards a light mixture. Whisking is important, too. In my early days, when the cook used to make a sponge sandwich without butter, using only flour, eggs and sugar, the eggs had to be whisked for half an hour with a wire whisk. That half an hour used to seem never-ending, and even when I was young my arm used to feel as though it was dropping off. Then for some reason or other the sugar had to be held up high and gradually poured in. I never knew the significance of this. Today, of course, many people use an electric mixer for sponges. I still whisk by hand, with a wheel beater which is easier to control. There's always a risk of over-beating with an electric mixer.

Really fresh eggs help to make a sponge light and fluffy, which I think is the reason so many farmers' wives have such good reputations as cooks. Make sure that the butter or the margarine and the sugar are properly creamed and made fluffy before the eggs are added. Unless you have a creamy smooth mixture, the eggs may take on a curdled appearance, and the cake becomes heavy. All the beating should be done before you add the flour. The flour should never be vigorously stirred; it should be folded in. If you beat once you've added the flour, it will make the cake heavy.

With fruit cakes, if the oven isn't hot enough quickly to set the cake mixture, the fruit will sink to the bottom never to rise again, but don't forget to lower the heat after the cakes have set, otherwise the outside will get hard and dry and the inside won't cook sufficiently. When you test to see if it's done, use a fine skewer or, better still, a steel knitting needle. Don't try a thick skewer and don't do it too often otherwise the cake will resemble a colander outside and a honeycomb inside

If cake-making bores you, or if you haven't got the time, you can buy packets of cake mix; most of them need only an egg or two to complete the mixture, and even if you can't say as you hand the cake to the guests, 'It's all my own work,' at least if it isn't a success you can blame it on the manufacturers. It is possible with these packet mixes to add that little extra: an extra egg or a few drops of almond or vanilla essence or an ounce of butter if it's one that is made without fat. You can make your own icings. I've given recipes for a number. You can make a quick and delicious cold pudding with a packet sponge: cover one half with raspberries or strawberries from a tin and then slightly thicken the juice with cornflour, pour it over and cover it with whipped cream; then put the other half on top, and leave it in the fridge to cool, and if you put half a wine glass of sherry over it, it's better still, and nobody will know that it started life as a packet sponge.

But fundamentally, I don't believe in these half-way measures. I like to make my cakes right from scratch or, if I haven't the time, buy one. I find these packet mixes have too much bicarbonate of soda in them, they taste peppery at times and many of them don't make the amount that is indicated on the packet. So I feel if I'm being cheated one way, I'm probably being cheated other ways as well, and, as you've probably gathered, I don't like being cheated.

BREAD

Bread Home-made

3½ lb. flour
½ teaspoon castor sugar
1 oz. yeast

2½ teaspoons salt
about 1¾ pt warm water

Warm the flour and put it into a large bowl with the salt; make a well in the centre. Cream the yeast and sugar, stir in about ¾ pint of warm water, pour this into the flour, cover with a sprinkling of flour from the sides of the bowl, put a cloth over and let stand in a warm place for about 20 minutes to 'sponge'. Now work in all the flour with the hands, adding enough warm water to make the flour an elastic dough; knead for 10 minutes. Cover the bowl again and leave in a warm place to rise for about 1½ hours, the dough should then have doubled its bulk. Turn on to a board and shape into the required size; put into greased and floured tins which should be half filled (if Cottage or Coburg loaves are preferred, place these on a baking tin). Leave in a warm place for about ½ hour to let the dough rise just to reach the top of the tins. If the dough is made into 3 loaves, then bake for 30 to 35 minutes in the centre of a hot oven. The oven should be heated for about 15 minutes before baking the bread.

Gas 7; Electricity 425°

Brown Bread

3 lb. wholemeal flour
2 oz. lard
1 oz. yeast

2 teaspoons salt
1 teaspoon castor sugar
1½ pt warm water

Mix the flour and salt together, rub in the lard and stand in a warm place. Cream the yeast with the sugar in a small basin, pour on to it about ¾ pint of warm water, cover and stand in a warm place for about 10 minutes. Pour the yeast mixture over the flour, mix with the hands, using more warm water to make an elastic dough. Set to rise until the dough has doubled its bulk. Then turn on to a floured board; knead well. Shape into loaves and put into greased and floured tins. Stand in a warm place to rise for ½ hour or longer to allow the dough just to rise to the top of the tins. Bake as for bread.

Currant Bread

1½ lb. flour
4 oz. currants
2 oz. butter
3 level teaspoons dried yeast

1 teaspoon sugar
¾ pt warm milk
1 teaspoon salt

Mix the sugar with ¼ pint of warm milk, sprinkle on the yeast and leave in a warm place for 20 minutes. Warm the flour and put it into a basin with the salt, rub in the butter, make a well in the centre, pour in the yeast, add enough warm milk to make into a dough. Knead well and leave in a warm place until the dough has doubled its bulk. Put on a board and work in the currants, kneading the dough until the currants are evenly distributed. Grease some bread tins, half fill them with the dough

and leave to 'prove' in a warm place for 20 to 25 minutes. Bake
for 40 to 45 minutes in the oven.

Gas 6; Electricity 400°

Baps

1 lb. flour	1 small teaspoon castor sugar
2 oz. butter	½ pt warm milk
2 level teaspoons dried yeast	½ small teaspoon salt

Use the method as for currant bread (see p. 197) to make the
dough, and after it has 'proved', knead lightly for a few minutes,
then roll into a square piece about ¾ to 1 inch thick. With a
knife dipped into flour cut the dough into 4-inch squares, put on
a greased and floured baking tin, dust the tops with flour, cover
with a cloth and leave in a warm place until light and puffy in
appearance. Bake in a hot oven—about the middle shelf—for 15 to
20 minutes; they should rise well but be only lightly brown.

Gas 7; Electricity 425°

Sally Lunns

12 oz. flour	½ oz. yeast
1½ oz. butter	1 gill milk
1 egg	½ teaspoon salt
1 oz. sugar	

Sieve the flour into a basin with the salt; melt the butter in a
pan, add the milk and warm to blood heat, about 98° F. Mix
together the sugar and yeast, add this to the milk with the beaten
egg, pour into the middle of the flour and beat well to a light
dough; if it seems too stiff, add a little more milk. Turn on to
a board, knead for a few minutes; grease two tins about 5 inches
wide by 3 inches deep, divide the dough into two and put into
the tins. Leave in a warm place until the mixture reaches the top
of the tins, then bake for 20 to 30 minutes in the oven; when
done brush over with melted butter while still hot.

Gas 6; Electricity 400°

SCONES

Brown Scones

Time: 12 to 15 minutes

½ lb. wholemeal flour
2 oz. butter
½ level teaspoon bicarbonate
   of soda

1 level teaspoon cream of
   tartar
milk
salt

Sieve the flour, bicarbonate, cream of tartar and a pinch of salt;
rub in the butter; add enough milk to mix into a soft dough.
Put on to floured board, roll out to about ½ inch thick and cut
into rounds. Put them on a greased baking tin, brush over with
milk and bake in the oven for 12 to 15 minutes according to size.

Gas 7; Electricity 425°

Drop Scones

Time: 8 to 12 minutes

¾ lb. flour
1 heaped teaspoon baking
   powder
1 large egg

¾ pt milk
3 tablespoons cream
salt

Sieve the flour and baking powder, add a pinch of salt. Beat the
egg with some of the milk, add the cream, make a well in the
centre of the flour, pour in the egg mixture, and beat well, add
enough milk to make into a fairly stiff batter. Grease a frying
pan and drop in spoonfuls of the batter, leaving a good space
between each; when brown, turn over and brown the other side.
Butter them and serve as quickly as possible after making them.

Sour Milk Scones

Time: About 15 minutes

½ lb. flour
1 teaspoon baking powder
3 oz. butter
2 oz. sultanas

1 gill sour cream
½ gill milk
salt

Sieve the flour, baking powder and a pinch of salt into a basin,
rub in the butter, mix in the sultanas. Add the sour cream and

enough milk to mix into a light dough. Put on a floured board
and roll out to about ¼ inch thick; cut into rounds, put on a
greased baking tin and bake in the oven for about 15 minutes.
Remove from oven, brush over with milk and return to oven for
a further 5 minutes.

Gas 6; Electricity 400°

Yorkshire Muffins

Time: 10 to 12 minutes

1¾ lb. flour	1 pt water
½ oz. fresh yeast	salt

Sieve the flour and ½ level teaspoon of salt into a basin;
cream the yeast with a wooden spoon, add the lukewarm water,
stir into the flour and beat for about 15 minutes; cover and put
into a warm place to rise for about 1½ hours. Turn the mixture
on to a floured board and knead with the hands for a few
minutes. Grease some large round cutters, half fill them with the
mixture and put on a greased girdle to cook and brown. When
they are done on one side, remove the rings, turn the muffins
over to cook the other side; when done, split open, butter, and
serve hot. The cooking takes 10 to 12 minutes.

CAKES

Angel Cake

Time: About 1 hour

2 oz. flour	4 oz. castor sugar
2 oz. cornflour	2 large eggs
2 oz. ground rice	1 teaspoon baking powder
4 oz. butter	salt

Sieve the flour with the cornflour, ground rice, pinch of salt and
baking powder; cream the butter and sugar, add the yolks of
eggs, one at a time. Stiffly-whip the whites of eggs and fold in
alternately with the flours to the egg mixture. Well-butter a
square cake tin, sprinkle with flour, put in the cake mixture and
bake in the oven for about 1 hour.

For the first 20 minutes: Gas 5, Electricity 375°; then Gas 4,
Electricity 350°, for the rest of the cooking time.

Christmas Cake

Time: 5 to 6 hours

1 lb. flour
¾ lb. butter
½ lb. sugar (castor or soft
  brown)
1 lb. sultanas
1 lb. currants
6 oz. mixed peel (chopped)
¼ lb. glacé cherries (chopped)
6 large eggs

¼ lb. almonds
1 teaspoon grated orange rind
1 tablespoon black treacle
1 level teaspoon baking
  powder
½ teaspoon mixed spice
1 wineglass (or more) of
  brandy

Sieve the flour with the baking powder, spice and a pinch of salt. Blanch the almonds and finely chop; chop the peel or put through a mincer, quarter the cherries. Put the butter into a bowl, warm it slightly, beat with a wooden spoon, add the sugar and continue to beat until the mixture is light and fluffy. Beat in the eggs, one at a time, using a level dessertspoon of flour as each egg is added, then stir in the treacle. Add half the rest of the flour, all the fruit, almonds and orange rind, put the other half of the flour on top, stir and mix well but do not beat. Put in the brandy; if the mixture seems too stiff add a little milk —the mixture should drop easily from the spoon. Prepare a cake tin about 10 inches in diameter; grease the tin, then line with buttered grease-proof paper high enough to come 2 to 3 inches above the top of the tin. Put in the cake mixture, slightly press in the centre to make the cake rise evenly, stand the cake on a layer of crushed salt on a baking tin, this will prevent the bottom becoming too brown before the cake is cooked. Have the oven pre-heated at Gas 4, Electricity 350°; put the cake not higher than the centre of the oven—just below if possible—lower the heat at once to Gas 2, Electricity 300° for 1 hour, then lower the heat to Gas 1, Electricity 275°. The cake will take from 5 to 6 hours to cook; test with a warmed fine skewer or knitting needle after 5 hours. After removing from oven, leave in tin for ½ hour, then turn out on to wire rack, remove the paper. After about 12 hours, wrap in double sheets of grease-proof paper and store in a tin with tightly-fitting lid until required for icing.

If preferred, the cake can be baked at Gas 3, Electricity 325° for 1 hour, then turned to Gas 1, Electricity 275° for the rest of the time.

Coconut Meringues

Time: About 35 minutes

3 whites of eggs
6 oz. desiccated coconut
5 oz. castor sugar

cochineal
rice paper

Whisk the whites to a very stiff froth, fold in the coconut and
sugar. Divide the mixture into halves, colour one half pink;
cover a baking tin with the rice-paper, pile the mixture into small
pyramids on the paper; bake in the oven for about 35 minutes.

Gas 1; Electricity 275°

Dundee Cake

Time: 2 to 2½ hours

½ lb. flour
6 oz. castor sugar
6 oz. butter
4 oz. sultanas
2 oz. peel
3 oz. seeded raisins
6 oz. currants

3 large eggs
2 oz. glacé cherries (chopped)
3 oz. almonds
½ teaspoon baking powder
½ teaspoon ground cinnamon
½ lemon
½ gill brandy

Sieve the flour with the baking powder and cinnamon. Cream the
butter and sugar in a bowl, add the eggs one at a time, adding a
dessertspoon of flour to the mixture with each egg; add the
brandy and beat well. Mix in the rest of the flour, fruit, grated
rind of ½ lemon, add half of the blanched almonds, chopped;
do not chop the other half. If the mixture seems too stiff, add a
little milk, but the cake must not be too moist. Grease a cake
tin 7 to 8 inches in diameter, line with buttered paper, put in
the mixture, put on the rest of the almonds, split into halves.
Bake in the oven—Gas 4, Electricity 350°—for 1 hour, then
Gas 1, Electricity 275° for the rest of the time.

French Gâteau

Time: About 1¼ hours

4 oz. flour
7 oz. castor sugar
4 eggs
3 extra whites of eggs

apricot jam
pistachio nuts
1 wineglass sherry

Break the 4 eggs into a bowl, beat for 5 minutes, add 4 oz. of
the sugar, stand the bowl over a pan of hot water and beat for
another 10 minutes, remove from the heat and continue to beat
until the mixture is quite thick. Lightly stir in the sieved flour
and put into a greased and lined cake tin about 6 inches in
diameter; bake for 1 hour at Gas 3 to 4, Electricity 325°–350°.
When cooked, partly cool before turning out. When quite
cold, make holes in the top with a skewer and pour in the sherry.
Stiffly-whip the whites of eggs, fold in the other 3 oz. of sugar,
cover the whole cake with this meringue, sprinkle with the
chopped nuts, make a well in the centre. Put the cake on the
bottom shelf of the oven for 15 to 20 minutes to set the meringue,
then fill the well in the centre with apricot jam.

Genoa Cake

Time: About 2½ hours

½ lb. flour
6 oz. castor sugar
3 large eggs
¼ lb. sultanas
¼ lb. currants
¼ lb. mixed peel
3 oz. cherries

6 oz. butter
2 oz. almonds
1 level teaspoon baking
   powder
½ lemon
milk
salt

Sieve the flour with the baking powder and a pinch of salt.
Cream the butter and sugar, add the eggs one at a time, using a
dessertspoon of flour with each egg, beat well. Add the rest of
the flour with the chopped peel and cherries, currants and sultanas and the grated rind of ½ lemon. Mix well together; if it
seems too stiff, add a little milk. Grease a cake tin, line with
buttered paper, the tin should be about 7 inches in diameter, put
in the mixture, sprinkle with the blanched and chopped almonds
and bake in the oven for 2 to 2½ hours.

Gas 2; Electricity 300°

Gingerbread, Rich

Time: 50 minutes to 1 hour

8 oz. flour
4 oz. soft brown sugar
8 oz. black treacle
4 oz. lard
2 eggs
6 oz. seeded raisins

little milk
1 teaspoon ground ginger
¼ teaspoon bicarbonate of
   soda
½ teaspoon mixed spice

Sieve the flour with ginger and spice. Cream the lard and sugar,
add the yolks of eggs and beat well. Put in the treacle, flour,
raisins and the bicarbonate of soda mixed with 1 to 2 tablespoons
of milk, mix well together. Stiffly-whip the whites of eggs, fold
them into the mixture. Put into a greased and lined oblong tin,
bake in the oven for 50 minutes to 1 hour. When cooked,
remove from oven, leave in tin to cool for 20 to 30 minutes,
turn on to a board and cut into squares.

Gas 4; Electricity 350°

Macaroons

Time: About 25 minutes

3 oz. ground almonds	almonds
6 oz. castor sugar	almond essence
1½ teaspoons ground rice	rice-paper
2 whites of eggs	

Mix together the ground almonds, ground rice and sugar, add
a few drops of almond essence and the unbeaten whites of eggs,
mix to a fairly stiff paste—if too stiff, add a little water. Mix all
well together, cover a baking tin with rice-paper, put teaspoons
of the mixture on it. Brush lightly with water, place half a
blanched almond on each one and bake in the oven for about
25 minutes.

Gas 3; Electricity 325°

Madeira Cake

Time: 1 hour 10 minutes

6 oz. flour	½ teaspoon baking powder
4 oz. castor sugar	1 lemon
4 oz. butter	milk
3 eggs	salt

Sieve the flour with the baking powder and a pinch of salt,
cream the butter and sugar, beat in the eggs one at a time,
adding a dessertspoon of flour with each egg until the mixture
is thick and smooth. Stir in the rest of the flour, add the grated
lemon rind and enough milk to make the mixture drop easily
from the spoon. Grease and line a tin about 5 to 6 inches in
diameter, put in the cake mixture and bake in the centre shelf
of the oven for 1 hour 10 minutes.

Gas 4; Electricity 350°

Munster Cake

Time: 45 to 50 minutes

2 oz. flour	1 oz. peel
2 oz. cornflour	1 lemon
3 oz. castor sugar	1 teaspoon baking powder
4 oz. butter	1 teaspoon coffee essence
2 large eggs	1 dessertspoon rum
4 oz. grated chocolate	almond paste (see p. 209)
1 oz. glacé cherries	glacé icing (see p. 210)

Sieve the flours with the baking powder. Cream the butter and sugar, add the chocolate, coffee essence and the grated rind of the lemon. Beat in the eggs one at a time, adding a dessertspoon of flour between each egg, add the rest of the flours, the chopped peel, cherries quartered and the rum; mix carefully together. Grease and line a cake tin about 6 inches in diameter, put in the mixture and bake for 45 to 50 minutes in the oven, when cooked remove and leave for a few minutes to cool before turning out. When cold, cover with almond paste and ice with glacé icing flavoured with lemon.

Gas 4 to 5; Electricity 350° to 375°

Orange Layer Cake

Time: 1 to 1¼ hours

4 oz. flour	1 large orange
2 oz. cornflour	1 small teaspoon baking powder
4 oz. castor sugar	butter icing (see p. 210)
4 oz. butter	glacé icing (see p. 210)
3 large eggs	

Sieve together the flour and cornflour. Cream the butter and sugar, add the eggs one at a time, using a dessertspoon of flour with each egg, add the grated rind of the orange and half of the juice. Fold in the rest of the flours. Grease and line with buttered paper a cake tin about 7 inches in diameter, put in the cake mixture and bake in the oven for 1 to 1¼ hours. When cooked, remove from oven, leave until cold, then cut into 2 or 3 layers and spread with butter icing flavoured with orange, then cover the whole cake with orange glacé icing.

Gas 4; Electricity 350°

Sand Cake

Time: 1 to 1¼ hours

¼ lb. flour
¼ lb. potato flour
¼ lb. castor sugar

¼ lb. butter
2 eggs
½ lemon

Sieve the flour with the potato flour. Cream the butter and sugar, beat in the yolks of the eggs one at a time and the grated rind of ½ lemon. Stir in the flours, fold in the stiffly-whipped whites of eggs. Grease a cake tin, line with buttered paper, put in the cake mixture, bake in a moderate oven for about 1 to 1¼ hours. The oven needs to be hot for the first 20 minutes: Gas 5–6, Electricity 375°–400°, then turn to Gas 4, Electricity 350°.

Scotch Bannocks

Time: 30 to 40 minutes

1 lb. flour
½ lb. butter
¼ lb. castor sugar

¼ lb. chopped mixed peel
2 oz. almonds

Put the butter and sugar on to a board and mix together by hand, knead for a few minutes, then gradually work in the sieved flour, peel, and blanched and chopped almonds; knead until it is quite smooth. When ready, enclose in grease-proof paper, leave for 12 hours, or until the next day. Unwrap, knead a little, divide into 2 or 3 pieces, roll into rounds and bake in the oven for 30 to 40 minutes.

Gas 3; Electricity 325°

Scotch Shortbread

Time: 40 to 45 minutes

¾ lb. flour
¼ lb. ground rice
½ lb. butter

¼ lb. castor sugar
almonds
salt

Sieve the flour with a pinch of salt into a basin, rub in the butter to a very fine texture, add the sugar. Put on to a floured board and knead until smooth, then roll into 2 rounds or squares about ½ inch thick. Pinch the edges with finger and thumb, prick all over with a fork and put a few blanched and split almonds on the top. Put the round or squares on pieces of oiled, grease-proof paper, stand on a baking tin and cook in the oven for 40 to 45 minutes. When done, remove from oven, but leave on tin until it cools—it is less likely to break.

Gas 3; Electricity 325°

Simnel Cake

Time: 4 to 4½ hours

½ lb. flour	⅛ teaspoon bicarbonate of
¼ lb. butter	soda
½ lb. castor sugar	1 dessertspoon milk
4 eggs	almond essence
6 oz. currants	½ lemon
6 oz. sultanas	salt
¼ lb. mixed peel	almond paste for outside
¼ lb. glacé cherries	(see p. 209)
2 oz. almonds	glacé icing (see p. 210)

Almond paste for inside:

3 oz. icing sugar	6 ground almonds
3 oz. castor sugar	almond essence
1 egg	

To make the paste: Mix together the icing sugar, castor sugar and ground almonds, add a few drops of almond essence and enough beaten egg to make a fairly soft mixture; knead a little and roll to a round the size of the cake tin.

For the cake: Sieve the flour with a pinch of salt. Cream the butter and sugar, beat in the eggs one at a time, using a dessert-spoon of flour with each egg. Put in the rest of the flour with fruit, chopped peel, cherries (quartered), blanched and chopped almonds, grated rind of ½ lemon and the bicarbonate dissolved in the milk with a few drops of essence; mix all well together. Grease a cake tin about 9 inches in diameter, line with buttered paper, put in half of the cake mixture, cover with the round of almond paste, put the rest of the cake mixture on top. Bake in the oven for 1½ hours: Gas 3, Electricity 325°, then Gas 1, Electricity 275° for another 2½ to 3 hours. When done, remove from oven, leave to cool for a short while before turning out. When cold, cover the top with thick almond paste leaving a space in the centre, brown in the oven or under a grill; leave to get cold, then fill the centre space with white or pink icing and decorate with glacé cherries.

Soda Cake

Time: About 1½ hours

¼ lb. flour
¼ lb. butter
¼ lb. soft brown sugar
2 eggs
2 oz. currants
2 oz. sultanas
1 oz. peel

½ teaspoon bicarbonate of
  soda
1 dessertspoon vinegar
¼ nutmeg (grated)
1 tablespoon milk
salt

Sieve the flour with a pinch of salt, rub in the butter, add all the dry ingredients except the bicarbonate of soda. Dissolve this in the milk, add to the cake mixture with the beaten eggs and the vinegar; mix well together. Put into a greased and lined cake tin and bake in the oven for about 1½ hours.

Gas 4; Electricity 350°

Victoria Sandwich

Time: 20 minutes

¼ lb. flour
¼ lb. castor sugar
¼ lb. butter

2 large eggs
1 teaspoon baking powder
vanilla or almond essence

Sieve the flour, cream the butter and sugar, add the eggs one at a time, using a level dessertspoon of flour with each egg. Add the rest of the flour, baking powder, few drops of essence and about 1 tablespoon of tepid water, mix well but do not beat. Grease 2 sandwich tins and coat with flour, lay a piece of buttered paper in the bottom of the tins. Divide the mixture between the 2 tins and bake in the oven for 20 minutes. When cooked, remove from oven, let cool in tins for about 5 minutes, then turn out on to sugared paper. When cold, put together with jam or butter icing (see p.210).

Gas 5; Electricity 375°

Walnut Cake

Time: About 1 hour

4 eggs, their weight in butter,
  sugar and flour
2 oz. chopped walnuts
few whole walnuts

1 teaspoon baking powder
vanilla essence
glacé icing (see p. 210)
butter icing (see p. 210)

Sieve the flour with the baking powder; cream the butter and sugar, beat in egg yolks one at a time, using a dessertspoon of flour with each yolk, stir in the rest of the flour with the chopped walnuts and a few drops of vanilla essence. Stiffly-whip the whites of eggs, fold into the mixture. Grease a cake tin about 6 inches diameter, line with buttered paper, put in the mixture and bake in the oven for about 1 hour. When cooked leave in tin for a short time before turning out. When quite cold cut in half, cover one half with butter icing flavoured with a few drops of vanilla essence, put on the other half and cover the whole cake with glacé icing. Decorate with halved walnuts.

Gas 4–5; Electricity 350°–375°

ICINGS

Almond Paste

1 lb. ground almonds	almond essence
½ lb. icing sugar	1 teaspoon orange flower
½ lb. castor sugar	water
3 egg yolks	1 large teaspoon lemon juice

Mix the ground almonds in a basin with the castor and icing sugar and make a well in the centre. Put the yolks in a cup, add the lemon juice, orange water and a few drops of essence. Stir this into the ground almonds, a little at a time, until it becomes a stiff paste; if too dry, add a little water; put on to a board, sprinkle with icing sugar and knead for a few minutes. The paste should be perfectly smooth and just soft enough to work easily over the cake. Level the top of the cake, then turn upside down to make a perfectly flat surface. Roll out the almond paste to about an inch in thickness, brush the top of the cake with white of egg, put a large enough layer of paste on the cake to cover the top and reach about an inch down the sides. Roll quite smooth with a rolling pin. If the sides of the cake are to be coated with the paste, brush first with a little warm jam, roll the paste into a strip the depth and circumference of the cake and press round the sides, making the edges as smooth as possible where it joins the top layer. The royal icing must not be put on until the almond paste is dry and set.

Butter Icing

6 oz. icing sugar   flavouring as required
3 oz. butter

Use unsalted butter; put into a basin and beat with a wooden
spoon until creamy, then add gradually the sifted icing sugar.
Continue beating until the mixture is soft and creamy, then add
vanilla, almond or coffee essence, orange or lemon peel grated,
or any other flavouring as desired.

Chocolate Glacé Icing

10 oz. icing sugar   ½ gill (or slightly more) of
4 oz. plain chocolate (grated)   water
few drops vanilla essence

Put the chocolate and water into a pan over a low heat until the
chocolate has melted, stirring occasionally, then let it boil for
5 minutes. Remove from heat for a few minutes, then add sieved
sugar and essence; stir for a minute or two over a very low heat,
then pour over the cake.

To make coffee icing, use 1 tablespoon of coffee essence instead
of the chocolate, and a very little water.

Frosting

½ lb. loaf sugar   ½ gill water
1 white of egg   ½ teaspoon vanilla essence

Put the sugar and water into a pan, stir over a low heat until the
sugar is dissolved, then boil it to 238° F. Whisk the egg-white
in a basin until stiff, pour over the sugar syrup whisking all the
time; add essence and use quickly.

Glacé Icing (or Water Icing)

1 lb. icing sugar   colouring or flavouring as
4 to 6 tablespoons water   required

Sieve the sugar into a pan, gradually add the water, stir with a
wooden spoon until the sugar melts, do not let it get too hot; it
should be just thick enough to coat the back of a spoon, if not

thick enough add more sugar. Pour it quickly over the cake and if the sides are not completely covered, dip a knife into hot water and scoop up the icing that has run on to the plate and spread it round the sides. Do not touch the top once it has been coated or it will not look smooth. Glacé icing must not be made too hot, otherwise it will not look smooth and shiny.

Royal Icing

1 lb. icing sugar   1 lemon
2 whites of eggs   water if needed

Sieve the sugar into a basin, make a well in the centre and pour in the slightly-beaten egg whites, add a little lemon juice and mix to a stiff paste, adding more lemon juice if required. The icing must be beaten until perfectly smooth, it takes about 10 minutes. Be careful not to add too much lemon juice as the icing must be stiff enough for the spoon to stand up in the mixture. If it seems too stiff, add a few drops of water, if not stiff enough, add more sugar. If not required for immediate use, cover with a clean damp cloth.

To ice the cake: If it is not covered with almond paste the cake must be quite flat. Use a revolving cake-stand if available, if not, stand the cake on an inverted plate. Have ready a jug of hot water and a palette or broad-bladed knife. Put as much icing on the cake as you think will cover it, dip the knife into the water and smooth the icing over the cake until it is perfectly even, turning the stand or plate round at the same time. The knife should be brought across the icing in one direction. To ice the sides of the cake, place some icing at intervals round the sides, dip the knife into the water, then, holding the knife against the sides, slowly turn the stand or plate until the icing is smooth all round.

For a wedding or christening cake, two or three layers of icing may be used, but each layer must be dry before the next one is applied.

17

Egg Dishes

Mrs Beeton wrote that the quality of eggs depended upon the type of birds, the way they were housed and the variety of the food they ate; and that new-laid eggs are the more easily digested. So Mrs Beeton wouldn't rate our present-day eggs very highly. Since I've quoted Mrs Beeton, I won't go on about them. Nevertheless, tasteless though they seem, I presume they have the same nutritive value that the old ones had—according to dieticians, eggs have the same food value as meat; whether that's true or not, they still make very good omelets. Omelet making is not really difficult, but it requires a little practice. Your first efforts may have the consistency of rubber, be over-cooked and full of holes, but don't despair. Practice makes perfect. And there is such a variety that one can make, which adds to the pleasure of cooking and eating them. Practically any left-overs can be used in an omelet: remains of game or chicken, bits of asparagus, mushrooms, cheese, shrimps and even herbs make lovely dishes.

The choice of a pan requires consideration. In service I used a heavy aluminium one, but whatever type you decide on, copper, steel or silicon-coated, one that is non-stick, it should be kept only for omelets and not used for frying other things, and never washed unless absolutely necessary. It should be cleaned after use with kitchen paper and a dry cloth, or if by chance bits of eggs have stuck to the pan, sprinkle a little dry salt in it and rub it round with kitchen paper. Should something absolutely disastrous happen, such as the pan and its contents getting burnt, you should season it before using it again by heating a little fat in it, when hot pour the fat away and wipe the pan over with paper.

Don't beat the eggs too much; it's a common fault. People think that the more eggs are beaten the lighter the omelet will be. It's nonsense. They should be beaten so that they blend well together and so that no bits of white can be seen. You can add a tablespoonful of water or cream to the mixture of two or three eggs to make a larger omelet. Always use butter in the cooking but not too much. Don't think the more butter the better the omelet—too much only makes it greasy; and don't forget to have any ingredient that you're using prepared beforehand. It's no good suddenly deciding to chop up a bit of ham, and then having to get the asparagus tips or shell shrimps after you've got the omelet in the pan. And finally, have a hot dish ready to serve it on. Omelets need serving and eating immediately; it's certainly not something that you can keep warm and still find edible—not edible under the name omelet, at any rate. Two or three eggs are sufficient for two people if it's going to be a subsidiary course, but if it is in lieu of a main course you will need more. You must have a flexible palette knife to shape the omelet in the pan, and though some people use a spoon to stir the mixture as it starts to cook, I prefer a fork because a fork, by its nature, lets the air through. I have a fork from which the middle prong has been broken and I find this just the thing. Finally, using the palette knife, shape the omelet into a light oval cushion.

It is surprising the unappetizing concoctions served under the name of scrambled eggs. A few years ago, one of my daily jobs was at a boarding house where the unfortunate boarders were served scrambled eggs twice a week, on Mondays and Fridays. There were ten of them and they all sat round one large table. I used to make ten rounds of toast, put them on a large oval meat dish on which the landlady poured ten portions

H

of what she called scrambled eggs. Never in my life have I seen anything so revolting.

She diluted the eggs with milk and water so that not only were the pieces of toast soaked in the fluid, but it was floating all round the dish too; as for the eggs, they were a pallid-looking mess, all separate lumps. I used to hate taking it in and placing it on the table. One morning I'd just gone into the dining-room with these scrambled eggs when one of the lodgers said, 'Hello, Mrs P., been mucking out the calves' shed again?' Well, I couldn't help laughing. I didn't know Madam had followed me in. The lodger left that morning.

Yet scrambled eggs are a very pleasant dish and they're easy to do. Not more than a tablespoonful of milk or single cream should be added to four eggs; these should then be beaten together, seasoned and, with an ounce of butter, stirred over a low heat until the white begins to set. Then remove them because the heat of the saucepan will complete the cooking. It's a dish that is simple to make and yet so many people fail with it. I sometimes think that the cause of failure in cooking the simplest dishes is because they are simple.

Alpine Eggs

4 persons. Time: 10 to 15 minutes

4 eggs
2½ oz. grated cheese
¾ oz. butter
2 tablespoons cream

1 teaspoon mixed herbs
½ teaspoon parsley (chopped)
pepper, salt

Well butter a fire-proof dish and carefully break the eggs into it, sprinkle with seasoning, the herbs and half the cheese; pour over the cream. Cover with the rest of the cheese and the parsley, dot a few pieces of butter over and bake for 10 minutes in an oven or until the eggs are set. Serve in the dish they were cooked in.

Gas 6–7; Electricity 400°–425°

Baked Eggs

1 or 2 eggs per person

Well butter individual dishes or a large dish, break the required amount of eggs into the dish, or dishes. Sprinkle with salt and pepper, put a small dot of butter on top, and cook in the oven for 8 to 10 minutes to set. Sprinkle with chopped parsley before serving. Grated cheese can be put on the eggs before baking; or put mushrooms or cooked ham or tongue at the bottom of the dish, and break the eggs over, then cook in the same way.

Gas 6; Electricity 400°

Curried Eggs

4 persons. Time: 15 to 20 minutes

4 eggs (hard-boiled)	lemon
4 oz. rice (Patna)	curry sauce

Wash the rice, drain well, put into a pan of lightly-salted boiling water, add 1 teaspoon of lemon juice, boil until tender, about 10 to 15 minutes. Drain, and run under the cold tap to separate the grains, put in the oven to keep warm. Cut three of the eggs into halves and heat them in the curry sauce, cut the other egg into small pieces to use as a garnish. To serve, put the eggs into a dish, pour over the sauce, put the cut-up egg on top and put the rice as a border all round.

Curry Sauce

Makes ½ pint

1 level dessertspoon curry powder	½ oz. flour
1 small onion (chopped)	½ teaspoon brown sugar
1 small apple (chopped)	½ pt stock
1 tomato	1 sprig parsley
1 oz. butter	½ teaspoon lemon juice
	½ level saltspoon salt

Melt the butter in a pan, add the onion, parsley and tomato cut into small pieces; stir over a low heat until brown. Add the curry powder and flour and brown that also; add lemon juice and salt, gradually pour over the stock. Keep stirring until boiled, then add the chopped apple and sugar and simmer until the sauce is thick—about 20 to 30 minutes. Strain and use.

Eggs au Gratin

4 to 6 persons. Time: 15 to 20 minutes

6 eggs (hard-boiled)
1½ oz. Parmesan cheese
2 egg yolks
1 oz. butter

½ oz. flour
1 gill milk
1 tablespoon cream
paprika pepper

Cut the hard-boiled eggs in half lengthwise and put into fire-proof dish. Melt the butter in a pan, blend in the flour, stir over a low heat for 1 minute, add the milk and 1 tablespoon of water. Stir until it boils, simmer for 2 or 3 minutes, add seasoning and 1 oz. of the cheese; remove from heat, add the yolks of eggs one at a time and the cream, stir well and pour over the hard-boiled eggs. Sprinkle with the rest of the cheese and bake for 10 to 15 minutes. Serve with croûtons of fried bread.

Gas 6; Electricity 400°

Egg Kromeskies

4 to 5 persons. Time: About 20 minutes

3 eggs (hard-boiled)
1 oz. cooked ham
4 streaky rashers
2 egg yolks

white sauce (see p. 140)
frying batter
frying fat or oil
pepper, salt

Shell the eggs and roughly chop. Put 1 tablespoon of white sauce into a pan, add the finely-chopped ham, the eggs and the 2 raw yolks, season and stir well over a low heat until the mixture is hot, but do not let boil or the yolks will curdle; put on a plate and leave to get cold, then shape the mixture into 6 or 8 pieces roughly cork-shaped. Remove the rind from the rashers, cut into halves, wrap a piece round each cork-shaped egg mixture. Have ready a deep pan of fat, and when hot enough so that a faint blue smoke rises, dip each kromeski into the batter and drop into the hot fat; fry to a golden brown, drain on soft paper, and garnish with fried parsley (see p. 142).

Egg Oysters

1 per person

1 new-laid egg
½ teaspoon lemon juice

cayenne pepper
salt

216

Break an egg into a glass without breaking the yolk. Add the lemon juice and seasoning to taste. The egg must not be broken but swallowed whole like an oyster. It is a good pick-me-up.

Eggs with Truffles

3 to 4 persons. Time: About 10 minutes

5 to 6 eggs (hard-boiled)
1 small tin truffles
1 small onion
1 oz. butter

1 to 1½ gills brown sauce
(see p. 130)
pepper, salt

Cut the cold hard-boiled eggs into thin slices. Finely chop the onion and truffles, fry them in the butter to a pale brown, add the sauce and seasoning. Put in the eggs, make very hot and serve on large croûtons of fried bread.

Savoury Egg Custard

2 to 3 persons. Time: 15 to 20 minutes

3 eggs (large)
1 small shallot
¼ small bunch chives
1 oz. ham (cooked)

1 pt white stock
½ gill cream
pepper, salt

Beat the eggs in a basin, add the stock and cream. Finely chop the chives, shallot and ham, add to the eggs with the seasoning, mix well. Butter some small moulds or one large one, pour in the egg mixture, cover with grease-proof paper and steam for 15 to 20 minutes, or until set. If using a large mould allow slightly longer time to set.

Scotch Eggs

3 to 6 persons. Time: 15 to 20 minutes

3 eggs (hard-boiled)
about 6 oz. sausage meat
1 egg

frying fat or oil
breadcrumbs
pepper, salt

Thinly coat the eggs with the sausage meat; make the fat or oil hot in a deep pan, dip the eggs into the beaten egg, coat with breadcrumbs and drop into the pan of hot fat. Fry until a golden brown—about 15 to 20 minutes; drain on soft paper, cut into halves. If to be eaten hot serve each one on a croûton of fried bread, hand a brown or tomato sauce (see p. 139). If to be served cold garnish with watercress and cut lemon.

Scrambled Eggs

3 to 4 persons. Time: About 5 minutes

4 eggs   buttered toast
2 tablespoons cream or milk   pepper, salt

Break the eggs into a basin, beat lightly, add the seasoning. Melt the butter in a pan, put the eggs, cream or milk in and stir over a low heat until the eggs are just beginning to set. It is important to remove the eggs from the heat as they just set; the heat of the pan finishes the cooking. Serve on rounds of hot buttered toast.

OMELETS

Plain Omelet

1 to 2 persons. Time: 3 to 5 minutes

3 eggs   1 teaspoon chopped parsley
½ oz. butter   pepper, salt
1 tablespoon water

Break the eggs into basin, beat lightly, add the seasoning, parsley and 1 tablespoon of cold water. Melt the butter in an omelet pan, make hot, then quickly pour in the eggs; give a couple of stirs then hold the pan over a low heat, and as it begins to set slip a knife underneath and let some of the uncooked liquid run to the edges. As soon as the omelet is set lightly at the bottom and soft on top, slip the palette knife round the side nearest to the handle and double the omelet over; work it into a semi-circular shape with the knife, let it cook for a moment to set any egg that may have run out, then turn on to a hot plate so that the underneath side is on the top. It should look smooth and yellow outside and be soft and creamy inside.

Asparagus Omelet

2 to 4 persons. Time: About 5 minutes

5 eggs	1 oz. butter
½ tea-cup cooked asparagus tips	paprika pepper, salt
	1½ tablespoons water

Separate the yolks from the whites of the eggs, lightly beat the yolks, add the asparagus tips, seasoning and 1½ tablespoons of cold water. Beat the whites to a stiff froth and fold them into the yolks. Melt the butter in an omelet pan and cook as for plain omelet.

Cheese Omelet

2 to 4 persons. Time: 5 to 6 minutes

5 eggs	1 oz. butter
1½ oz. grated cheese	1½ tablespoons cold water

Follow the recipe as for plain, but add 1 oz. of cheese to the eggs; when the omelet is cooked, turn it on to a fire-proof plate, sprinkle on the rest of the cheese and put under the grill for a minute or two to brown.

Ham Omelet

2 to 4 persons. Time: About 5 minutes

5 eggs	1 teaspoon chopped parsley
4 to 6 oz. ham (cooked)	1½ tablespoons water
1½ oz. butter	pepper, salt

Prepare the eggs as for asparagus omelet, but using finely-chopped or minced ham and parsley; cook as for plain omelet. Minced or chopped tongue or chicken can be used instead of ham.

Mushroom Omelet

2 to 3 persons. Time: 3 to 5 minutes for omelet

3 eggs	½ teaspoon mixed herbs
2 oz. mushrooms	pepper, salt
1 oz. butter	

Peel the mushrooms and remove the stalks, dry, chop finely. Melt 1 oz. of the butter in a pan, put in the mushrooms and cook for about 5 minutes, add the herbs and seasoning, keep warm. Make the omelet according to recipe for plain omelet and, just before folding it over, add the mushroom mixture; fold and finish cooking.

18

Preserves, Bottling and Cordials

The most important thing in making jams is choosing the fruit. It should be firm, just ripe, and not damaged in any way because it is liable to ferment and the jam won't keep. Another thing to remember is that, after the sugar has been added and dissolved, the jam must boil fast otherwise it won't set well. It must be stored in a cool dry place, for if it gets too warm there's always the danger that it will ferment; this applies even to shop-bought jams. If by some misfortune you do get a layer of mould on the top of the jam, it is possible to take it off, put the jam back into a saucepan and re-boil it, then jar it up again, but if the whole jar seems to be affected, nothing can be done and you must throw it away.

People say to me that jam is so cheap to buy it's not worth making. I don't agree. There is no comparison. I can't help feeling that cheap jams are adulterated by adding bulk—carrots, I think, are used, and certainly colouring is. In any case, the difference in the texture and flavour is obvious, so

221

that by making your own you're getting tip-top jam for cheap jam price.

Your preserving pan should be thick-bottomed, otherwise the jam will stick and burn. When I was in service we used a thick-bottomed copper pan, but now I use a heavy aluminium one. Remember to have your jars absolutely clean and dry. I find that it's advisable to warm them slightly to make sure that no damp remains, because if it does the jam will quickly deteriorate. I always warm the sugar before adding it to the fruit. One of the cooks I worked with passed this tip on to me. She said it made the jam brighter and clearer, and if her jams were anything to go by, it certainly did.

I use preserving sugar if it's readily available, but granulated seems to do just as well, and it isn't much dearer. Fruits that have plenty of pectin, such as gooseberries, blackberries if they're not too ripe, plums and damsons, won't require the addition of tartaric acid or lemon juice. Where necessary, you use one or the other. I use lemon juice; I don't know why, but I just feel that lemon juice is a natural product and tartaric acid isn't. I believe that when using either, the results are the same. Fruits like strawberries, cherries and raspberries require this addition; it works on the fruit and extracts the pectin which eventually will set your jam. In the making, do keep skimming. You'll find that as jam is boiling the scum keeps rising to the top; if you don't remove it, it will sink down again and although it may not detract from the taste, it certainly discolours it. To know if the jam has boiled sufficiently, put a spoonful on a cold plate and leave for a few minutes. If it is ready you will find that a thin skin has formed on the top and that it has set on the plate.

With fruits like blackberries, raspberries and red currants, I think making jelly is preferable to making jam. Raspberry jam may not be so bad, but even that has too many pips for my taste.

For jellies always use fruit that is slightly under-ripe; this contains more of the pectin which is needed to set them, and jelly must set firmer than jam. If you use over-ripe fruit it will make it syrupy and no matter how much you boil it, it won't change. If, despite this, your jelly is syrupy, the only thing to do to save it is to add gelatine, about half an ounce to one pint of the juice; but it won't keep for very long.

PRESERVES

Blackcurrant Jam

4 lb. blackcurrants   1 pt water
4 lb. lump sugar, or slightly
    more if liked sweeter

The blackcurrants should be ripe and quite dry. Wash the fruit, remove the stalks, put the fruit into a pan with the water, place over a low heat until it boils, simmer for about 20 minutes. Add the sugar, stir all the time until it boils, let it boil for 25 to 30 minutes or until it quickly sets when a teaspoonful is tested on a cold plate. While it is cooking, frequent stirring is needed as the jam easily boils over the pan. Leave to cool, then put into clean dry jars and when quite cold seal with parchment paper or Cellophane covers.

Grandmother's Damson Cheese

damsons   castor sugar

Wash the damsons, put them into an earthenware pot, sprinkle lightly with castor sugar to bring out the juice, leave overnight. Cook them in the oven until the fruit is soft, and while still warm rub through a hair sieve. Measure the pulp; to every 1 quart of pulp add 1 lb. of sugar. Put sugar and pulp into a pan over a very low heat and simmer for 1¼ to 1½ hours. Leave to cool, put into small pots and when quite cold put on parchment paper or Cellophane covers and store in a dry place.

Green Gooseberry Jam

4 lb. gooseberries   1 pt water
3 lb. granulated sugar

The gooseberries should be fully grown but still green. Wash, top and tail the gooseberries. Put the sugar in a pan with the cold water, put over a low heat until the sugar has dissolved, then bring to the boil and simmer for 15 minutes; remove any scum that rises. Put in the gooseberries and boil for about 40 minutes, or until it quickly sets when tested on a cold plate. Leave to cool, then put into jars and when quite cold seal with parchment paper or Cellophane covers.

Old Hannah's Apple and Cinnamon Jam

6 lb. cooking apples
2 lemons
1 quince
4½ lb. preserving sugar

2 saltspoons ground cinnamon
3 gills water

Peel, core and slice the apples, put them into a pan with the sugar, grated rind and juice of lemons, cinnamon and the water; wipe the quince, remove the core, and coarsely grate the quince, peel included, into the pan. Put over a low heat, bring to the boil, simmer gently until the apples are pulp, stirring frequently and removing any scum. Leave to cool, put into clean dry jars. When quite cold put on parchment papers or cover with Cellophane. Store in a cool dry place.

Old Hannah's Pumpkin Jam

3 lb. pumpkin (after peeling
    and removal of pips)
2¼ lb. sugar

1 orange
2 lemons
1½ oz. bruised ginger

Peel and remove seeds from the pumpkin, cut the flesh into dice. Grate the rinds of the orange and lemon, put into a pan with the juice, diced pumpkin, sugar and the ginger tied in a muslin bag and leave overnight. Then pour the juice off into a pan, bring to the boil, add the pumpkin and simmer for about 1 to 1¼ hours or untill the pulp becomes almost transparent and the syrup quickly sets when tested on a cold plate. Leave to cool, then put into jars. When quite cold put on parchment papers or Cellophane covers.

Plum Jam

3 lb. plums (any type)
2¼ lb. sugar or (if liked
    sweeter) use extra ¼ lb.

½ pt water

Wash and dry the plums, either remove stones or cut plums across and take out the stones as they rise in the pan. Put the plums into a pan with the water, place over a low heat; when it reaches boiling point, simmer gently until soft, stirring from time to time. Add the sugar, stir until boiling again, then boil quickly until the jam rapidly sets when tested on a cold plate. Leave to cool, put into dry jars; when quite cold seal with parchment paper or with Cellophane covers.

Strawberry Jam

4 lb. strawberries   juice 4 lemons
3½ lb. sugar

The strawberries must be fresh and dry; wet mushy fruit will be extremely difficult to set.

Remove the stalks from the fruit; wash and leave to drain until all the water has gone. Put into a large bowl alternate layers of sugar and strawberries and leave in a cool place overnight. Then put into a pan, add the lemon juice and put on a low heat; slowly bring to the boil, stirring carefully to avoid breaking the fruit, then boil quickly for 30 to 35 minutes, skimming when necessary. When it is ready the fruit will sink and the scum will not rise. It is a good idea to add a small piece of butter at this stage to dispel the scum. Test on a cold plate to see that it sets well; then leave to cool for a while in the pan before putting into jars; this helps to prevent the fruit rising to the top. When quite cold, cover with parchment paper or Cellophane covers and store in a cool, dry place.

Strawberry Jam (another method)

3 lb. strawberries   2 lemons
3 lb. sugar (granulated or   ½ teaspoon tartaric acid
  preserving)

Put the sugar on to a large dish and place in a cool oven to get slightly warm. Remove stalks from the fruit, wash and leave to drain until all the water has gone. Put them into a pan with the juice of the lemons and the tartaric acid, place over a low heat and bring to the boil slowly, let simmer for 20 minutes. Add the sugar, stir until it dissolves, then boil quickly for 25 to 30 minutes, or until it sets when tested on a cold plate. Put into jars and make airtight; store in a cool, dry place.

Mrs Clydesdale's Apricot Marmalade

sound ripe apricots   (¾ lb. sugar to 1 pt apricot
granulated sugar   pulp)
water

Cut 4 lb. of apricots into halves, take out the stones, rub the fruit through a wire sieve. Measure the pulp, and, allowing the right amount of sugar, put the pulp and sugar into a pan with 3 gills of water—or just under. Put the pan on a low heat and stir until the sugar has dissolved, then fast boil for 20 minutes. Remove some of the kernels from the apricot stones, add to the marmalade and boil for another 5 minutes or until it quickly sets when tested on a cold plate. Leave to cool, then put into clean, dry jars and cover with parchment paper or Cellophane covers.

Great-Grandmother's Crab Apple Marmalade

crab apples   cloves
sugar   water
lemon

To every 3 lb. of apples allow ½ doz. cloves and the juice of a lemon. Wash the fruit, cut into quarters without peeling or coring, put into a pan with the cloves and lemon. Cook over a low heat until soft, then rub through a sieve. To each lb. of pulp allow ¾ lb. of sugar and ½ gill of water, put into the pan, bring to the boil, stirring all the time, then boil for about ¾ to 1 hour. Stir frequently, leave to cool, then put into jars and cover with parchment paper or Cellophane covers.

Lemon Marmalade

2 lb. lemons   2 pts water
4 lb. loaf sugar

Wipe the lemons with a clean dry cloth, put into a pan with the water, bring to the boil and continue boiling for 2 hours, changing the water once and replacing with the same amount of boiling water. Leave to cool slightly, then thinly slice the lemons and remove the pips. To each 1 lb. of sugar allow ½ pt. of the water in which the lemons were boiled, put into a pan over a low heat; when the sugar has dissolved, add the fruit and boil for about 30 minutes, or until the marmalade sets quickly when tested on a cold plate. Leave to cool a little, put into jars, make airtight and store in a cool, dry place.

Orange Marmalade

1 doz. Seville oranges	preserving sugar
2 lemons	

Wash and wipe the oranges, peel thinly, remove the pith and pips. Weigh the peel and fruit and to each 1 lb. add 3 pints of cold water; leave in an earthenware pan for 1 to 2 days, then put into a preserving pan, bring to the boil and simmer until soft. Leave to cool a little, then to each 1 lb. of fruit add 1 lb. of sugar, bring to the boil again and continue boiling until the fruit sets when tested on a cold plate. Leave to cool, then put into clean dry jars and when quite cold seal with parchment paper or Cellophane covers.

BOTTLING

Method of Bottling in Syrup

Use patent jars and make sure that the rubber rings are in good condition; always scald the jars, rings and glass tops in boiling water. When the fruit is ready to go into the oven fix on the rubber rings, put on the glass tops and adjust the screw top loosely. Stand the jars on an asbestos mat, or cardboard would do, on about the fourth runner from the top, leaving a space between the jars. When the jars have been in the oven for the required time, remove them one at a time and quickly tighten the screw tops. To test if they are properly sealed, wait until the jars are cold, remove the screw top and lift the jar by the glass top; if it does not come away then the sealing is all right.

If, however, the glass top does come off, the fruit must be sterilized again. To do this add a little more syrup to bring the level within 1 inch from the top, put back the rubber ring, glass top and the screw top loosely as before, put back in the oven for the same time plus an extra 5 to 6 minutes and finish off in the same way.

In all bottling care must be taken to see that the jars are completely sealed, otherwise the fruit will not keep.

Syrup for Bottled Fruits

Granulated sugar is the best for this, and the amounts vary from ¼ to 1 lb. sugar to every 1 pint water. Pour the cold water over the sugar and leave for about 15 minutes. Then put into a pan over a very low heat until the sugar has dissolved. Bring to boiling point, strain through 2 or 3 folds of muslin, reboil before pouring over the fruit.

Blackcurrants Bottled in Syrup

To make the syrup allow 1 lb. sugar to 1 pint water, allow this amount for each 3 lb. jar. The blackcurrants must be fresh and dry; wash them, remove the stalks, leave until they are well drained. Put into the hot jars, pack in as many as possible by shaking the jars, pour the boiling syrup to within an inch of the top. Then follow the instructions as given at the beginning of this section. Redcurrants can be done in the same way.

Time in oven 1 hour. Gas ½; Electricity 250°

Cherries Bottled in Syrup

Make the syrup by allowing ¼ lb. sugar to 1 pint water. Choose fresh, dry cherries, remove stalks, wash and leave to well drain. Then put the cherries into a pan with the syrup, bring to the boil over a low heat and leave overnight. Put the fruit into hot jars, pack in as many as possible by using two long sticks, reboil the syrup and pour over the fruit to within an inch from the top. Then follow the instructions as given at the beginning.

Time in oven ½ hour. Gas ½; Electricity 250°

Gooseberries Bottled without Syrup

Top and tail the fruit, wash and leave to drain. Put into hot scalded jars packing in as many as possible with the aid of two long sticks; cover with the glass lid only. Put the jars in the oven standing on cardboard or an asbestos mat, about the fourth runner from the top, leave a space between the jars. When they have been in the oven for the necessary time remove the jars one at a time and fill to the top with boiling water; put on rubber rings, glass and screw tops as quickly as possible. When cold, test seal as for bottling in syrup.

Time in oven ½ hour. Gas ½; Electricity 250°

Peaches Bottled in Syrup

Make the syrup with ½ lb. sugar to 1 pint water. The peaches should not be too ripe. Put them into a basin, cover with boiling water for a few minutes to loosen the skins, then peel, cut into halves and take out the stones. Put the fruit into the hot jars, packing in as many as possible without crushing the fruit. Pour over the boiling syrup to within an inch of the top then follow the instructions at the beginning of the section.

Time in oven 1 hour. Gas ½; Electricity 250°

Pears Bottled in Syrup

Make the syrup with ¼ lb. sugar to 1 pint water. Choose sound pears, not too soft, peel and cut them into halves, remove the core without breaking the fruit. Put the fruit into the hot jars, packing in as many as possible; pour over the boiling syrup to within an inch of the top. Follow the instructions as at the beginning of the section.

If bottling apricots these are left whole and are not usually skinned.

Time in oven ¾ hour. Gas 1; Electricity 275°

Plums Bottled without Syrup

Choose plums that are not too ripe, remove the stalks, wash and leave to drain well. Put into hot jars, pack in as many as possible, using two long sticks to arrange them. Cover with the glass lids only, stand the jars on cardboard or an asbestos mat in the oven about the fourth runner from the top. When they have been in the oven the necessary time, take out the jars one at a time and fill to the top with boiling water; put on the rubber rings, glass and screw tops as quickly as possible. When cold, test seal as in syrup bottling.

Time in oven ¾ hour. Gas ½; Electricity 250°

Raspberries Bottled in Syrup

Make syrup with 1 lb. sugar to 1 pint water. Dry, firm fruit is needed. Put into the hot jars without squashing, cover with only the glass lids, place in oven for 20 minutes. Take the jars from oven and refill to the original amount by taking fruit from one of the jars, leave a space for the syrup. Pour over the boiling syrup to within ¾ inch from the top and, following the instructions at the beginning of this section, leave the jars in the oven for another 35 minutes.

Gas ½; Electricity 250°

CORDIALS

Cherry Brandy

Morello cherries
granulated sugar
brandy

peach or apricot kernels
if available

(To each 1 lb. of cherries allow 7 oz. of sugar and ½ doz. kernels.)

Wash the cherries, leave about ½ inch of stalk, roll them in a clean dry cloth, then prick well with a darning needle. Put the cherries into clean, dry, wide-necked bottles—about half-filled—add the sugar and kernels in the right proportions, then fill the bottles with brandy. Closely cork, cover the top with melted wax, keep in a cool dry place for 3 months before using, occasionally shaking the bottles.

Cowslip Wine

4 qts cowslips
4 qts water
2 lemons
1 orange

4 lb. lump sugar
1½ teaspoons brewer's yeast
¼ bottle brandy

230

Put the water into a large pan, add the sugar, bring to the boil, simmer for ½ hour, removing any scum that rises. Thinly peel the lemon and orange, put this into a large earthenware bowl with the juice of 1 lemon and the orange, pour on the boiling syrup and leave until lukewarm, then put in the flowers of the cowslips and the yeast spread on a piece of toast. Leave to ferment for 3 to 4 days, then put into a clean, dry cask, add the brandy and let it stand for about 2 months; it can then be bottled and used as required, but the longer it is kept the better it is.

Damson Wine

2 qts damsons	¼ pt brandy
2 lb. loaf sugar	2 qts water

Wash the damsons and remove the stalks, put the fruit into an earthenware bowl, pour over the boiling water, cover with a cloth and leave for 4 days, stirring occasionally; add the sugar and brandy. When the sugar has dissolved pour it into a clean, dry cask. Cover the bung hole with several thicknesses of cloth. When fermentation has ceased, bung tightly and leave for 1 year in a moderately warm place. Then pour into bottles, well cork, store in a cool dry place. It will keep for several years.

Dandelion Wine

2 qts dandelions	1 lemon
1½ lb. lump sugar	½ tablespoon brewer's yeast
1 orange	2 qts water

Put the petals into a large bowl, pour over the boiling water, stir well, cover with a cloth and leave for 3 days, stirring from time to time. Then strain into a pan, add the thin rind of the orange and lemon, the lemon cut into slices, and the sugar. Boil slowly for about ½ hour, leave to cool. Put in the yeast spread on a piece of toast, let it stand for 2 days, then put into a dry cask, well bunged down. Leave for 2 months, then bottle and use as required.

Elderberry Wine

4 lb. elderberries	6 qts water

Wash the fruit and remove stalks, put the berries into a large container, pour over the boiling water and leave for 1 day. Then well bruise the berries and strain through a hair sieve. To each gallon of liquid allow:

3 lb. lump sugar	½ doz. cloves
1 lb. raisins	½ oz. ground ginger
1 gill brandy	¼ teaspoon brewer's yeast

Put the liquid, raisins, ginger, cloves and sugar into a pan, bring to the boil, simmer gently for 1 hour, skimming if required. Leave until lukewarm, then stir in the yeast and pour into a clean, dry cask. Place a thick cloth over the bung-hole and let it stand for 2 weeks, then stir in the brandy and tightly bung. Leave for 6 months, then pour into bottles and cork.

Mrs McIlroy's Quince Liqueur

Ripe quinces	cinnamon
sugar	ginger
brandy	

Wipe the fruit carefully on a cloth, remove the cores, then grate them on a coarse grater, unpeeled, into a bowl, cover tightly and leave for 3 days. Then squeeze the pulp through a piece of fine linen and measure the juice, then add ⅔rds of the amount in brandy. To every 1 pint of this mixture add ⅔rds teaspoon of cinnamon, ¼ teaspoon of ginger and ¼ lb. of sugar. Put into bottles and leave for at least 2 weeks, then strain and rebottle.

Sloe Gin (Old recipe from a cook)

2 lb. sloes	1 qt gin
1 lb. sugar candy	½ doz. bitter almonds

Well bruise the sloes, put them into a small cask, add the gin and the crushed sugar candy; blanch the almonds and finely chop, stir into the cask. Mix well and leave in a fairly warm place for 3 months, then strain through fine muslin, put into bottles and securely cork.

19

Pickles

Pickles are fairly simple to make. They do not need much explanation; this is contained in the recipes themselves. Because pickles are cheap to buy, people today are not generally prepared to take the trouble to make their own, but they are like any of the things that are made on a mass scale, they haven't the flavour that you get when you do them yourself. Then there is a certain satisfaction in pickling that you don't get when preparing a meal; you continue to see the results of your labour.

The first point I must make is that only the best malt vinegar should be used; it's false economy to use any other, and of course the same applies to the ingredients—if they are not in the best condition when they are pickled, they will most certainly not keep.

Another point is that an enamelled pan is the best to use when you're boiling vinegar. If you use a metal pan it is apt to cause discoloration. Similarly, use a wooden not a metal spoon for stirring.

Bottle in dry stone or glass jars, and if you find that, after a while, some of the vinegar has evaporated, top it up, remembering to use vinegar that has been boiled and left to get cold. Never put in vinegar straight out of the bottle.

Whatever kind of pickles you are making, the liquid should be about an inch above the vegetables. The jars should be covered so that they are absolutely airtight. We used parchment paper when I was in service, but now, if you are not using screw-topped jars, there are Cellophane covers sold specially for the purpose. As with preserves or jams, the jars should be stored in a cool, dry place. Remember some pickles keep longer than others; for instance, if kept too long, red cabbage can lose both its colour and its crispness. Whereas pickled walnuts and some chutneys can be kept for a year or two and, like wines, their flavour improves.

Apple Chutney

1 doz. sour green apples	½ oz. ground ginger
3 oz. seeded raisins	¼ oz. mustard seed
1 small onion	¼ oz. garlic
½ lb. demerara sugar	cayenne pepper
1 pt vinegar	

Peel, core and slice the apples, put them into a pan with the sugar and vinegar, cook gently until the apples are soft. Wash and dry the mustard seed, put into a mortar with the ginger, garlic, onion and raisins chopped; pound well together. Add them to the cooked apples with a pinch of cayenne, stir and mix well and put into small jars or bottles and either cork or cover with parchment paper or Cellophane covers.

Green Gooseberry Chutney

3 pts green gooseberries (must not be ripe)	1 qt vinegar
	½ oz. mustard seed
½ lb. seeded raisins	1 oz. ground ginger
1 medium apple	½ level saltspoon cayenne
¾ lb. onions	pepper
¾ lb. demerara sugar	salt

Top, tail and slice or roughly chop the gooseberries, peel and chop the apple and onion, chop the raisins. Put all the ingredients into a pan with ½ oz. of salt, pour over the vinegar and bring to the boil. Simmer for 1 hour, stirring frequently, leave to get cold, then put into jars and either cork or tie down with parchment paper or Cellophane covers.

Pickling Vinegar

1 qt vinegar
1 onion (not too large)

2 oz. pickling spice
1 teaspoon salt

Tie the spice in a piece of muslin and put into a pan with the onion, salt and vinegar. Bring to the boil and keep boiling for 5 minutes; remove the spice and use the vinegar as required.

Onions Pickled

shallots or small button onions

pickling vinegar

Peel the outer skins from the onions, using a silver knife; a steel one is apt to discolour them. Put them into a large stone jar, or several small ones, pour over the cold pickling vinegar. Keep for at least 2 weeks before using.

Mrs McIlroy's Chutney

4 medium-sized green apples
2 medium-sized onions
½ lb. seeded raisins
½ lb. ripe plums (not over-ripe)
1 qt best malt vinegar

1 lb. soft brown sugar
¼ lb. green ginger
2 oz. dry mustard
1 clove garlic
1 oz. salt

Peel and chop the onions, peel and thinly slice the apples, wash and stone the plums, cut into small pieces. Cook the apples, onions, sugar, garlic, salt and vinegar in a pan until soft, then rub through a hair sieve. Add the raisins, plums, thinly-sliced ginger and mustard, mix well together, leave in a warm place until the next day. Then give a thorough mixing, put into clean, dry, wide-necked jars and make air-tight. This will keep for some months.

Tomato Chutney

3 lb. ripe tomatoes
1½ lb. green apples
½ lb. demerara sugar
½ lb. onions

1½ pt vinegar
1 oz. pickling spice
1 teaspoon salt

Put the tomatoes into boiling water for a few minutes to loosen the skins, then peel and cut up. Peel the apples and onions, chop them, tie the spice in a piece of muslin and put all the ingredients into a pan. Put over a fair heat until it boils, stirring frequently, then simmer gently until thick and tender. Remove the spice, leave to cool, then put into wide-necked jars and either cork, or cover with parchment paper or Cellophane covers.

Vegetable Marrow Pickle

To each 2 lb. of marrow—weighed before salting—but after peeling:

4 oz. lump sugar
1½ oz. white ginger
6 chillies

1 clove garlic
1 oz. mustard flour
vinegar

Peel the marrows, remove the seeds, cut the flesh into pieces, sprinkle with salt and leave overnight, then drain on a clean cloth. Crush the ginger small, mince the garlic and then put all the ingredients—except the marrow—into a pan and boil for 2 to 3 minutes, add the marrow, bring to the boil again and simmer gently for 20 to 30 minutes, leave to cool. Put into dry, wide-necked jars and make air-tight.

Melon can be done in the same way.

Walnuts Pickled

walnuts
pickling vinegar

salt
water

The walnuts need to be young enough so that an inside shell has not formed. Make a brine, using 4 pints of water to 1 lb. of salt; shell the walnuts and soak them in the brine for 10 to 12 days, changing the brine during that time 2 or 3 times. Then drain and leave the walnuts on flat dishes until they are quite black; put them into jars and pour over the pickling vinegar hot. Cover and keep for a few months before using.

Index of Recipes

237